The State
OF
Black Progress

Introduction by Star Parker

Encounter
BOOKS
New York • London

First American edition published in 2024 by Encounter Books,
an activity of Encounter for Culture and Education, Inc.,
a nonprofit, tax-exempt corporation.
Encounter Books website address: www.encounterbooks.com

Manufactured in the United States and printed on
acid-free paper. The paper used in this publication meets
the minimum requirements of ANSI/NISO Z39.48–1992
(R 1997) (*Permanence of Paper*).

FIRST AMERICAN EDITION

LIBRARY OF CONGRESS CATALOGING-IN-PUBLICATION DATA IS AVAILABLE

Information for this title can be found at the Library of Congress
website under the following ISBN 978-1-64177-341-6 and LCCN 2023058714.

Edited by Star Parker and Marty Dannenfelser

CONTENTS

INTRODUCTION

by Star Parker

In the 1860s, black America was promised emancipation but continued to experience subjugation. In the 1960s, black America was promised equality but was frequently exploited. Racial discrimination played a role, but misguided progressive policies and reparationist ideology played a bigger one. By failing to live up to American ideals, our nation undermined the opportunity for many black Americans to realize the American Dream.

Black Americans have now arrived at the height of their cultural prominence. In politics, entertainment, academics, and nearly every sphere of influence, "black issues" dominate the discussion. Yet the average black American is suffering worse than ever from the blight of poverty, physical and mental health struggles, lack of opportunity, and failing schools. Anti-American sentiment and societal resentment are at an all-time high.

The Center for Urban Renewal and Education (CURE) has partnered with scholars and luminaries who believe that what has been lost can be recovered. If our nation recognizes the history of our current predicament, embraces America's founding principles that made her an economic powerhouse, and commits to a program of restorative fiscal, education, and social welfare policies, black Americans can overcome the struggles that most impact their communities.

The State of Black Progress details the role of government and the courts in overcoming racial discrimination, but explains how they have since become key obstacles to black progress in America. The contributing scholars address this dilemma in light of American values and the history of constitutional jurisprudence.

The book is comprehensive in scope, covering black history in our nation from America's founding to current times. The authors address the history and current state of affairs for black Americans on education, health care, housing, community development, and private investment including Social Security reform. They explain how we got here and offer concrete policy solutions that highlight the importance of equal opportunity, personal responsibility, and limited government.

Dr. William Allen, Emeritus Professor of Political Philosophy and Dean of James Madison College at Michigan State University and former Chairman of the United States Commission on Civil Rights, details black history in America from Reconstruction to the present. Dr. Allen says policies that separate out community members, rather than integrating them (e.g., targeted admission, contracting, appointment procedures) "ought to be abandoned and replaced by practices that work hand-in-glove with self-motivation to profit from a breadth of opportunity consistently offered and made highly visible."

Janice Rogers Brown, a former judge on the United States Court of Appeals for the D.C. Circuit, argues that the U.S. Supreme Court in its 1873 *Slaughterhouse* decision subverted the protections in the Fourteenth Amendment, turning "what was meant for bread into a stone." In commenting on a later Supreme Court decision, Judge Brown said, "In the Framer's constitution, equality and liberty were two sides of the same coin—complements, not opposites."

Grace-Marie Turner, President of the Galen Institute, testifies regularly before Congress and has been instrumental in developing and promoting ideas to transfer power over health care decisions to doctors and patients through a more competitive, patient-centered health sector. Turner's essay, "The Dignity of Private vs. Public Insurance," argues that the Left has a "disguised agenda" and sees Medicaid as "a platform upon which to build their government-run health care system."

Sally Pipes is President, CEO, and Thomas W. Smith Fellow in Health Care Policy at the Pacific Research Institute. Her essay, "The State of Black Health Care in America," traces how federal welfare programs have failed black American enrollees by saddling them with subpar health care coverage and penalizing them for trying to climb the economic ladder. She offers market-based solutions that will benefit Americans of all races—black Americans in particular.

Ian Rowe is a Senior Fellow at the American Enterprise Institute (AEI), where he focuses on education and upward mobility, family formation, and adoption. He is the cofounder of Vertex Partnership Academies, a network of character-based International Baccalaureate high schools in the Bronx. With his book *Agency*, Mr. Rowe seeks to inspire young people of all races to build strong families and become masters of their own destiny. His essay addresses an unintended consequence of the U.S. Supreme Court's historic *Brown v. Board of Education* decision—the demise of the privately funded Rosenwald schools that educated more than 700,000 black children over four decades. Mr. Rowe's dedication to equal opportunity and strong families has led him to the forefront of a movement for rigorous, character-based education.

Leslie Hiner is Vice President of Legal Affairs for EdChoice, leading their Legal Defense & Education Center. In her essay, "K–12 Education: The Imperative of Empowering Parents," Leslie explains how the COVID-19 experience has caused many parents to become painfully aware of something Frederick Douglass recognized more than 100 years ago: When children do not receive a proper education, "there is no light or liberty."

Howard Husock is a Senior Fellow in Domestic Policy Studies at AEI. Mr. Husock's essay, "How Public Housing Has Harmed Black America—And Still Does," argues that public housing advocates (as far back as Eleanor Roosevelt) have ignored "the possibility that government intervention has helped create the 'problems facing inner cities' and that steering blacks time and again into subsidized housing deepens those problems." He believes it is "far better for government to do what it is meant to do: to take the steps [e.g., safe and clean streets, good schools, available parks and recreation] required to ensure that poor neighborhoods are good neighborhoods and can serve as the launching pads for upward mobility."

Edward Pinto is Senior Fellow and Director of the Housing Center at AEI. Pinto argues that after "spending incalculable sums of money, after many millions of foreclosures, and after the destruction of large areas of our cities, the federal government has little positive to show for its attempts to help black households and neighborhoods." He believes there is a "growing consensus" that the best way "to make housing more affordable is to increase supply, not to ease credit, increase government subsidies, or suppress interest rates." Pinto says even "a few progressive think tanks and cities have come around to this view."

Craig Scheef cofounded Texas Security Bank in 2008 and serves as Chairman and CEO. Mr. Scheef's essay, "The Impact of Economic Stability in Marginalized Zip Codes," argues that "poverty is man-made" and "reversing poverty is man-made, as well." Scheef says that free enterprise "has proven to be the vastly superior economic system for reversing poverty" and that socialism and communism have proven to be responsible for creating poverty. He suggests that each stakeholder in the free enterprise ecosystem (e.g., nuclear family, all areas of education, investors, financial institutions, entrepreneur/business owners, all levels of government) needs to know its role and responsibilities. "Poverty is reversed and marginalized zip codes are stabilized when the stakeholders of the free enterprise system fly in formation," Scheef says.

Curtis Hill has served as Attorney General of the State of Indiana and as chief prosecuting attorney in Elkhart County, Indiana. In his essay, "Marginalized Communities Didn't Just Happen," Hill says, "Our American values of freedom and equality can be realized through instilling conservative principles into our daily practices with our families, faith communities, and the work that we commit to in transforming our local communities."

Stephen Moore is a Senior Economist at FreedomWorks, a Distinguished Fellow at the Heritage Foundation, and a *Fox News* analyst. In his essay, "Social Security Robs Black Americans of Their Lifetime Savings—There's a Better Way," Moore says, "Few federal programs have had a more a deleterious effect on the economic advancement and wealth accumulation opportunities of minorities in America than Social Security." He further states, "Every year we wait to give workers the option of choosing an individual 401(k) type of account, the potential for building up ownership and wealth is further diminished."

Raheem Williams is a former CURE Senior Policy Analyst and a member of the Louisiana Advisory Board for the U.S. Commission on Civil Rights. His essay, "Social Security Reform and Market Alternatives," argues that Social Security "has arguably done nothing to reduce racial wealth inequities by forcing the limited funds that people of color have into a subpar retirement program." He says today's Social Security status quo "has not allowed low-income black workers to accumulate the savings necessary for a secure retirement or to provide their children with an equal opportunity for a more prosperous future."

The State of Black Progress highlights the interaction between public policies and community development. It aims to explore the latest scholarship into the character, shape, and tendencies of life in the United States for black Americans.

Given the right set of policies and incentives, including minimal interference by government, Americans of all races can make substantial progress. Where problems exist, and where progress is disappointing, invariably, government has been the problem, not the solution.

I

COUNTER-RECONSTRUCTION: A LINGERING INJUSTICE

W. B. Allen

The term "racial equality" falsely describes the human situation, inasmuch as there is no such thing as an equality of races. There is rather only one race—the human race—within which there is a moral equality of persons. The advent of Reconstruction at the end of the Civil War aimed to reinforce that central truth, a truth embedded in the realization that every human person is subject to the rigorous exactions of nature. Reconstruction began with the broad argument made by Senator Lyman Trumbull (Illinois) in favor of the Freedmen's Bureau Bill. In defense of that legislation, he reminded that:

> Before the Civil War the slave states had slave codes which denied to slaves certain legal rights which all of the free persons had. Slaves had no right to sue or be sued in court; they had no right to make or enforce contracts; they could not testify in any case in which a white person was a party; they could not obtain or own real or personal property; they did not have the same legal protection as free persons; and they were subject to punishments and offenses to which free persons were not subject. Even children, women, and aliens (with the exception of owning real estate) had these

rights, and in most of the slave states free Negroes had almost all of these rights.

The rights enumerated in Trumbull's bill were, in general, only denied to slaves. Trumbull's theory was that the amendment abolishing slavery gave Congress the right to pass laws eliminating state laws which denied rights common to all persons except slaves, who were considered "unpersons." His position was that those laws incidental to the status of a slave were "badges" or signs of slavery, and that *in abolishing slavery Congress could abolish laws made to keep persons unemancipated. This theory* becomes clearer when it is kept in mind that *a person* who cannot make a contract, such, for example, as a contract to work (without which he cannot get a job), who cannot buy or own property (such as food or clothing), who cannot own or lease real property (such as a home), and who cannot sue in court or otherwise obtain legal protection of his person or property, or recover his wages, *must necessarily be dependent on someone else for his food, clothing, and shelter. . . . The only other person so dependent is an infant, who is considered in law an unemancipated minor.*[1] (Emphasis added.)

The legislative process initiated with this argument carried through the Fourteenth and Fifteenth Amendments and several civil rights bills shepherded by the Republican majority in Congress. Throughout the entire process, stout resistance arose from the former Confederate states as well as from skeptical parties in the North. The resisters consisted of those who deliberately sought to preserve the subordinate status of American blacks (the freedmen in particular) and also others who were motivated by fear of racial intermixing. Throughout the process, the resisters never gave voice to an underlying theory in accord with which they sought to direct policy. But they had a clear tacit theory, a theory of Counter-Reconstruction.

Ulysses S. Grant ascended to the presidency in 1868 and took up the mantel of Reconstruction with a vigor worthy of Lincoln himself. Grant met at first with violent resistance throughout the unreconstructed South. He accomplished much in the face of that resistance to empower freed persons to assume the full status of citizenship in the United States. His accomplishments, however, proved elusive in the face of continuing resistance, and once the initial wave of the Ku Klux Klan and white supremacists was over-come, the resisters settled into patterns of civil, political, and legal subterfuge to accomplish the purposes sought through rampant violence initially. The resisters acquired the abetting support of wearied and cynical Northerners (Democrat and Republican) who wished to reintegrate the South politically without continuing to safeguard the rights of black citizens. Consequently, by the end of Grant's second term, Reconstruction was all but entombed though discernibly dead.

What replaced Reconstruction was no longer direct and immedi-ate violence (though very much of that would persist for another sixty years), but a deliberate attempt to construct a wardship relationship of blacks to the non-black majority, to be superintended at first by secessionists returning to political authority and, eventually, by the entire national political architecture. That wardship is what I have designated Counter-Reconstruction theory, and that is the theory of the dependent, unemancipated minor identified by Trumbull in the foregoing passage. It is reminiscent of the argument by John Stuart Mill, to the effect that peoples in their "nonage" could not be vested with rights of autonomy or self-government. As such, the theory goes beyond the legal terms of citizenship evinced by Trum-bull and embraces a general cultural perspective that holds peoples in their nonage to be excluded from the privileges and opportuni-ties of an advanced culture. Such theories remain present today in those forms of social science that argue concerning descendants of

Africa in particular that they bear the continuing influence of non-individualist, animist cultures and are not capable of performing and achieving in individualist, rational cultures such as those spawned in Europe. The aim (and theory) of Reconstruction had been directly opposed to this theory, and it is for that reason that we now term the response to Reconstruction "Counter-Reconstruction." For the latter theory proposes quite opposite terms of association for life in the community, terms in accord with which some are confined as wards of the others (hence, wards of the State).

To surface the theory of Counter-Reconstruction we must distinguish it from the practices of violent intimidation, disguised peonage, and deliberate segregation. All of those practices had racial animus at their foundations, but they were also part of a broader pattern of resistance to the goals of Reconstruction. Those broader goals are highlighted above in the passage from Trumbull's argument—namely, real emancipation and not just freedom from slavery, understood as elevation from the condition of infantile dependence. In other words, the theory of Reconstruction was to clear the path for the formerly enslaved to emerge into full, self-respecting independence and mature citizenship (real emancipation and not just liberation). The theory of Counter-Reconstruction sought to perpetuate the status of dependent wardship, a guardian class established in permanent authority to oversee "dependent cultural minors." In that respect, the Counter-Reconstruction theory aimed to create for American blacks a de facto status equivalent to the legally defined status of American Indians as "dependent sovereigns" (albeit without a fig-leaf pretense of sovereignty).

The theory of Counter-Reconstruction, accordingly, required the development of the infrastructure of civil polity (as opposed to terrorist intimidation) under the aegis of which the participation of American blacks in the civic and cultural life of the nation could be regulated by a guardian authority in which American blacks did not exercise a determining authority or even influence. (Note: This generalizes the denial of personal agency to individuals to the communal experience of an entire segment of society.) The first signs of that infrastructure emerged in the area of public education (the enforced segregation of public transit being an inessential dimension of the system precisely because, while it sought to exclude American blacks from valuable resources, it did not directly deprive them of means of self-advancement). In public education, on the other hand, the means were found to enforce differential standards of personal development, the point of which was to deprive American blacks of the necessary tools of self-advancement. And that system became especially meaningful when, in the guise of offering education, enforcement of Jim Crow restrictions led jurisdictions in the South especially to co-opt the indigenous educational efforts that had sprung up in the aftermath of slavery. The thousands of Rosenwald schools founded under the aegis of Booker T. Washington and Julius Rosenwald[2] were brought within the ambit of majority-directed public school systems, starved of resources, and developed as "reservations" in which American blacks were to receive an education short of emancipatory development (no "Greek and Latin"; no "silk and satin"). Under the guise of providing necessary resources, in other words, the architecture of a permanent wardship was created.

What this review means is that we have been mistaken to speak in terms of Reconstruction and Post-Reconstruction. Reconstruction failed precisely because the theory of Counter-Reconstruction prevailed. Now, more than 150 years later, the reality that shapes the "state of Black America" is the enduring presence of Counter-Reconstruction theory driving public policy. That is, the relationship between the larger culture and American blacks remains the relationship of guardian to ward. It has been disguised because of the intervention of "benign guardianship" rather than "malign guardianship." It has as a result seemed to be a different system,

one that has responded to legal challenges and social developments to overcome the most egregious injustices of the earlier
phase of Counter-Reconstruction. But that apparent change only
disguises the underlying reliance upon guardianship to govern
relations. That was signaled in *Brown v. Board of Education*,[3] when
Chief Justice Warren wrote that, respecting freedmen, "Education
of Negroes was almost non-existent, and practically all of the
race were illiterate." In proportion as that observation increasingly became the foundation of common opinion on the subject,
principled discussion of civil rights (not just liberation but full
emancipation) became less likely. Warren's observation was not
true in any meaningful or non-trivial sense. Nevertheless, it served
to perpetuate the myth of a backward people needing help to
catch up instead of the truth of a people being held back. That
is the perspective—the disadvantaged group perspective—that
ultimately infected all discussion of civil rights, even after the
designation of so-called "disadvantaged groups" had been extended
beyond American blacks. On that foundation, the guardian-ward
relationship was cemented in public policy. A concrete example
of this cultural edifice occurred once when I had a seat-mate on a
commuter flight in the Midwest. He was the president of a major
research university who, in the course of our conversation, referred
often and glibly to "our minorities." He was not conscious of the
possessive denotation and meant no offense. It was merely second
nature for him to think and speak so.

To understand the relevance of these observations to the current
state of black America, we can revisit the fundamental meaning of
civil rights as I have previously expressed it, and we begin with what
all mankind would likely recognize. Thus, the dictionary definition
of "civil rights" stands: "the rights that belong to *all individuals* in a
nation or community touching property, marriage, and the like." In
that definition the term "rights" may be further expanded to mean

"legitimate claims," following the definition of right as law—as "a claim or title or interest in anything whatever that is enforceable by law."[4] This definition applies with minimal distinction of regimes intruding and therefore without the host of recent complications in the United States that create the impression that civil rights have somewhat to do with pluralism or so-called "racial equality." Previously, the generic definition was thought to exhaust the meaning of the term in the United States. Witness James Wilson's pithy version of the early 1790s:

> Under civil government, one is entitled not only to those rights which are natural; he is entitled to others which are acquired. He is entitled to the honest administration of the government in general: he is entitled, in particular, to the impartial administration of justice. Those rights may be infringed; the infringements of them are crimes.[5]

When distinguishing between natural rights and acquired rights (the latter coming to be for the sake of the former), we readily discern a "fair play" formula that is well captured by an ethic of non-discrimination on the part of public officers. In the context of racial tensions in the United States, the ethic of non-discrimination came to assume particularly the form of prohibiting to public officers recourse to race in the performance of their duties.

The ideal of holding race irrelevant in the "administration of government in general" and in the "administration of justice in particular" eventually spawned parallel concerns respecting gender, religion, ethnic background, age, and physical or mental handicap. "Disadvantaged groups" had been extended beyond American blacks. This proliferation did not fully occur, however, until after the equal opportunity standard implicit but fundamental in the ethic of non-discrimination had been challenged by an implicit equality of results standard. That challenge appeared most openly and decisively in President Lyndon Johnson's commencement address at Howard University in 1965. In that speech, Johnson maintained that the equality of opportunity defended only the year before in the landmark "1964 Civil Rights Act" was not enough. Black people in particular, he maintained, required positive efforts on their behalf in order to enable their enjoyment of the rights otherwise enjoyed by *mature* citizens. In this, however, Johnson reinforced the Counter-Reconstruction theory. For the idea that equality was not enough rested upon the assumption that black people could not do what people in an advanced culture had done—namely, advance by dint of their own exertions.

Those dynamics were reinforced in *Bakke v. University of California*[6] by Justice Lewis F. Powell's introduction of the "diversity rationale," in which that Virginia patrician no less than the Texas redneck affirmed a continuing guardianship by the majority culture. And what appeared to be an opening chink in the underlying Counter-Reconstruction theory proved to be an illusion, when Justice Sandra Day O'Connor's 2003 *Grutter v. Bollinger* opinion mused about the possibility of a looming emancipation from dependent minority status "in 25 years." It was after that nod in the direction of the original goal of Reconstruction that a powerful stream of Diversity-Equity-Inclusion emerged to reinforce the claims of Counter-Reconstruction.

In light of the definition offered by James Wilson, one could properly inquire what more than an ethic of non-discrimination is needed for *any individual* to enjoy the honest administration of government in general and the impartial administration of justice in particular. That question would expose Johnson's premise of equality of results and also an unannounced redefining of civil rights to include an active role on the part of government to *produce and maintain* an equality of result (now termed "equity" and founded upon "positive discrimination"). That is by now far more nearly the operational definition of civil rights in the United States. It entails a permanent wardship for American blacks and a permanent guardianship for the larger society.

This radically untenable and unstable relationship further requires the guardian authority to reduce ever larger segments to the same wardship status, in order to maintain its continuing authority. For the evident differences in treatment between the wards and the non-wards will unavoidably feed resentments and social pressures for reform. Only when all citizens are wards can there be any hope for stability on the theory of Counter-Reconstruction.

We have abundant evidence of these dynamics in the relevant polling of opinions *and* attitudes that focus on the differential estimates of the value of American citizenship on the basis of race. The Pew Research Center routinely analyzes American trends with recourse to a randomly selected panel of participants who respond to surveys. In Pew's last published survey[7] on "Divisions in Americans' Views of Nation's Racial History—and How to Address it," one observes a stark divide between blacks and others along the most important dimension of analysis. By a factor of two to one black respondents "say that in order to ensure equality for all Americans regardless of their racial or ethnic backgrounds, most *major U. S. institutions need to be completely rebuilt* because they are fundamentally biased against some racial and ethnic groups." (Emphasis added.) That telling response is a measure of alienation from the majority culture. It would be a mistake, however, to think that it measures capacity to function in the majority culture. What it measures is an intelligent response to the manifest evidence that the majority culture propagates dependence that can only be seen as "disadvantage." That necessarily means that no matter what material advances occur, the persistent cultural relationship will always convey disadvantage.

Moreover, this measure of alienation explains the phenomenon of a deficient expression of patriotism in black communities. It would be surprising if people who believed that the entire civil polity needs to be refounded were to express patriotic attachment to the existing arrangement. The sense that white people hold advantage over others because of their race emerges from the conflation of their putative majority status with their race. In fact, however, the advantages that accrue derive not from the prejudice of race but from the effects of the theory—Counter-Reconstruction theory—on which civil relations are founded. This is a difficult relationship to disentangle, but a great deal depends upon doing so. For this is not a mere subtlety. To believe that the manifest differences that exist derive from the prejudice of race diverts attention from the necessary reform that is required—namely, the elimination of the guardian-ward relationship.

That reality would be obvious if we consistently recalled how present usage derived from the 1936 *Carolene Products* footnote 4, which identified "discrete and insular minorities" who were unable to benefit from the ordinary operations of republican government.[8] What that argument meant derived from the heart of Counter-Reconstruction theory—namely, cultural deficiency. On the strength of that argument, we generated the notion of "protected classes," that is, the status of dependent minority for identified segments of the society. The "protected classes" are the wards of the guardians who, themselves, operate on the basis of republican principles of government.

The same line of analysis explains why some respondents to the Pew survey say that "enough has been done" to address problems of inequality in the society. The perspective from which they assess the situation is one that conflates their assumed emancipated status with the formal provision of legal protections, and they do not observe that the legal protections embed a permanent subjection to guardianship. Increasingly, however, such respondents in other terms are responding to populist appeals for restraining governmental direction and mandates in their own lives. But they do not connect the burgeoning regulation of their lives with the dynamics of sustaining a guardian society, which grow entirely out of Counter-Reconstruction theory.

Eventually, if matters continue in their present train, they will come to see that they are directly imperiled by the alienating effect of the guardian society on the wards of society. While non-blacks in some measure perceive increasing emphasis on the history of slavery and race as a danger to the country, they respond in fact not to the effect of historical attention but to the reality of contemporary dynamics of social organization. To call this "systemic racism" is false and misleading. While it gives free play to racist formulations, its systemic character is the logic of a guardian-ward relationship that is color-blind and will ultimately encompass all without respect to race. That is the most compelling reason that I have strenuously argued that the most urgent need in this society today is for a surge in black patriotism, which can lead the way out of the cul-de-sac created by Counter-Reconstruction policy. Of course, such a development would depend upon an almost supererogatory transcendence of present appearances by American blacks in order to grasp and advance a healing affect.

For years now, the present state of affairs has been projected and anticipated with worry by insightful observers. I, too, on numerous occasions have sought to post monitory alerts to the danger ahead. It would be fair to say that we have now arrived at the foreboding moment. That should lead us to inquire whether recourse to any of numberless positive proposals for reform can yet avail.

One needs a very special exception to write race-regarding-, gender-regarding-, and sexual-orientation-regarding rules, and that exception is a legal atmosphere created by the history of adjudication of the Fourteenth Amendment that created protected groups in society—not, I want to be clear, protected individuals, but protected groups. One earns title to these protections only to the degree that one creeps within the shadow of the protected group.

This is where the question of the loss of confidence in American liberty arises, for American liberty is predicated upon assuring protection to individuals. The original, multicultural impulse was designed to say that we could, on the strength of protecting individual liberty, bring to the fore a flourishing of various cultures in the United States. Nathan Glazer wrote in *The New Republic* over three decades ago an essay on multiculturalism—a defense of multiculturalism harkening back to an older view—in which he pointed out, "Surely there is no objection to broadening the horizon of our academic curricula. That, in addition to all things else, would include material representative of African [blacks] and, indeed, of the experience of American blacks; that would add material indicative of the experience of women; that would add material indicative of the experience of Hispanics: that would add material indicative of the experiences even of homosexuals—if one wants to insist upon segregating homosexuals as a group."

No objection to that. This is wholly compatible with the idea of a university education. But, of course, Nathan Glazer himself, responding at the time to an attack on a recent curricular reform in the State of New York, went beyond that verb we have used repeatedly, "add." For now, the prevailing wisdom is: substitute, not add. The thought is that there has been previously a predominant white, European, male-oriented view of the world, which, in its principles, oppresses people whose backgrounds and origins are not white, European, and male. And how does it improve the white, European male's point of view by adding to it? One can only improve it by replacing it, as the theory goes.

The reason one can only improve it by replacing it is straightfor-wardly articulated: namely, cultural views are mutually exclusive. Cultural backgrounds are mutually exclusive. Ethnic heritages are mutually exclusive. There is not, as the leading thinkers in the move-ment of deconstruction argued, a notion of common humanity. In fact, the very notion of humanity is an instrument of oppression used to marginalize those not defined or described as fitting the stereotypical characteristics of what is called humanity. The only way to overcome the marginalizing impact of reason, the reason in accordance with which the notion came to prevail in the Western World, is to displace it altogether. So, now we talk of various, centric curricula: Euro-centric, Afro-centric, Hispano-centric, etc.—all mutually exclusive.

This is a new era. When, therefore, we speak of racism on cam-pus,[9] we must learn to speak correctly. What we're really talking about is the reemergence of ethnocentrism as a moral horizon with a vengeance and as the only legitimate reference to humanity. We no longer admit references to common humanity as prevailing moral authority. As a result, we elide any notion of moral equality descending from human nature. Hence, the central claim of the Declaration of Independence must be rejected in order to sustain this perspective.

The various regulations and provisions, therefore, which seek to punish people for infelicitous comments are based on that insight. It is not whether people know that they do harm or not, it is whether what they do, knowingly or not, causes harm to an alien universe, an alien perspective; that is the concern of this movement. As long as universities are in the grips—I paraphrase a passage from Eugene Genovese's essay, "Heresy Yes, Sensitivity No"—as long as universities are in the grips of administrators, faculty, and others who make decisions on the basis of absolute oppositions of culture, absolute differences, and not on the basis of common humanity, racism on campus will grow. And that observation now applies to the entire landscape of the guardian class—not only universities but also corporations, military branches, and governmental agencies. The conquest of Counter-Reconstruction theory is complete.

It is a dubious claim that the task of repairing the historical injuries of slavery and discrimination more than justifies burdening innocent persons, even if they did (and by no means did all) profit from the past. Proponents of this view often try to reduce it to the idea of a sacrifice in the interest of the common good—or a greater good—the same, say, as if someone had to accept the unpleasant fate of a noisy roadway situated next to the home that she had, perhaps, purchased for its quiet. Immediately, of course, the examples do not differ at all, so long as a citizen were no less eligible for the one sacrifice as the other. But that condition cannot be satisfied. For, while all persons may be liable, without regard to race, to suffer the inconvenience of the roadway, only some, designated by race, must suffer the unfairness of racial preferences.[10]

These excuses for racial injustice would be more patently clear if we placed them in juxtaposition with policies and practices everyone experiences and understands. But what is better understood than the progressive income tax? American society has accepted that people differently situated will pay taxes in different ratios, hence unequally. This is deemed in the common interest and thought by most to be fair. The reason, in brief, is that the distinction producing different treatment under the law is adventitious rather than invidious—it could theoretically happen to anyone. Thus, they who are situated so as to pay more make a sacrifice for the common good.

Suppose, however, that the progressive tax scale were calculated rather by race than by level of income—call it the affirmative action tax. Historically, the differences would be statistically imperceptible. Whether one said white folk or rich folk had to pay more, one would still be collecting largely from the same people. Thus, the same practical result would follow. Does the same moral result follow? Does it not matter that at least some of the white folk are actually poor, while at least some of the black folk are actually rich? A progressive tax based on actual income affects people equally, as to race, while the other is unequal and unfair. The question is not whether but how sacrifices are made in the common interest. Under a "jurisprudence of minorities" sacrifices are made unevenly—and based on invidious distinctions, which deny by imputation the existence of a common good.

A series of court decisions three decades ago prefigured the nature of the dilemma. In *Richmond v. Croson*, the majority maintained the legitimacy of set-asides. Justice O'Connor expressed the problem squarely: "we confront once again the tension between the 14th Amendment's guarantee of equal treatment [under law] to all citizens, and the use of race-based measures to ameliorate the effects of past discrimination on . . . minority groups in our society."[11] O'Connor resolved that tension in favor of policy instead of principle, while I insist that policies without firm principles are merely arbitrary.

O'Connor raised, without settling, the question of the fate of the ethic of non-discrimination. Justice Kennedy, in *Patterson v. McLean Credit Union*, stepped right through that open door, albeit cautiously. He introduced in a key role in a majority opinion of the Supreme Court for the very first time the language from Justice Harlan's 1896 dissent in the "separate but equal" case. "The law regards man as man and takes no account of his color when his civil rights as guaranteed by the supreme law of the land are involved."[12]

Justice Kennedy's caution was shown by his stopping one phrase short of the controverted language, the "Constitution is color-blind." His boldness shone, however, in his willingness to use the citation the Court has shied away from for two generations. He indicated thereby a judgment that there existed a firm national policy and sense of justice that supports prohibiting racial segregation and discrimination. On that basis, the Court upheld *Runyon v. McCrary.* (If the Court had not unwisely limited the ruling too severely, it would have served as a beachhead for color-blindness in our laws. Instead, we got new legislation that moved us away from rather than toward that goal.)

Some of Justice Kennedy's argument on behalf of color-blindness, however, was rather wish than reality. There was no clear consensus that "race-based measures" are no less discriminatory than old Jim Crow. Accordingly, there remained a need to build the consensus for which Justice Kennedy longed, and to do so in a manner that could resolve positively Justice O'Connor's tension.

A proper policy goal would be to eliminate once and for all routine references to race and gender in surveys, plans, projections, and other official accounts of private and public workforces—wherever the logic of the profession itself does not impose such categorizations. The fact that such usage is pervasive and deeply rooted describes the nature of the task we face—the first thing that must fall, accordingly, is the very concept of group representation or, more precisely, "protected groups." All Americans must be protected by freedom, or, in the end, none will be.

Summarizing, based on a principled approach, I have called for several legislative or judicial initiatives since 1987. In summary, these reforms are:

1. Complete the reaffirmation that the Constitution is color-blind. This is the work of the Court and well within the reach of the Court's resources.[13] At a stroke this would deprive Congress of the resort to race and thus foster greater creativity in dealing with questions of civil rights.
2. Complete the elaboration of the nexus between economic liberty and civil rights, making the right of contract a more

robust source of protection. This, too, falls initially to the Court to effect.[14]

3. Extend recourse to tortious litigation as the principal means to defend individuals against the impermissible deprivation of legitimate powers and privileges, and, therefore,

4. Replace legislated obstacles to litigation with recognition of the principle that individual injuries, whatever other reparatives may be encouraged, ought always to be compensable by means of such litigation. Congress alone can accomplish these tasks.

5. Re-codify the jerry-rigged structure of civil rights laws with a coherent, self-consistent code, enunciating principles by which any citizen may discover his salvation in the protections of the law. This falls no less to Congress than the foregoing.

Such reforms as these are straightforward. Nevertheless, it is safe to say that they are unlikely to be accomplished without some degree of reassessment of our general approach to civil rights.

For example, in 1988 Congress enacted the Fair Housing Act Amendments, in which they gave increased space to elements of the third and fourth proposals above. Congress, though, simply added them onto new administrative obstacles, including a new layer of administrative judges. Congress also obscured the definition of an injury (i.e., denial of contract) by seeking to specify classes of injuries to deal with the non-accommodation of the handicapped. On balance, therefore, the 1988 Act was not an advance.

Two arguments frequently oppose reliance upon tortious processes as the preferred response to impermissible discrimination. The first argument asserts the obstacle of excessive costs both to initiate litigation and, more importantly, in the realm of prospective awards or settlements. This argument is spurious and stands rather as an expression of temporizing hesitance than of logical propriety. The second argument warns that dependence on compensatory and punitive damages to deter discrimination will surely inspire employers or contractors to rely on the practice (as opposed to a legislated policy) of racial or gender preferences as the surest defense against the risks of litigation and liability. This argument is serious and by no means disposed of by mere logical analysis. Nevertheless, its chief error lies in its statement of the terms of analysis.

The cost argument separates into one argument about the cost of litigation for plaintiffs (who are supposedly too poor to pursue their cases) and another argument about so-called social costs.

Respecting the former argument, it is manifest that the availability of adequate counsel is directly dependent on the prospects for real financial gain in this realm no less than in the realm of personal injury litigation. The cost of initiating litigation, therefore, is a barrier only to frivolous litigation. As it turns out, however, in order to make the litigation worthwhile for plaintiffs, it is necessary greatly to increase the liability exposure of defendants. Just as cost explosions in other of areas liability coverage have traumatized the United States, it is feared that a like result will occur in discrimination cases. It is often maintained that society could not bear the cost of large settlements in discrimination cases.

In 1985, I participated in a conference on affirmative action, where I posed the following question to an author of the "1964 Civil Rights Act": "Just why did you design the Act in such a way as to discourage private litigation with attendant compensatory and punitive damages?" The response was curt but complete: "Are you kidding? That would bankrupt the society!" I maintained then, and I do so no less now, that I could not comprehend how a transfer of whatever magnitude between two members of a single society could bankrupt that same society. My interlocutor's premise must rather have been that the perpetrators of discrimination and the victims of discrimination in fact constituted two distinct societies. That is, he worked on the basis of Counter-Reconstruction theory. Be that as it may, the social cost argument against reliance upon private tortious litigation with large awards or settlements as a deterrent to discrimination is plainly spurious.[15]

What, then, must one make of the propensity of likely defendants in such private litigation to shield themselves from exposure through the practice of racial preferences? This would unfortunately be a necessary consequence of such an approach, as predictable as the raising of automobile insurance rates when states impose mandatory insurance laws, provided there were any available shield adapted to the purpose. The assumption that employers or contractors could hire black people by preference and thus shield themselves, for example, is however entirely undermined by the false premise that only "minorities and women" should be protected by these legal procedures. The moment one provides, however, against racial or gender discrimination altogether, there is in fact *no such preference* that can survive—for what is a racial or gender preference, after all, but implementation of an impermissible discrimination? In other words, abandoning the theory of protected groups (guardian-ward relations) would necessarily undermine slighting non-blacks or males, where non-blacks or males had the same access to these legal procedures as all other folk.[16]

At all events, in proportion as a society relies upon tortious litigation to deter impermissible discriminations, and despite any possible private schemes of preference that evolve, to that degree it will be found unnecessary to retain vast and costly administrative structures to supervise the integration of society. Further, legislated policies of affirmative action would be contraindicated (as under-cutting, deliberately perhaps, peoples' opportunities to vindicate their own claims).

One America for All Americans

There is a different course heretofore eschewed; it may be summed up rapidly. The tone was set in an old study that expressly recognized that the decision in *Croson*,[17] far from dismantling set-asides, only limited the licenses of states and municipalities to impose them.[18] The point, they held, is that the means themselves neither produce the desired end nor are just. "The notion that it is an outcome that is either just or unjust, rather than an individual's actions," they wrote, "leads to conclusions that contradict many of our common notions of justice. For example, the rule seems to say that we may discriminate against a black person yesterday, pay a different black person for the injury today, and call it even. Under this principle, one black person is pretty much the same as another."[19] The point is precisely to move our polity toward the day when "one black, one woman, one minority" is not pretty much the same as another. When people see only in black and white, they miss all the color in the world. While it would exaggerate the power of language to insist that only the correct use of language can inform solutions to the dynamic social problems that we address, it would be a mistake to underestimate the importance of getting the language right.

The problem of distinguishing when our obligations to others ought to shape the "permissions" of public policy and when public policy may leave a wide sphere of discretion for decisions or actions that affect others constitutes the entire foundation for differences of opinion over diversity and inclusiveness. The debate, however, narrows significantly when we discuss what public bodies or agencies (that is, our common government) may do. Persons who act in the name of the state exercise less liberty than ordinary citizens because of the sufficient constraints that derive from the relationship between the citizens and their "limited government."

The commitment to equal rights enshrines equality as the principle of public treatment of all persons without respect to race, gender, ethnicity, religion, or national origin. It clearly establishes a positive command of inclusiveness. That means that public bodies or agencies may be monitored in their performances to assure that their policies and practices are consistent with the promise of equality.[20]

Changing Policies and Practices

Policies that separate out rather than integrate community members (such as targeted admission, contracting, or appointment procedures and provision for interest or constituency representation at the expense of exposure to mission-related professional challenge) ought to be abandoned and replaced by practices that work hand-in-glove with self-motivation to profit from a breadth of opportunity consistently offered and made highly visible. In this area we must be excruciatingly precise.

An admissions, contracting, or appointment policy that rewards the exertions of applicants (such as first come, first served or lowest bid) is worth infinitely more than a procedure that renders applicants dependent upon the discretionary authority of faceless gnomes. But such a policy or practice cannot be understood as passive; it requires the greatest exertion and redirection of budget by an order of magnitude toward outreach in order to reinforce equality of opportunity in our society. The payoff, however, is greater still, since it will far more surely build a single community of self-respecting, emancipated individuals.

We struggle today with what was once called political correctness and is now known as "wokeness" in large measure because a subtle transition has occurred. Namely, there has been a transition from emphasizing cultural plurality, in which we honestly believed it was possible for us mutually to share one another's backgrounds, mutually to be enriched by various heritages, mutually advanced, therefore, toward a conception of common humanity—that is what we thought.[21]

But we made a transition from that to emphasizing, instead, not common humanity, but cultural marginality. At every pen stroke, work devoted to proving the argument of cultural marginality drives a wedge into the argument in favor of plurality. The one argument is the enemy of the other. Ultimately, the diversity that succeeded multiculturalism destroyed multiculturalism.

To state it in political terms, the argument in favor of diversity is the enemy of the notion of a common heritage in the United States as well as among all citizens of the United States. The diversity argument has been so thoroughly absorbed that Barbara Herrnstein Smith wrote—without apparent irony or regret—in response to E. D. Hirsch's proposal to develop the "cultural literacy" of American youth, that:

> There is, however, no single, comprehensive macro culture in which all or even most of the citizens of this nation actually participate, no numerically preponderant majority culture in relation to which any or all of the others are 'minority' cultures, and no culture that, in Hirsch's term, 'transcends' any or all other cultures.

When, therefore, we speak of diversity, what we're really talking about is the reemergence with a vengeance of ethnocentrism as a moral horizon and as the only legitimate reference to humanity. We no longer admit references to common humanity as prevailing moral authority. And as a consequence, racial conflict and separatism.

Recovering Fairness

We began this chapter by observing that the critical issue was the correct application of terms of association among the members of any harmonious community. We close by observing that unless we can navigate the transition from diversity to inclusion, our social conversation will continue to be tortured by discussions of race and gender relations and the embedded practice of affirmative action preferences even when otherwise legally and constitutionally impermissible.

The controlling principles of this presentation, and our future hopes, are to mine our policies and practices for conscious awareness of "what persons owe to others." That is the fruit we reap when we treat persons as ends rather than as means. Today, the fundamental principle of equality that amplifies the American commitment to self-government most of all highlights the imperative of inclusiveness as an alternative to preferences. Inclusiveness and not diversity reflects the standard of fairness that underscores and promises the benefits that properly accrue to those most directly affected by public policies and practices.

2

BREAD INTO STONES

Janice Rogers Brown[1]

The American Founders thought they had caught lightning in a bottle. They were right. Still, they could not invent quite the future they envisioned. Perhaps they were far too hopeful. Freedom only flickers now and then. Consider what is probably "the most famous single sentence ever written in the Western Hemisphere," according to the late Leszek Kolakowski: "'We hold these truths to be self-evident, that all men are created equal, that they are endowed by their Creator with certain unalienable rights, that among these are Life, Liberty, and the Pursuit of Happiness.'"[2] But as Kolakowski goes on to say, "what seemed self-evident [at the Founding] would appear either patently false or meaningless and superstitious" to most of the great men who keep trying to "shap[e] our political imagination."[3]

The Founders' Constitution

Jefferson described the Declaration of Independence as reflecting "the harmonizing sentiments of the day, whether expressed in conversation, in letters, printed essays, or in the writings of Aristotle, Cicero, Locke" and other thinkers within the Aristotelian tradition.[4] The Declaration was not designed to "find out new principles, or new arguments, or say things which had never been said before; but to place before mankind the common sense of the subject, in terms so plain and firm as to command their assent."[5] In other words, the American Mind recognized the deep connection between the natural world and political organization; that the laws of nature rendered God-given rights and consent-based government "self-evident" truths.

The Founding generation had a deep understanding of the way the axioms and first principles of moral reasoning were integral to the telos that defined American constitutionalism. The drafters of our constitutional documents assumed that any good regime must respect the nature of the creature to be governed. Man was a creature of the logos, whose rational nature, created by the God of the logos, was guided by the moral law engraved on every heart. The mistake of the French revolutionaries, in John Adams's view, was not contempt for tradition, it was contempt for man.[6] Natural rights "rightly understood" were a framework for governance that respected man's immutable nature. The distinctive achievement of the American Revolution was the establishment of the Constitution "as a formal instrument or code giving existence to government and prescribing and limiting the exercise of its powers."[7]

In those early days, however, not everyone loved the governmental blueprint adopted virtually unanimously by the constitutional convention. The Anti-Federalists took issue with several aspects of the Constitution. Writing as Brutus, New York judge Robert Yates warned that the independent and unaccountable judiciary created by the Constitution would lead inevitably to judicial supremacy. Brutus worried the judiciary would have the power to resolve all questions of constitutional interpretation—not just the meaning of the words but "according to the reasoning spirit of it."[8] The core of Brutus's critique was his dismay that the Constitution's commitment to judicial independence meant judges would be limited and constrained only by their sense of honor and judicial duty. Noting there would be no power above them; no authority that could remove them for ordinary malfeasance as they were placed outside legislative control, he predicted: "Men placed in this situation will generally soon feel themselves independent of heaven itself."[9]

The Federalists countered with a plea of necessity. Besides, Hamilton explained, having neither the purse nor the sword, the judiciary was clearly "the least dangerous branch." Time has proved this notion culpably naive. Hamilton was too optimistic and may have been foolish to trust the virtue of men so completely. But parchment cannot compel more. Time has validated Brutus's skepticism, but he could not have predicted that whether judges abused the spirit of the Constitution or refused to acknowledge it, the result might be equally harmful to the body politic.

Brutus's doubts notwithstanding, the American Constitution was greeted with approbation by most of the civilized world. The Declaration's stirring words that "all men are created equal" and that the only just government was "government by consent" were a model celebrated and eagerly emulated by nascent democracies. The Founders themselves were enormously proud of their achievement. John Adams confided to his diary in 1765, that he always considered "the settlement of America with reverence and wonder as the opening of a grand scene and design in providence for the illumination of the ignorant and the emancipation of the slavish part of mankind all over the world." George Washington's June 1783 Circular Letter to the States declared:

> The foundation of our Empire was not laid in the gloomy age of Ignorance and Superstition, but at an Epoch when the rights of mankind were better understood and more clearly defined, than at any former period, the researches of the human mind, after social happiness, have been carried to a great extent, the

Treasures of knowledge, acquired by the labors of Philosophers, Sages and Legislatures, through a long succession of years, are laid open for use, and their collected wisdom may be happily applied in the Establishment of our forms of Government;...above all, the pure and benign light of Revelation, [has] had ameliorating influence on mankind and increased the blessings of Society. At this auspicious period, the United States came into existence as a Nation, and if their Citizens should not be completely free and happy, the fault will be entirely their own.[10]

John Quincy Adams, speaking at the Constitutional Jubilee (fifty years after its ratification), urged Americans to keep the principles of the Declaration of Independence and the Constitution in their hearts and souls; to remember the day of its ratification with the same reverence and profound thanksgiving the Israelites exhibited in recalling their escape from bondage in Egypt. Americans should, he said, "bind [the principles of the founding documents] for signs upon [their] hands,...—teach them to your children...write them upon the doorplates of your houses, and upon your gates—cling to them as to the issues of life..."

It is possible to go on at length quoting the Constitution's framers in this vein. Indeed, the Constitution's connection to natural rights and natural law was forthrightly acknowledged for more than 150 years. On the eve of the Civil War, when President Lincoln lamented that we might "meanly lose or nobly save the last, best hope of earth," he was speaking of the American notion of human freedom. But why would this be so? In Lincoln's view, constitutional principles—"conceived in liberty and dedicated to the proposition that all men are created equal"—were a sacrosanct inheritance we were obligated to preserve.[11]

It is accurate to say that American political thought subsequent to Lincoln, for the most part, undermined Lincoln's (and the Founders') conception of American constitutionalism and the philosophical proposition on which it rests. After the Civil War, the Court was not content to chip away at the constitutional foundations. Where the freedmen were concerned, the Court went after the remedies fashioned by the radical Republican legislators with steam drill and blasting caps.

The Souls of Black Folks and the Founders' Constitution

For black people in America, the stirring words of the Declaration always promised more than they delivered. Nevertheless, for a very long time, and despite decades of disappointment, black people did all in their power to cash the "promissory note" tendered by America's founding documents. The Constitution was not, as critics then and now assert, a pro-slavery document; it was a pragmatic outline of governing principles. A decade before a bloody Civil War would be fought to prove the Constitution's anti-slavery bona fides, Frederick Douglass defended it as "a GLORIOUS LIBERTY DOCUMENT" containing "principles and purposes, entirely hostile to the existence of slavery."[12] Douglass lived to see slavery abolished, but the dream of full citizenship never became a reality in his lifetime.

Although courts in free states regularly complied with the intrusive requirements of the Fugitive Slave Act, slaves and free black people could take some solace in the fact that the federal courts' rigorous enforcement of the Act as a kind of vigilante license with minimal protections for an alleged slave was somewhat offset by the personal liberty laws enacted in Northern states to "strike some balance between the rights of slaveholders and the rights of free Negroes" threatened by the Act's loose evidentiary requirements and the lack of due process.[13] The possibility existed that a slave who resided in a free state might be deemed a free man.

However, even these small mercies were nullified by Justice Roger Taney's infamous *Dred Scott* decision.[14]

The perspectives of three men—Thaddeus Stevens, Frederick Douglass, and John Marshall Harlan—who were closely acquainted with the Founding era, acute observers of the political scene, and who had a front row seat for the political shenanigans that precipitated the Civil War and the proxy wars that troubled the nation's peace thereafter, illuminate and indict the wayward course of Supreme Court jurisprudence during this critical period. A fourth, Abraham Lincoln, perhaps the best natural law lawyer of the nineteenth century, did not live to experience the attempt to reconstruct the shattered union. He did articulate, with an unmatched homespun brilliance, why the Founders' universal insight about human equality provided the unique, irreplaceable basis for self-government, "the last, best hope of earth."

In *Dred Scott*, Chief Justice Taney went out of his way to declare that neither Scott, nor any other person of African descent, whether slave or free, could be a citizen of the nation or any state. Moreover, Scott did not gain his freedom when he was taken into free territory by his owner because Congress lacked the power to prohibit slavery in the territories.[15]

Dred Scott did not—as the Court and President Buchanan seemed to think it might—settle the slavery question. Mr. Lincoln never accepted the notion that human beings could be chattel. "Slavery," he said, "is founded in the selfishness of man's nature—opposition to it in his love of justice."[16] Lincoln rejected the reasoning of the *Dred Scott* decision "as a political rule"[17] and pledged to work to overturn it. In that same speech, Abraham Lincoln identified the notion of human equality at the philosophical core of American constitutionalism: "I think the authors of that notable instrument [the Declaration of Independence] intended to include all men, but they did not intend

to declare all men equal in all respects. They did not mean to
say all were equal in color, size, intellect, moral developments,
or social capacity. They defined with tolerable distinctness, in
what respects they did consider all men created equal—equal
in 'certain inalienable rights, among which are life, liberty and
the pursuit of happiness.'" The differences among men were
less "fundamental than the natural equality of human beings
qua human beings, which gives rise to their rights.[18] As Lincoln
acknowledged on the way to his first inaugural: [He] "never
had a feeling politically that did not spring from the sentiments
embodied in the Declaration of Independence."[19] Even before
he became president, Lincoln urged his countrymen to re-adopt
the Declaration and the policies and practices that "harmonize
with it" because in doing so "we shall not only save the Union;
but we shall have so saved it, as to make, and keep it, forever,
worthy of the saving."[20]

The Radicals in Congress were often impatient with Lincoln's
cautious, statesman-like weighing of alternatives. The Republicans
were a relatively new party. Lincoln's election was the alleged catalyst for the South's move into active rebellion. The prosecution of
the war and its complicated aftermath forced Mr. Lincoln and the
Radical Republicans into the role of reluctant and distrustful allies.
One of those skeptical allies was Thaddeus Stevens.

Stevens was a complex and enigmatic figure—the radical Republican most viciously reviled as the scourge of the South. Stevens,
who along with Charles Sumner, became the main architect of
Southern Reconstruction after the war, was born with a club foot.
His lameness, his legion of enemies insinuated, was "hell's seal of
deformity," the mark of a demon in human form. Perhaps, because
he was branded an outcast from an early age, he felt more empathy
for others who were branded because they were different. He was
shackled by his lameness as slaves were shackled by color and caste

as well as iron; Stevens, though, never sang in his chains. He was master of a powerful invective that could be withering to friend and foe alike.

Stevens's criticism of *Dred Scott* and the justices that signed on to Taney's opinion was a great deal less circumspect than Lincoln's. Stevens accused Taney of writing a false chapter into the country's history to sustain his partisan views; damaging the reputation of the founding generation by perverting their "immortal words" to suggest that the authors of the Declaration of Independence "while inaugurating a new and startling epoch in the science of govern-ment—an epoch of liberty and equality—were preparing a system which denied that a whole race of God's immortal creatures" had any rights a white man was bound to respect. Taney and six other justices "had promulgated a doctrine more infamous than the divine right of kings—the divine right of color."[21]

Lincoln was a strict constitutionalist who was always anti-slavery but not an abolitionist. In fact, as a senator, he tried to dampen the ardor of the abolitionists. Senator Lincoln cautioned against too great a zeal in doing good. An imprudent devotion to a perfect society fails to accommodate the opinions, beliefs, and prejudices of the community. The rule of the self-righteous is an acute problem for self-government. Though Lincoln agreed with the abolitionist cause, he co-sponsored a resolution that strongly condemned slavery but noted that the "promulgation of abolition doctrines tend[ed] rather to increase than to abate its evils."[22]

In contrast, Stevens was an abolitionist decades before abolition-ists had a party. His most insightful biographer describes him as "a humanitarian lacking in humanity; a man of boundless charities and vindictive hates; a Calvinist convinced that all men are vile who nevertheless cherished a vision of the Promised Land where all men should be equal before the law."[23]

In 1858, Lincoln had expressed little confidence in the Negroes' capacity for citizenship. He did not advocate social or political equality between the races, declaring he was "not in favor of making voters or jurors of negroes" and believed physical differences would "forever forbid the two races living together" on terms of equality.[24] As president, his evolution on these questions was rapid. He was impressed by his firsthand acquaintance with articulate groups of black petitioners and "even by the fighting record of the Negro soldier."[25] When a portion of Louisiana was organized with a loyal Union government, Lincoln diffidently suggested to the newly elected governor that the elective franchise might include some of the "very intelligent colored people," especially "those who have fought gallantly in our ranks." He added: "They would probably help, in some trying time to come, to keep the jewel of liberty within the family of freedom."[26] Shortly before his death, President Lincoln openly advocated Negro suffrage for this group and in private correspondence suggested he was "seriously considering universal suffrage." The Radical Republicans gave him only grudging credit. As Wendell Phillips put it: If Lincoln was able to grow, "it is because we have watered him."

Despite years of posturing and threats by Southern congressmen, bragging of their willingness to "shatter the republic from turret to foundation stone" to preserve slavery, the North seemed oddly unprepared for the rupture when it came. Even while forts, arsenals, customs houses, and navy yards fell into the hands of the secessionists, Northern politicians still thought concession, humiliation, and compromise might prevent war; others advocated disunion, arguing that peace would be better than coercion. Horace Greeley advised the South to "depart in peace." After Lincoln was inaugurated and confirmed his determination to prosecute the war vigorously, confusion still reigned. Were the wayward states still part of the Union and whose citizens were protected by the Constitution? Were they enemy combatants, subject only to the laws of war? Was the object of the war to preserve the Union or to eliminate slavery? Were Union generals authorized to make whatever provisions they wished for the fugitive slaves that swelled the ranks of the Union Army? Was compensation to be paid to the rebels for any slaves emancipated? Could the fee and title of the rebel landholders be confiscated? When the war ended, many of these questions had not been answered.

Lincoln had issued the Emancipation Proclamation, but it left large sections of the slave territory untouched. The president began seeking a constitutional amendment abolishing slavery in December 1862, but Democrats defeated several attempts, still hoping for a negotiated peace "irrespective of the fate of the Negro,"[27] and despite Lincoln's repeated urgings, the Thirteenth Amendment was not passed until January 13, 1865. Lincoln praised the amendment as a "great moral victory," and deemed it "the central act of [his] administration" and "the great event of the nineteenth century."

President Lincoln did not live to see the Thirteenth Amendment ratified or the passage of the Fourteenth Amendment. He was succeeded by Andrew Johnson, a man who had no sympathy for the black race. Johnson's hostility to even the most moderate Reconstruction measures and his conciliatory attitude toward the rebels strengthened the South's resistance to Reconstruction. In May 1865, President Johnson issued a Proclamation of Amnesty, pardoning most former Confederates and permitting them to recover any of their lands which had been confiscated or occupied.[28]

It was left to Congress to finish the task of emancipation. Thaddeus Stevens's clear objectives were anathema to rebellious Southerners and conservative Democrats. He wanted the freedmen to have liberty, the ballot, free schools, and the forty acres and a mule many had been promised.[29] The latter promise Congressman Stevens would have kept by confiscating the property of the South's agrarian aristocracy and making it available to the newly freed slaves.

Stevens thought it would be best to provide for economic survival first, then education, and finally—after a delay of several years—

the right to vote. Still, he recognized the legitimacy of Frederick Douglass's complaint that the "schoolhouse door would never open unless the Negro had the ballot." Douglass was quick to point out the obvious double standard. The ignorance that barred the black man from voting presented no impediment to the illiterate white man.

Douglass requested only that "whatever rule the [reconstruction governments] adopted, whether of intelligence or wealth, as a condition of voting" be applied equally.[30]

Dred Scott was ever considered a ghastly error which helped to kindle the conflagration that engulfed the nation a few years later, but it was only the end of a series of unconscionable compromises and the beginning of an epoch of judicial infamies. It gave black men—whether slave or free—good reason to dread the pronouncements of the Supreme Court. And it sealed the determination of the post–Civil War Congress not to rely on the "dogmas of [the]Court upon any question touching the rights of humanity."

The preference for action by Congress instead of the courts is strongly manifested by the Reconstruction Amendments. The Radicals "did not trust the judiciary in general and the Supreme Court in particular."[31] Indeed, *Dred Scott* had been so bitterly etched into abolitionist memory that Senator Sumner even sought to bar the customary memorial placement of Chief Justice Taney's bust in the Supreme Court Chamber. Taney was an object of obloquy whose name, the senator insisted, should be "hooted down in the pages of history." Thaddeus Stevens went further, damning the late chief justice to everlasting infamy and "everlasting fire."[32] Alas, the dawn of the new birth of freedom did very little to lift the heavy burden of centuries of bondage from black people. The Reconstruction Congress enacted three broad constitutional amendments— abolishing slavery, declaring birthright citizenship for slaves and their descendants, and prohibiting racial discrimination in voting rights. However, beginning with the *Slaughterhouse* case in

1873[33] and continuing well into the twentieth century, the Court proceeded to nullify most of the benefits the Civil War Amendments had intended to confer on the freedmen and, with the end of Reconstruction, did more than any other federal institution to snatch defeat from the jaws of victory. Although the South had lost the Civil War, the Court made sure "it had conquered the constitutional law."[34]

In the *Slaughterhouse* case, the Supreme Court majority managed to resurrect much of the discredited dogma of *Dred Scott*. The Fourteenth Amendment's definition of citizenship was limited to preventing the denial of state citizenship to a citizen of the United States.[35] Justice Miller acknowledged that state laws that discriminated against the newly emancipated slaves with gross injustice and hardship were "the evil to be remedied." The "protection of the newly-made freeman and citizen from the oppression of those who formerly exercised dominion over him" was the pervading purpose of the amendment.[36] He nevertheless held that a citizen of a state must look to the state for protection, thus aborting what he himself had declared to be the enactment's main goal: to protect the Negro from the evil of the Black Codes. He callously returned the free man "back to his oppressors."

In dissent, Justice Field insisted the privileges and immunities of the United States were broadly defined and secured against abridgment in any form by any state. If the amendment accomplished no more than the majority claimed, he said, "it was a vain and idle enactment which accomplished almost nothing."[37] Justice Swayne went further. The construction adopted, he said, defeated "the intent of those by whom the instrument was framed and those by whom it was adopted. To that extent it turns...what was meant for bread into a stone." That meme described the pattern of the Court's civil rights cases for the next thirty years. Avid court watcher Frederick Douglass agreed the Court had eviscerated the Privileges and

Immunities clause. Douglass's bitter conclusion: "dual citizenship means no citizenship."[38]

Passage of the Civil Rights Act of 1866 was one of the first Acts of the Reconstruction Congress. Section 1 of that Act prohibited racial discrimination in "civil rights or immunities," mandated that inhabitants of every race should have the same contractual and inheritance rights, the same treatment in courts of law, the same property rights, and the right to "full and equal benefit of all laws and proceedings for the security of person and property." Fearing that a future Congress might repeal these protections, Congress enacted the Fourteenth Amendment primarily to constitutionalize the Act.[39] Section 1 was a specific response to the perceived evil of the Black Codes, which the more radical Republican members of Congress saw as an attempt to undo emancipation, restore the shackles of the Slave Codes, and return freedmen to serfdom. As Senator Trumbull explained, the bill sought to "destroy all these discriminations." The debates surrounding the bill and the Fourteenth Amendment demonstrated a broad, sympathetic understanding of the "damnable violence," "fiendish oppression," and "barbarous cruelties" the newly freed slaves faced. These legislators did not have to leave the legislative chamber to know that the scions of the Confederacy were committed to the continuance of their proxy war against former slaves.[40]

The Reconstruction Congress expressed great skepticism about the commitment of the courts to the cause of emancipation; and in case after case, the Supreme Court showed that their distrust was entirely justified. In *People v. Cruikshank*,[41] a mob broke up a political meeting of black people in Louisiana. Both sides were armed; several of the black men attending the rally were killed. The Enforcement Act of 1870[42] provided criminal sanctions against groups that banded together or conspired "to injure, oppress, threaten or intimidate any citizen to... prevent or hinder his free exercise and enjoyment of any right or privilege" granted by the Constitution.

The *Cruikshank* case provided the perfect opportunity to apply the Enforcement Act. Incredibly, the Court decided the right to peaceably assemble was not a right granted by the Constitution. Furthermore, while the Fourteenth Amendment did prohibit a state from depriving any person of life, liberty, or property without due process of law, the Court concluded it did not reach conduct by one private citizen against another. This was quintessential constitutional doublespeak; "the States would not protect the civil rights of Negroes: the court would not permit Congress to do so."[43] The Court had literally issued the Ku Klux Klan a license to kill.

The Court put any doubt to rest in 1883, in *United States v. Harris*.[44] In that case an armed mob took black prisoners from the custody of a Tennessee sheriff, killed one, and severely beat others. The Court concluded that when the laws of a state are facially neutral and no state institution is involved in the mob action, the amendment "imposes no duty and confers no power upon Congress...." The equal protection clause prohibited sins of commission by the state, but a federal law punishing individuals for mob violence intended to prevent black people from exercising citizenship rights was invalid.

Various explanations and excuses have been given for impudence, imprudence, and perfidy of the Court during this shameful period. One allegedly extenuating circumstance absolves the Court of being motivated by pure racial animus. Arguably, the Court was "merely implementing the semi-tacit 'Compromise of 1877,' which returned the race problem to the states" and acknowledged the failure of Reconstruction.[45] "It was as easy for these men to tolerate the evils of the burgeoning Jim Crow system as it was for the Founding Fathers to accommodate slavery. And for the same reason: both had blinded their eyes with visions of other goals."[46] Perhaps. However, those who found a nation face a different task than a court that purports to be interpreting a written (and recently amended) constitution. It was not for the Court to implement a political compromise. Moreover, the contested election of 1876 made Rutherford B. Hayes president. It was Hayes who appointed John Marshall Harlan to the Supreme Court. And Harlan never seems to have been blinded by the light that affected his brethren.

John Marshall Harlan was the sixth child and fifth son born to James and Eliza Harlan. James, who was said to have a passion for the law, named the boy for the renowned and most influential chief justice of the U.S. Supreme Court. The Harlans were not wealthy, but they were firmly ensconced in the Kentucky Gentry and owned a modest number of slaves who served mainly as household servants. One of the enslaved was a young boy, Robert Harlan, in whom James took a special interest. Although he was rebuffed in his initial attempt to send Robert to the neighborhood school, James continued to believe Robert was destined for better things—a faith Robert amply justified—despite the handicap of being a slave who was permitted to receive a half-day of formal education—by achieving success as a barber, business owner, gold prospector, horse owner and trainer, and later as an articulate black spokesman for the Republican cause.

John Marshall Harlan grew up in the same house with Robert and seemed to take pleasure in his adventures and personal triumphs. The two maintained cordial relations throughout Robert's life, and Robert sometimes interceded to smooth John's path in the black community.

Kentucky was neutral during the War Between the States, but many of her citizens did choose sides, and John Marshall Harlan joined the Union Army. He viewed the war as a fight not only for the Constitution but for freedom itself. Exhorting his fellow Kentuckians to enroll for service, he said: "All that is most glorious in human government is now at stake, and every true man should come to the rescue."[47] Although Harlan had supported slavery until the South erupted in open rebellion, after the war, when the rise of the Klan fueled a culture of mob violence, he reluctantly acknowledged that the abolition of slavery was an "affirmation of the constitutional values of freedom and equality" he had always revered. As W. E. B. DuBois would later summarize the despair and confusion of former slaves and their descendants: neither freedom, nor book-learning, nor the power of the ballot provided relief from the "vast despair" that shadowed "the very soul of the toiling, sweating black man."[48] Nowhere was the Supreme Court's mockery and ridicule of black aspirations more evident than in the justices' treatment of the Civil Rights Act of 1875.

The Supreme Court's Coup

The Court's 1883 decision, holding the 1875 Civil Rights statute unconstitutional, was one in a long line of disappointments stretching from the enactment of the Civil War Amendments in the 1860s to the 1930s. One of the plaintiffs in the *Civil Rights* cases[49] was an irascible fellow named Bird Gee. He was the grand-uncle of the same Loren Miller cited by Fehrenbacher.[50] Miller seemed particularly well positioned to write such a chronicle since he dedicated the book to his father, who was born a slave, and chronicles his grand-uncle's disappointment.

Bird Gee was not alone in his quest to vindicate the 1875 Civil Rights law.[51] A young newspaper agent, William R. Davis Jr., was turned away from the New York Grand Opera; George M. Tyler, a San Francisco theatergoer, was denied his orchestra seats; the railroad refused to honor Sallie Robinson's first-class ticket between Grand Junction, Tennessee, and Lynchburg, Virginia; while W. H. R. Agee, a delegate to the Missouri Republican Convention, was expelled from the Nichols House Inn because of the complaints of other guests, who refused to share quarters with him. Bird Gee objected to his ejection from a frontier rooming house in Hiawatha, Kansas. Together these cases illustrated the routine disparagement and daily humiliations experienced by black people.

The cases were considered together by the Supreme Court. Despite the high hopes of black communities all over the nation, the Court showed no sympathy for the plaintiffs' plight. Having drawn a distinction between state laws and the discriminatory actions of individuals in *Cruikshank*, the Court proceeded to open a loophole in the *Civil Rights* cases through which the whole unwieldly apparatus of segregation, separation, and general disdain for the black race could pass without hindrance. The Court's decision was a cause for widespread celebration, especially among white Southerners. The mood was much otherwise in black neighborhoods.

Bird Gee was allegedly so disgusted by the Court's action that he spent the rest of his life in Indian Territory, among the heathens, where there was no discrimination. By all accounts, Bird Gee did well enough in life after abandoning the civilized world. Certainly, he was not more disappointed by the Court's betrayal in his case than those who denounced the Court's decisions in mass meetings across the nation. The Supreme Court, they complained, had begun its interpretation of the Fourteenth Amendment by "substantially repudiating it."[52]

Bishop H. Turner[53] of Atlanta compiled a record of the sentiments expressed at a mass meeting of colored citizens at Lincoln Hall in Washington, D.C. In his caption to these collected speeches, he decried "the barbarous" decision of the Supreme Court which disrobed "the colored race of all civil protection. The Most Cruel and Inhuman Verdict Against a Loyal People in the History of the World."

A local newspaper reported Lincoln Hall was filled. There was no standing room and "scarcely even breathing room" when Frederick Douglass took the stage. Douglass spoke more, he said, "in sorrow than in anger," acknowledging that the occasion called more loudly for silence than speech. Nevertheless, he gave one of the most eloquent and anguished orations of his long career. The 1875 bill was "a voice against popular prejudice and meanness" which appealed to "the noble and patriotic instincts" of the American people and told them they were all equal before the law and belonged to a common country. If such a bill was an attempt to impose social equality, the same criticism must apply to "the Declaration of Independence which declares that all men have equal rights; so is the Sermon on the Mount, so is the Golden Rule, that commands us to do to others as we would that others should do to us, so is the Constitution of the United States, and so are the laws and customs of every civilized country in the world." The Court's betrayal must have been especially bitter for Douglass. He had personally recruited free black men in the North, helping to enlist some, including his own son, in the newly formed 54th Massachusetts Regiment.[54] Douglass thought that once black men fought to preserve the Union, "no power on earth [could] deny that they [had] earned the right to citizenship in the United States."[55] Although "[l]iberty [was] now the base line of the republic," Douglass concluded, it had failed to supplant "the spirit or power of slavery. Where slavery was strong liberty is now weak." He expressed the longing for a Supreme Court that would be "as true to the claims of human liberty as the [S]upreme [C]ourt formerly was to the demands of slavery." When that day comes, as it will, Douglass told his audience, "a civil rights bill will not be declared unconstitutional and void, in utter and flagrant disregard of the intentions of the national legislature . . . and the rights secured by the [C]onstitution."

Douglass was not the only one to notice the Court's blatant contradictions. Justice John Marshall Harlan, in a powerful dissent, complained that "the substance and spirit of the recent amendments of the Constitution have been sacrificed by a subtle and ingenious verbal criticism." Noting that the "power of Congress, by legislation, to enforce the masters' right to have his slave" returned was only implied from the recognition of slavery in the Constitution, Justice Harlan pointed out that the power of Congress to enforce the Thirteenth Amendment, by appropriate legislation, was expressly granted by a change in the fundamental law. How then could any court that was not being obstinate, impudent, and lawless conclude that Congress's exercise of this express power was unconstitutional? The burden badges of servitude that excluded people from the stream of everyday life and commerce were part of the very foundation of slavery. In Justice Harlan's view, the burden of discrimination imposed by Jim Crow laws could not be "sustained; except upon the assumption that there is, in this land of universal liberty, a class which may be discriminated against, even in respect to rights of a character so necessary and supreme, that deprived of their enjoyment in common with others, a freeman is not only branded as one inferior and infected, but, in the competitions of life, is robbed of some of the most essential means of existence." Douglass later praised Harlan's lonely dissent, saying "one man with God is a majority."[56]

Colonel R. G. Ingersoll, who shared the podium with Douglass at Lincoln Hall, insisted the analysis need go no further than the enactment of the Thirteenth Amendment. The adoption of that amendment had made slaves free men and citizens. Thus, he said, the civil rights legislation was authorized by the Thirteenth Amendment because that amendment abolished not only slavery, but every "badge and brand and stain and mark of slavery." It abolished all distinctions on account of race or color. "From the moment of adoption of the Thirteenth Amendment the law became color blind."[57]

The Supreme Court did not think so and would soon wipe away the last sliver of protection it had once pretended to offer from discrimination on account of race or color. In 1869, Louisiana law prohibited racial segregation by public carriers. In his critique of the Court's decision in the *Civil Rights* cases, Col. Ingersoll cited *Hall v. DeCuir.* Mrs. DeCuir purchased passage from New Orleans to Hermitage, a trip which began and ended within the State of Louisiana. Refused accommodation because of her color, she sued the steamship company and recovered $1,000 in damages. The Supreme Court of Louisiana sustained the judgment. The defendant took the case to the United States Supreme Court, where the judgment was overturned. Even though the state had acted in accordance with the constitutional amendments, the high court declared: "If the public good required such legislation, it must come from Congress and not from the States."[58] But in 1883, in the *Civil Rights* cases, the Court declared just the opposite: "If the public good requires such legislation it must come from the States and not Congress."[59]

In 1892, when Homer Plessy took a seat in the "white" railroad car running between New Orleans and Covington, Louisiana, state law, known as the Separate Car Act,[60] required racial separation of passengers on railroad trains. The Creole aristocracy, a group that generally lived a life of freedom and privilege in New Orleans, was deeply affronted by the Separate Car Act. As head of a hastily convened Louisiana Citizens Committee, Louis Martinet, a Creole doctor, lawyer, and publisher of the *Crusader* newspaper, called for a legal assault on the new law.

However, freedmen and their descendants understandably deemed lynchings and Ku Klux Klan attacks more urgent, existential threats. Martinet's correspondence with Frederick Douglass received a discouraging response. Douglass felt no good would come of such a challenge and he would not support it.[61] The Court's decision in the *Civil Rights* cases was close enough to a fatal blow. Douglass would trust no more in the wisdom or humanity of the Court.

Martinet enlisted the aid of Albion Tourgee, a lawyer, a former judge, and best-selling novelist, who believed that the Civil War represented a "fundamental reordering of the relationship between the states and the federal government and between the races"[62] to devise a legal strategy. Homer Plessy, whose French grandfather had emigrated to New Orleans when Haiti was overrun by a slave rebellion, was not discernibly black. His light skin made him an ideal candidate for Martinet and Tourgee's test case. Having played his well-scripted part, Mr. Plessy was ejected, arrested, and criminally charged with violating Louisiana's Jim Crow law. When the case reached the Supreme Court, Tourgee offered a spirited argument, arguing that the Act represented a legalization of caste and quoting Justice Harlan's dissent in the *Civil Rights* cases: "Justice is pictured blind," said Tourgee, "and her daughter, the Law, ought at least to be color blind."[63] Carried away by his own eloquence, Tourgee seemed to forget that Homer Plessy could not be physically distinguished from any white man.

Justice Henry Billings Brown, writing for the 7–1 majority, made short shrift of Plessy's complaint.[64] "A statute which implies merely a legal distinction between the white and colored races...has no tendency to destroy the legal equality of the two races . . ." He added:

> Laws permitting, and even requiring separation [of the races] in places...have been generally, if not universally, recognized as within the competency of the state legislatures in the exercise of their police power.

The flaw in Plessy's reasoning, according to Justice Brown, was his "assumption that social prejudices may be overcome with legislation, and that equal rights cannot be secured except by an enforced commingling of the races." Rejecting that proposition, Justice Brown offered the willfully obtuse observation that any badge of inferiority imposed by such a separation was the result of black sensitivity—perceiving insult where none existed.

Douglass had been prescient. "Rather than invoke the Constitution to quell racism, [Justice] Brown invoked racism to quell the Constitution."[65] The decision evoked Taney's dictum that the "unhappy black race" was separated from the white race by "indelible marks" and, Justice Harlan pointed out in a blistering dissent, like *Dred Scott*, the Court's rewriting of the Constitution would haunt the nation's history.

As the lone dissenter, Harlan reminded the Court of the essential purpose of the Civil War Amendments, which "removed the race line from our governmental system." He declared that in "the view of the Constitution, in the eye of the law, there is in this country no superior, dominant ruling class of citizens. There is no caste here. Our Constitution is colorblind, and neither knows nor tolerates classes among its citizens." Harlan did not allow the majority to hide behind its pitiful fig leaf. This was not a routine rubber stamping of state police powers. The decision, he said, upended the Constitution and gutted the principle of equal protection. He predicted the decision would not only "stimulate aggressions, more or less brutal and irritating, upon the admitted rights of colored citizens, but would encourage the belief that it is possible, by means of state enactments, to defeat the beneficent purposes which the people...had in view when they adopted [the Civil War] amendments." What, he asked "can more certainly arouse race hate...than state enactments that proceed on the grounds that colored citizens are so far inferior and degraded that they cannot be allowed to sit in public coaches occupied by white citizens?" His prognosis was spot on. *Plessy*'s unconstitutional recognition and approval of the color-caste system as entirely compatible with the amended Constitution unleashed a flood of Jim Crow legislation and domestic terrorism that would not abate for seventy years.

Harlan's dissent in *Plessy* cemented his place in the pantheon of saints as far as black folks were concerned. His dissents were rumored to be the Rosetta Stone that inspired Thurgood Marshall in his quest for equal educational opportunity for black students. Not everyone lauded Harlan's effort. An Asian scholar took offense to a portion of Harlan's dissent that identified "a race so different from our own that we do not permit those belonging to it to become citizens of the United States." His point was simply that even the exotic Chinese, who could not become U.S. citizens, could ride in the same passenger coach as white passengers. It was a powerful rhetorical point. Obviously, Louisiana's separate carriage law could not have been implemented only to prevent friction among the races as the state claimed. The dissent was intended to highlight the unequal treatment of black citizens, not to support discrimination against Asians.[66] Still, the distinction may have revealed a flaw in Harlan's otherwise comprehensive understanding of constitutional principle. It raised a question that later cases dealing with racial discrimination did not answer.

As bad as its record was, the Court was still not quite done. In *Plessy*, Justice Brown insisted legislation is powerless to eradicate racial instincts. "If the two races are to meet in terms of racial equality, it must be the result of natural affinities, a mutual appreciation of each other's merits, and a voluntary consent of individuals." But when that case came along, the Court decided states could prohibit voluntary associations, too. Berea College in Kentucky declared in its corporate charter that it was established to "promote the cause of Christ" and to provide general and nonsectarian instruction to "all youth of good moral character." The college was open to all races, and the interracial association was entirely voluntary. Kentucky enacted a statute requiring that a school could teach both races only if it maintained separate branches at least 25 miles apart. In *Plessy*, the state claimed that it was necessary to prevent the involuntary mingling of the races in order to prevent racial conflict. In Kentucky, the state said citizens had no right of choice in their interracial associations. The law protected something more important than choice: the preservation and purity of the races. When the case reached the Supreme Court, Justice Brewer, writing for a five-judge majority, held that states could prohibit interracial association for innocent purposes. States could now order the exclusion of Negroes from places where a welcome had been extended. States and municipalities were not slow to accept the invitation and pass ordinances forbidding innocent association of Negroes and whites in hotels, barber shops, ball parks, pools, auditoriums, toilets, contests, and games. This was worse than Jim Crow; it harkened back to the Black Codes of the slave era.

Once again, Justice Harlan was the sole, plaintive voice of reason. "Have we," he asked, "become so inoculated with prejudice that an American government, professedly based on principles of freedom, charged with the protection of all citizens alike, can make distinction between such citizens in the matter of their voluntary meeting for innocent purposes simply because of their respective races?" The answer to his rhetorical question was a resounding "yes." And so, with limited exceptions, the law remained until the mid-fifties.

The Court had deftly and deliberately opened a loophole which rendered the whole unwieldy apparatus of Jim Crow permissible. The lesson was not lost on the rising generation of politicians—North or South. As President, Woodrow Wilson dismissed the ringing phrases of the Declaration as "Fourth of July sentiments." His criticism of the flaws of the Founding are eerily reminiscent of the condemnations that animated the defenders of slavery before the Civil War. Though he certainly would not have advocated the resurrection of the South's peculiar institution, Wilson strongly empathized with the South's resistance to Reconstruction. In his five-volume history of America, Wilson spoke approvingly of the domestic terrorism unleashed against black people in the South. It was understandable, he said, that white men "aroused by the mere instinct of self-preservation" would seek to rid themselves "by fair means, or foul, of the intolerable burden of governments sustained by the votes of ignorant negroes...."[67]

This was no accidental, off-the cuff observation. Progressives claimed they wanted to make government less corrupt and more democratic, but Progressive anti-corruption reforms often reduced democratic participation. Disenfranchisement of black voters in the Jim Crow South was justified as an anticorruption measure.[68] Jim Crow was needed, Professor Wilson told *Atlantic Monthly* readers, because otherwise black Americans "were a danger to themselves as well as those whom they once served." The freedmen were "unpracticed in liberty, unschooled in self-control, never sobered by the discipline of self-support, never established in any habit of prudence...insolent and aggressive, sick of work, [and] covetous of pleasure."

A number of prominent Progressives agreed with him. According to John R. Common, black suffrage was not an expansion of democracy but a corruption of it. Ignoring the valor and sacrifice of black soldiers who served in the Civil War, Common complained that the black race had obtained the boon of citizenship and suffrage through the cataclysm of a war in which they took no part.[69] Edward Ross mocked the voting aspirations of black folks: "One man, one vote does not make Sambo equal to Socrates." When President Wilson came to Washington, he wasted no time in resegregating the federal administration and "hounding from office large numbers of black federal employees."

A Change Is Gonna Come

Most people can remember exactly where they were and what they were doing when a great national tragedy or triumph occurred. There may still be a few people who can remember Pearl Harbor. More who recall the Kennedy assassination with great clarity. The death of Malcolm X; that of Martin Luther King; the *Challenger* disaster. And a great majority recall the horror of 9/11. I have a similarly vivid and indelible memory of the moment I learned about the now iconic *Brown* decision.[70] The rural electrification project had not yet reached my grandparents' home. My grandmother and her sister had married two brothers. They built their homes on adjoining acreage that was eventually bisected by the main road. My grandfather's brother, my Uncle Ed, was a veteran of World War I. A popular song from that era asks: "How you gonna keep 'em down on the farm, after they've seen Paree." I don't know if Uncle Ed made it to Paris. He did get far enough out of Alabama to contemplate new possibilities in plumbing.

When he returned, he added a pump house with a generator to his property. His house had all the modern amenities, electric lights, indoor plumbing, and the unbelievable luxury of a television.

Being unsure whether a television was strictly compatible with Christian praxis, my great-aunt Loretta did not watch frivolous entertainment. She did, however, faithfully watch NBC's *Huntley-Brinkley News Hour*. My grandmother would go over to her house every afternoon. They would watch the news together. Our house sat on a hill, at the top of a long sloping driveway. Loretta's house sat directly across the road, much closer to the highway because the county repeatedly relied on its powers of eminent domain to lop off large portions of her front yard.

One afternoon, a few days after my fifth birthday, I was standing in the yard when I heard the screen door slam as my grandmother left her sister's house. Perhaps I was waiting for her because I was looking in that direction. And this was the amazing thing. My grandmother was running. Never in my short life had I seen her run. She didn't usually move slowly. She was brisk and purposeful in her actions; impatient with indolence. But she was a gray-haired matron, and she did not run. On this day, though, she practically sprinted across the road and all the way up the driveway. I was transfixed. She stopped in front of me. There were tears in her eyes.

She said: "They did it. They did it. Thank the Lord, they did it." It was May 17, 1954. "They," as it turned out, referred to the U.S. Supreme Court; "it" was the decision in *Brown v. the Board of Education.*

On one side there was jubilation; on the other rage and enmity. For many people of goodwill in the muddled middle, the mood was consternation and confusion. For Loren Miller, judgment day for *Plessy* v. *Ferguson* was cause for celebration. It felt like redemption; justice at long last. The headline of *The New York Times* editorial discussing the ruling was "Justice Harlan Concurring."[71] Over the years, the decision achieved iconic status. It changed, perhaps forever, the role of judges, recasting them as heroic agents of change.

The scholarly criticism of *Brown* was cogent but muted. Professor Herbert Wechsler, a notable constitutional scholar, said the decision failed to embody any "neutral principle of constitutional law" and was "read with less fidelity by those who praise it than by those by whom it is condemned." And Professor Harry Kalven Jr., one of the preeminent legal scholars of the twentieth century, and author of *The Negro and the First Amendment,* described how the civil rights litigants' "almost military assault on the Constitution" had succeeded "as a strategy to trap democracy in its own decencies."[72] Judge Learned Hand noted the lack of constitutional basis for the decision.[73] Learned Hand, perhaps one of the most revered American judges in history, was critical of the Court's apparent activism in the *Brown* case, calling the Supreme Court a "third legislative chamber."[74] Hand delivered his critique at the Holmes Lecture in 1958. The following year Professor Wechsler responded to Hand, strongly supporting the idea of judicial review, but cautioning that constitutional decision-making "must be genuinely principled...[with] reasons quite transcending the result." Without such a standard, Wechsler warned that: "The man who simply lets his judgment turn on the immediate result...implies that the courts are free to function as a naked power organ [and] that it is an empty affirmation to regard them...as courts of law." Wechsler's lecture, entitled *Toward Neutral Principles of Constitutional Law*,[75] set off a debate about the role of the judiciary in American democracy that still resonates.

But whatever *Brown*'s legal deficiencies, it seemed morally right. Scholar Derrick Bell described the school desegregation decision as the start of "the greatest racial conscious-raising the country has ever known."[76]

Whatever its constitutional or analytical infirmities, this much is certain: *Brown* was like an earthquake far out at sea that sets a tsunami in motion. The initial reaction to the decision was promising. Most border states complied even before the issuance of the decree. Governors in Southern states urged citizens to exercise restraint and preserve order. The few riots that cropped up were easily quelled. By 1958, however, Alexander Bickel, who served as Justice Frankfurter's law clerk during the 1954 term when *Brown* was decided and who, as a professor at Yale Law School, became one of the most astute observers of the Court, would describe the segregation problem in the South as looking "like the American Algeria."[77] The storm was apparently ignited by the Congressional Manifesto issued in March 1956. In it, the full membership of the Southern delegation declared war against the *Brown* decision, accusing the Court of "a clear abuse of judicial power" and commending the motives of the states that had pledged to "resist forced integration by any lawful means."[78] The White Citizens Council expanded exponentially. The Klan was resurgent. Even the turn to mob action might have succeeded. For, as Bickel noted, compulsory segregation, like states' rights, and the Southern Way of Life was an abstraction to most people. A neutral and vaguely sympathetic one. But the sight of grown men and women, confronting, cursing, hurling racial invectives and other missiles at a small band of "scrubbed, starched, scared and incredibly brave colored children" made the premises of segregation concrete.[79] "The moral bankruptcy, the shame of the thing, was evident," Bickel said.[80] Michael Klarman agrees that *Brown*'s contribution to the positive change in American race relations was perverse: By provoking an ugly and violent resistance to the desegregation of schools, it stimulated Northern backlash, which may have hastened the passage of national civil rights legislation.[81] When the white resistance engendered by *Brown* collided with the determination in the souls of black folks and the courage they had instilled in their children, the pillars of the earth shuddered. And slowly, oh so slowly, the world shifted on its axis.

By the time armed officers attacked 600 peaceful civil rights marchers on the Edmund Pettus Bridge near Selma, I no longer lived in Alabama. On March 7, 1965, marchers demonstrating in favor of voting rights were forced back across the bridge by mounted officers using billy clubs, old tires cut into pieces and studded with metal spikes, and tear gas. The confrontation was televised. I, along with millions of others across the nation and around the world, watched the melee. That broadcast is largely credited with creating a surge of support that led to passage of the Voting Rights Act.

A change did come. *Brown* may have represented a judicial *mea culpa* because segregation had prospered, indeed flourished, in reliance on decisions of the Court. The tragedy is that it came too late to fulfill the promise of the Founders' Constitution. *Brown* ignited the era of full-blown group entitlements which *Carolene Products* had only vaguely promised. It launched the modern era of judicial "reform," in which noble ends justify even the most constitutionally suspect ends.[82]

Abraham Lincoln may have been the most articulate defender of the old "American constitutional order and the principles it enshrined." Progressivism—a toxic combination of social Darwinism and philosophical pragmatism—undermined Lincoln's and the Founders' conception of a fixed constitution and with a big assist from the judicial branch has implemented a historicist view of the Constitution and constitutionalism.[83] This is emphatically not a distinction without a difference.

Mark Twain's dictum that history does not repeat itself but rather rhymes perhaps acknowledges that similar events have a certain symmetry. The shift from natural rights and natural law, from rights as a shield to rights as a sword, was a shift that would inevitably lead to rights as a bludgeon to beat down all opposition. America went from the sublime idea that, because of the fatherhood of God and the brotherhood of man, all human beings are equal and, consequently, no just rule can occur without consent of the governed, to the diabolical idea that all desires—no matter how destructive—are deemed equal, and that justice demands their imposition, without consent, by the state.

In a wonderful speech given in 1926 to celebrate the 150th anniversary of the Declaration of Independence, President Coolidge lamented that most of those who clamor for reform are "sincere but ill-informed." Were they more knowledgeable, he believed, they would realize America's foundation was spiritual, not material, and the founders were a people influenced by "a great spiritual development" who acquired "a great moral power."[84]

To Coolidge, only the exercise of God's providence seemed adequate to explain the Declaration of Independence. He concludes:

> It is often asserted that the world has made a great deal of progress since 1776, that we have had new thoughts and new experiences which have given us a great advance of the people of that day,

and that we may therefore very well discard their conclusions for something more modern. But that reasoning cannot be applied to the [Declaration]. If all men are created equal, that is final. If they are endowed with inalienable rights, that is final. If governments derive their just power from the consent of the governed, that is final. No advance, no progress can be made beyond these propositions. If anyone wishes to deny their truth and their soundness, the only direction in which he can proceed historically is not forward, but backward toward the time when there was not equality, not rights of the individual, no rule of the people. Those who wish to proceed in that direction cannot lay claim to progress. They are reactionary.[85]

President Coolidge concludes by reminding his audience, "The things of the spirit come first" and warns that if we hope to maintain the legacy bequeathed to us, we must be like-minded.

When it comes to the things of the spirit, the histories of the four men sketched here may be illuminating. Frederick Douglass was born a slave and became one of the most eloquent opponents of that vile institution. He knew of his own experience; indeed, he was living proof that the claims of black inferiority, cowardice, and brutishness, and the paeans to the positive good of slavery, were false. Douglass had begun his career as an abolitionist orator condemning the Constitution as a pro-slavery document, but had gradually become convinced that the Founders' claim about human equality was the only real hope for ending slavery.

Abraham Lincoln was never a slave owner and had always argued that slavery was abhorrent and contrary to principles of human equality articulated in the Declaration of Independence. But even when he had been elected president with the help of abolitionists, he continued to believe black people were inferior to whites and peaceful coexistence between the two races would always be impossible.

Lincoln's thinking evolved. He could acknowledge the intelligence and perspicacity of a man like Frederick Douglass, and the steady parade of articulate Negro petitioners who sought his assistance must have persuaded him that Douglass was no aberration. But it seems likely that it was the valor of the black troops who willingly fought and died in the country's cause that made their humanity and their courage undeniable.

Justice Harlan revered the Constitution even as a boy, but it may have been growing up in a household where a black man was raised almost as an older brother that helped shape his understanding of the true import of the Civil War Amendments. He had seen Robert Harlan, who admitted he had received only a half-day of education, succeed as a business owner and a horse breeder and secure a fortune in the Yukon gold rush, and Robert had celebrated the possibility of his appointment to the Supreme Court and done his best to help him secure it. Harlan knew and respected Frederick Douglass enough to attend his funeral.

Although an early and flattering portrait of Thaddeus Stevens shows an attractive young man with smiling eyes, he remained a lifelong bachelor, a loner, and a revolutionary scold who, in later years, is pictured with a perpetual sneer upon his lips. Perhaps, though, that was merely his public persona. For more than twenty years, Lydia Smith, a young mulatto widow, described as comely, highly intelligent, and entertaining, served as Stevens's housekeeper. She was widely believed to be his mistress. However, Thaddeus Stevens usually allowed these prurient insinuations to pass without response. He was remarkably immune to the many calumnies frequently published against him. He did express astonishment that Richard M. Johnson of Kentucky, admittedly guilty of slave trading, concubinage, and lechery, could still be elected vice president under Martin Van Buren. Ironically, Johnson's slaveholding sanctified his vices. While he, Stevens said, "with three times the ability and a thousand times the honesty" was barred from any hope of higher office because of a rumored liaison with his housekeeper. "What was forgiven when "sanctified by the slave-relationship was not forgiven in a free society."[86]

If he thought his rumored relationship with Lydia barred him from higher office, he never repudiated her. He commissioned a portrait of her by the same painter who had painted his youthful likeness. In his last illness he went to great lengths to make sure he would not be buried in a segregated cemetery. He provided a bequest for her in his will. Lydia chose not to share his final resting place, but she used a portion of her inheritance to ensure that his grave was maintained. Lydia was not the catalyst for his revolutionary ideas. His path had been set long before he met her. Perhaps his equalitarian philosophy made it possible for him to be devoted to a woman of color in an era when an illicit liaison could be accepted with a wink, while a marriage would have been scandalous. And maybe understanding the hopes and dreams and humiliations of such a human being was part of the reason for his determination to see protection for a despised race inscribed in the Constitution.

As Justice Miller acknowledged in the *Slaughterhouse* cases, the pervading purpose of the Civil War Amendments was the freedom of the slave race. Nevertheless, by 1900, the elaborate mechanisms to enforce equal rights had failed, and the Supreme Court had established itself—not Congress—as the primary enforcer of the Fourteenth Amendment—just what the Radical Republicans had tried to avoid. In the near-century that passed between the end of the Civil War and the beginning of the Civil Rights Movement, Brutus's intuitions proved prescient. The Court arrogated to itself the legislative power to authorize discrimination on the basis of race, contrary to the words and the history of the Civil War Amendments. When Justice Brown decided, in *Plessy*, that racial discrimination was a reasonable exercise of the police power, the Court confirmed the belated triumph of the Confederacy. "Rather than invoke the Constitution to quell racism, Brown invoked racism to quell the Constitution."[87]

Brown manifested a new, national determination to right this long-festering racial wrong. The dismantling of court-approved Jim Crow laws was long overdue. On one level, the general jubilation that greeted the case was warranted. Unfortunately, the case—though it is now legendary and iconic—could not turn the constitutional clock back to the beginning. The case did not consider whether the Founders or the Radical Republicans had any philosophy of government. It did not discuss the centrality of a claim about human equality to the question of natural liberty. Instead, the Court turned to sociology. The Court totaled up per pupil expenditures, numbers of buses, disparities in equipment and library books. The plaintiffs relied heavily on testimony from social psychologists, educationists, and sociologists to the effect that segregated education in itself, independent of the quality and quantity of facilities, was detrimental to those who were segregated. This suggests the wrong of discrimination was solely contingent on its effects. What if black children performed better in segregated schools? Was Dr. Martin Luther King mistaken when he complained that "all segregation statutes [were] unjust" because they "were out of harmony with the moral law"?[88] In the Framers' Constitution, equality and liberty were two sides of the same coin—complements, not opposites. In the end, *Brown* was a discussion about equity and not freedom.

Brown came after atheists and academics had rejected The Great I Am in favor of The Grand Sez Who; after American jurists had embraced Justice Oliver Wendell Holmes's revolt against natural law and objective concepts of right and wrong as the new gospel; after President Woodrow Wilson succeeded in dismissing the "abstract truth of the Declaration, applicable to all men at all times" as mere Fourth of July sentiments. The post-Reconstruction court adamantly refused to stay in its lane. The *Brown* court claimed the authority to build its own freeway. And that was a detour no version of textual originalism could ever cure.

3

THE DIGNITY OF PRIVATE VS. PUBLIC INSURANCE

Grace-Marie Turner[1]

There is no question that Americans are frustrated with our current health care system. Millions remain uninsured, and coverage and care cost too much. People are hurting, and they feel powerless against this system.

But political leaders tell us we should be happy about progress in the current system as the nation's uninsured rate has reached an all-time low.[2] However, there is a big problem beneath the headlines, starting with the disparity between uninsured rates for minorities and whites. The most recent data from 2019 showed that only 9% of whites were uninsured compared to 15% of blacks.[3]

And there are large disparities in the health status and health outcomes for black Americans compared to white Americans, according to the Office of Health Policy at the Department of Health and Human Services (HHS).[4] Chronic disease burden, morbidity, and mortality are all significantly higher among young adult black Americans than the U.S. population as a whole.[5] According to the U.S. Census Bureau, black Americans' life expectancy in 2020 was 3.6 years shorter than non-Latino white Americans.[6]

There also are big disparities in types of coverage. Pacific Research Institute President and CEO Sally Pipes explains in her chapter for this book that 52% of black Americans had private health insurance in 2019 compared to 74% of white Americans. And 37% of blacks were enrolled in Medicaid—the joint federal-state health insurance program for the poor—or other public insurance compared to only 19% of whites.[7]

The Biden administration boasts that 1.1 million fewer Americans were without health insurance in 2021 than in 2020. But what they don't tell us is that the number of people with *private* health coverage fell while enrollment in public programs, especially Medicaid, soared. Democrats in Congress used COVID to expand the welfare state, to the detriment of people who prefer and deserve the dignity of private health insurance.

"All told, more than half of Medicaid's beneficiaries are racial and ethnic minorities,[8] subject to the long waits, poor quality of care, and devastating outcomes endemic to government-run programs. If we want to improve health outcomes among black Americans, we'll have to start here," Pipes writes.

Mortality of black babies is another tragic disparity. Infant mortality is 10.8 per 1,000 live births for black mothers compared to 4.6 per 1,000 for whites.[9] More than half of all births in the U.S. are covered under Medicaid, and black women are disproportionately likely to be enrolled in this program for lower-income Americans. Black women are less likely to receive prenatal care and therefore more likely to experience maternal complications and are more likely to give birth to infants with low birthweight and congenital malformations.[10] The problem with Medicaid, especially the difficulty in accessing coordinated care, is a problem that manifests in these tragic disparities.

Access to mental health care among black Americans also is an important problem. The Office of Minority Health at HHS reports that black adults are more likely than white adults to report "persistent symptoms of emotional distress."[11]

"Black adults living below the poverty line are more than twice as likely to report serious psychological distress than those with more financial security," government data show. Despite the needs, only one in three black adults with mental illness receives treatment.[12]

This chapter will offer policy recommendations to address these inequities. But rather than the typical failed prescription of recommending new government programs, we believe that policies need to be directed at lifting all people up and creating a health sector that is efficient, dynamic, and relies on consumer power and competition to drive transformative change.

Promises Not Kept

While politicians have made many promises to black Americans and others, the reality is that the government "solutions" often relegate them to failing public programs. Medicaid recipients struggle to find physicians who can afford to take the program's low payment rates, and patients can find it especially difficult to get appointments with specialists to treat more serious health problems. Studies have shown there is little if any difference in outcomes between patients who are on Medicaid and those who are uninsured.[13] That is an insult to those who rely on the program and often have no other alternative.

Despite these failures, the Left isn't giving up and believes that all of these problems could be solved if the government were to control all of the health sector. They are proposing an alternative that would provide coverage for everyone, with no premiums, copayments, or deductibles—a new universal system run by the federal government.

As I will document, a government-run system would have many if not more of the problems we experience today because it would put even more health care decisions under control of government. Americans deserve better.

It is true that the United States does not have a properly functioning market in the health sector. It does not respond to the needs of consumers and their demands for lower costs and abundant choices as they are accustomed to receiving in other sectors of the economy. Too many people are priced out of the market for health insurance—they don't qualify for subsidies or public programs and can't afford private insurance. The costs of premiums can be prohibitive, and even those with policies say they face deductibles that are so high they might as well be uninsured.

Instead of being relegated to failing government programs, Americans deserve the "freedom to flourish," as Center for Urban Renewal and Education (CURE) founder and president Star Parker insists. All Americans, especially black Americans, deserve the dignity of private health insurance and a choice of physicians and care arrangements. That means offering coverage that gives them more options of plans that meet their needs. Creation and expansion of government programs is not the answer.

Opinion Polling Swings

The political dangers of the U.S. slipping into a national government controlled health system are very real. The Kaiser Family Foundation[14] regularly asks Americans about health policy issues as part of its Health Tracking Poll series. Its 2019 comprehensive survey found that 56% of Americans support a "national health plan, sometimes called Medicare for All" and an even larger 71% support the idea when told that it would "guarantee health insurance as a right for all Americans."

But then come the details. When the surveyors focused on the costs of this single-payer system, support for Medicare for All dropped below 40%. Support fell even further, to 37%, when Americans learned the plan would eliminate private health insurance and require people to pay more in taxes. And when they learned that some medical treatments and tests could be delayed, support dropped even further, to 26%.

More recent focus group testing has found that soaring inflation in our economy makes calls for more health spending and expansion of government programs "seem reckless, not compassionate."[15]

Political philosopher Thomas Sowell gets it right: "It is amazing that people who think we cannot afford to pay for doctors, hospitals, and medications somehow think that we can afford to pay for doctors, hospitals, medications and a government bureaucracy to administer 'universal health care.'"[16]

Too Much Government

Wharton School Professor Mark Pauly, in a paper published by the American Enterprise Institute, has important findings about the controlling role that the federal government already plays in our health sector today.[17] Pauly details how the federal government shapes a much larger share of spending than the portion it finances directly. He finds the share of "government-affected" spending in 2016 totaled nearly 80%—"not leaving much in the unfettered, market-based category."

The federal government finances nearly 55% of all "explicit and implicit" health spending, he reports—including Medicare, the federal share of Medicaid, Affordable Care Act (ACA) subsidies, and tax preferences for employer-sponsored health insurance, etc. The federal government controls even more of our health care through regulations and mandates it imposes on titularly private plans.

We are close to having the majority of Americans dependent on government for their health care and coverage. Liberals have gained government control over the health sector with step-by-step changes over nearly 60 years, never missing an opportunity to expand an existing government program and using the slimmest of political majorities to create new ones.

The passage of the Inflation Reduction Act (IRA) in 2022 is an example. It means that Washington will exert even more control over health care for millions more people and lead to greater dependency on taxpayer subsidies for health insurance.

Star Parker and the CURE team pushed back hard against passage of the IRA, arguing that the law would "plunge low-income Americans deeper into government dependency, undermine individual freedom, harm small business owners and individual contractors, substantially increase the national debt, and exacerbate already growing inflation."[18]

Star points out there are better options. "Following passage of welfare reform, child poverty fell, dependency shrunk, and millions of Americans moved from welfare to the dignity of work." Freeing people from dependency on government enriches opportunities for success.

The Left promises "free" health care with Medicare for All[19] and its derivative big-government, taxpayer-funded solutions. But we know nothing is free. Having an insurance card doesn't equal access to actual care. Putting everyone on one big federal plan would mean people would lose their employer health plans. Medicaid, Medicare, and Medicare Advantage would go away, and 330 million Americans would be competing for care from a shrinking number of physicians working for ever lower payment rates, with many being forced to close their doors.

While there are a few incentives in taxpayer-supported programs to moderate costs, at some point the expenses of these wasteful and inefficient programs must be addressed. In other countries with government-run healthcare systems, it's done through rationing of care, underfunding public institutions, and restricting purchases of the latest medicines and technologies.

The Congressional Budget Office (CBO) found that using Medicare payment rates for the entire U.S. health sector would substantially reduce income for physicians, hospitals, and virtually all others in the health sector.

CBO found this would likely "reduce the amount of care supplied and could also reduce the quality of care." It says that "decreases in payment rates lead to a lower supply" and "fewer people might decide to enter the medical profession in the future. The number of hospitals and other health care facilities might also decline as a result of closures, and there might be less investment in new and existing facilities."

According to CBO, the government's low payment rates "could lead to a shortage of providers, longer wait times, and changes in the quality of care, especially if patient demand increased substantially."[20]

Their Disguised Agenda

While Medicare for All is their moniker, the Left sees Medic*aid* as a platform upon which to build a government-run health care system.

Nearly 90 million Americans now are enrolled in this federal-state program designed for the poor. Medicaid is arguably the worst of U.S. public programs. It dramatically underpays doctors and hospitals and thereby restricts access to coordinated, quality care for patients.

Instead of reforming and improving government-funded health programs like Medicaid, Congress has pumped more taxpayer dollars into expanding enrollment.

COVID provided the opening for Congress to expand Medicaid dramatically and to enhance and expand ACA subsidies for two years. The federal government bribed states into expanding Medicaid enrollment by paying a bigger share of costs, and once people were enrolled, states were forced to keep them enrolled even if recipients no longer met program qualifications.

In the midst of COVID, Congress also lifted the cap on income eligibility for ACA subsidies and made premium subsidies richer. The Inflation Reduction Act of 2022 extended the expansion for three more years. These COVID expansions are a regressive use of taxpayer dollars since much of the benefit accrues to higher-income people.[21]

Most of those who will benefit from the added ACA subsidies are in the upper two income quintiles, many of whom drop private coverage to take advantage of the taxpayer subsidies. For example, a family of four with a 60-year-old head of household earning $265,000 could end up eligible for more than $7,800 or more a year in ACA subsidies, according to an analysis by Brian Blase, president of the Paragon Health Institute.[22]

With taxpayers footing most of the bill, there are few incentives for insurance companies to moderate costs. Premiums for insurance in the individual market increased by 143% over six years to 2019, and deductibles also have skyrocketed. The average annual premium plus deductible for a family of four with an ACA plan was about $25,000 in 2021. And that is for coverage with extremely narrow physician networks and often limited access to the best hospitals.

"Between 2000 and 2021 alone, premiums for individual coverage increased 213%, and premiums for family coverage increased 245%—much greater than the 60% increase in overall prices during this period," Brian Blase explains.[23] Government spending has been a primary contributor to health cost inflation. All of this pumps more taxpayer dollars into the health care system, further inflating premium and health costs for everyone. This makes it increasingly difficult for people to keep and afford private coverage and the choices of quality care it generally provides.

Galen Senior Fellow Doug Badger explains[24] that many people will lose their private coverage as a result of the Inflation Reduction

Act. Small businesses can't compete with government. Businesses with fewer than 50 employees aren't subject to the Affordable Care Act's employer mandate, and many will drop insurance coverage they currently offer to their employees and instead send employees to the government exchanges. That means millions more people will have policies through government programs where politicians and government bureaucrats, not doctors and patients, are making medical decisions.

Public coverage is inferior to private coverage because it pays doctors and hospitals less, making access to care more difficult. Providers and facilities throughout the health sector also are forced to respond to legislative and regulatory demands rather than to the needs and preferences of patients. Too many patients on public programs find that having an insurance card doesn't mean having access to care.

Small Business in the Crosshairs

Small businesses that have borne the brunt of cruel COVID closures lack the bargaining power of big companies to negotiate lower health insurance rates. New and bigger government programs fuel inflation and make it harder for these businesses to make ends meet, especially those that want to provide health insurance for their employees and need to offer benefits to attract good workers.

CURE president Star Parker stresses that "Health is essential to productive citizenship." Black entrepreneurs are especially challenged. Blacks comprise approximately 14% of the U.S. population, but only 2.3% of owners of employer firms. According to a 2022 Brookings Institute report, 2019 Census data show there were 3.12 million black-owned businesses in the United States, generating $206 billion in annual revenue and supporting 3.56 million U.S. jobs.[25]

Many want to offer health insurance to their employees and want to use the benefit to attract new employees in a tight labor market, but the costs of coverage and the enormous bureaucracy of running an employer-sponsored health program deplete the time and resources of most small businesses.

Wall Street Journal editorial writer and author Jason Riley got it right in his 2014 book, *Please Stop Helping Us: How Liberals Make It Harder for Blacks to Succeed.*[26]

CURE emphasizes the need to "provide our most vulnerable communities with the care they need."[27] Government policies can provide this strong safety net, but it needs to stop creating lifelong dependency on government programs and robbing people of the opportunity to be independent and succeed.

Shared Goals

While there are different views on how to reach that goal of a fair, affordable, quality health care system in the United States, there are important shared values:

- Everyone should be able to get health coverage to access the health care they need.
- Coverage and care should be affordable.
- We must guard the quality of care.
- People should be able to see the physicians and other providers of their choice.
- And most important, we must work together to protect the most vulnerable and marginalized communities.

So What Should We Do?

We have fresh ideas to allow people to obtain a wider variety of health insurance offerings, and that involves giving states more authority over approving policies that meet the needs of their citizens—not the dictates of Washington bureaucrats.

Health care is too local and personal for a Washington-driven, one-size-fits-all approach to work. Health care costs and spending are escalating, dependence on government programs is at an all-time high, and individuals and families have less control of their health care decisions.

The only way to help black Americans obtain better, more afford-able, more reliable, quality health coverage is to reform the health sector so consumers, rather than bureaucrats, are in charge.

A system that devolves power and control away from Washington to communities and ultimately to doctors and patients will better serve all Americans, including black Americans. Their needs are not being met in a system run by remote bureaucrats that are detached from their communities.

Texas state legislator Tan Parker writes in *Making American Health Care Great:*

> No policy area in America is more complex or more personal than healthcare. Protecting the health and wellbeing of our families is a top priority for us all. As Americans, we are blessed with the greatest medical practitioners and innovative technologies in the world, but hidebound government programs and endless bureau-cratic red tape hinder the innovative solutions desperately needed to make sure everyone can access the health care they need and have insurance coverage that is affordable.[28]

CURE has as one of its core pillars promoting "policies that give people freedom to flourish."[29] Star Parker stresses that "Ameri-cans deserve to make their own decisions about their health and healthcare."

Star is right. Eighty percent (80%) of voters say that individual Americans should be allowed to purchase any health insurance product approved by their state's health insurance commissioner. A Scott Rasmussen national survey found that 9% think they should not, and 12% are not sure.[30]

The survey also found that 45% of voters think that allowing each state to set its own health insurance guidelines would lower the cost of healthcare in America; 27% think it would not lower the cost, and 27% are not sure.

Rather than dramatically expanding the role of government through "Medicare for All" or other new or expanded taxpayer-supported programs, policymakers should focus on creating a functional health sector, emphasizing improved health outcomes for everyone. We should start by devoting resources to address the specific needs of those who are uninsured, focusing on those in marginalized communities and the most vulnerable. But these policies should lift people up, not force them into reliance on inadequate government programs.

We are offering better ideas that rely on market forces and consumer power, but we need a different political environment for those ideas to advance.

The goal must be to return power to doctors and patients. That is our task now and will be for many years to come. For starters, we just need politicians to stop making it worse.

The patient-centered plan supported by scores of health policy experts in the market-based community is called Health Care Choices.[31] It is built around changes to help patients have the dignity of private insurance in a system that is responsive to their needs.

States have decades of experience in regulating health insurance markets and can better assure citizens that policies offered balance the needs and resources of each state. Under our plan, states also would be able to set up new, better-funded risk mitigation programs, such as reinsurance, that help those with the greatest medical needs to get the care they need. Regulatory barriers would be removed that keep plans from specializing in treating those with chronic conditions. And people with chronic illness would be better able to manage their health care spending in accounts they own and control.

One Woman's Frustrations

The problems with government-run health care are not limited to Medicaid. A woman from Colorado recounted her story about the difficulty of getting the care she needs in the highly regulated Obamacare exchange marketplace:[32]

"Janet" reported to us that when she was diagnosed with Hepatitis C in 1999, she enrolled in Colorado's high-risk pool.

"My premiums in 2010 were $275/month with a total out of pocket of $2,500. [While I was on] this plan, my liver failed, and I needed a liver transplant. It was approved without a question," she said. "My $600,000 transplant was covered 100% with a $2,500 out of pocket maximum!"

When Obamacare went into effect, Colorado's high-risk pool was shut down. "I was forced into the regular marketplace." Her premiums rose to $450 right away, and eventually she was paying $1,100 a month with a deductible of $6,300.

But her anti-rejection meds weren't covered along with the cost of other necessary care. She now is spending $19,500 a year just in out of pocket costs before her insurance kicks in.

Too many families report their ACA plans do not provide them access to hospitals that specialize in the cancer care they need, the surgeries they require, or the medicines they must have.

Like Janet, they have "coverage" under the ACA, but access to care is often inferior to the state high-risk pool or other coverage they had before. We must do better for those who are most vulnerable and most need quality care.

Transformation to Lift People Up

"The only effective way to resolve persistent problems in health care is to leverage the power of personal choice and market competition," writes health policy expert Nina Schaefer of The Heritage Foundation:

> Congress should take the steps needed to transform the health care system away from a government micromanaged public utility model, as advocated by the Left, and instead embrace a patient-centered health care agenda that puts individuals and families, not the government, in control of health care decisions and subjects the health care sector to the discipline of market competition.[33]

There is an enormous amount of energy pent up in our economy among those who have transformative ideas for change in our health sector. But even the most entrepreneurial companies crash into barriers created by a government, which controls far too much of the spending and sets virtually all of the rules in our health sector. This government monopoly must end if we are to get to a system centered around doctors and patients with incentives for providers, hospitals, and manufacturers to compete on price and value and satisfy the needs of consumers.

Consumers gain control over resources and therefore choices in a system that supports "defined contributions" in private and public health plans. [34] Like school choice, patients can take the money devoted in public or private programs to support their coverage and give consumers a chance to obtain insurance that better supports their needs. Our Health Care Choices proposal also provides better support than the ACA or Medicaid for those who need assistance because of age, disability, or economic conditions by providing dedicated resources to states to provide for their care.

Defined contributions mean consumers can control and direct resources to the health care arrangements that suit them best.

The defined contribution model works in both private and public coverage. Being on Medicaid, the Children's Health Insurance Program (CHIP), or Obamacare exchange programs should not lock people into a lifetime of dependence on poorly performing, government-run health care programs. Americans, regardless of income status, should benefit from the innovations of the private sector.

"Congress should allow beneficiaries to apply the dollars that otherwise would have been spent on their care through the traditional Medicaid program to a private coverage option of their choice," Schaefer writes.[35] States have some flexibility to do this now by requesting mother-may-I waivers from Washington, "but Congress should remove burdensome requirements that act as barriers to making it more widely available to enrollees," Schaefer says.

Several administrations, both Republican and Democrat, have permitted states to have more flexible programs and policies. Congress should make these options more readily available without the need for administrative waivers.[36]

And choices should be extended to seniors on Medicare as well. While more than half of seniors have voluntarily enrolled in private Medicare Advantage plans, other options would be available if they could direct the value of their Medicare subsidies to other private coverage of their choice, such as Direct Primary Care where people have a private physician on call to coordinate their care.

A patient-centered system would put more focus on the needs and special health problems faced by black Americans.

Specialized Solutions

In a patient-centered system, providers would organize care to better serve patients rather than forcing them to follow Washington's detailed policy prescriptions. We would see more innovative options:

Kidney disease: Those with end-stage renal disease must submit three times a week to dialysis to cleanse their blood, which means regular hours-long visits to clinics and hospitals to undergo the procedure.

Innovation in this sector has lagged far behind the rest of medical technology largely because the federal government pays the lion's share of dialysis costs through Medicare. There are experiments with home dialysis, for example, but it is not widely available. The U.S. falls far behind other developed countries in access to home dialysis, with only 12.6% of U.S. patients using this treatment. And this is another disparity: Black and Hispanic people have even lower rates of use of home dialysis.[37]

Even still, dialysis is a stopgap measure that fails to fix a chronic problem. Dialysis clinics that profit from the government payments have for decades shirked responsibility to help patients get on kidney transplant lists to receive organs from living donors that would eliminate the need for the life-altering dialysis treatments.

A patient-centered system would empower patients by giving them more options for treatment and would encourage the industry to innovate to be more responsive to their needs.

New and better medicines: The Inflation Reduction Act that Congress passed in August of 2022 will have a seriously detrimental impact on future pharmaceutical innovation. The law's supporters cheered that it allows the federal government to "negotiate" Medicare drug prices with pharmaceutical companies. But this is just another name for price controls, which Europe has painfully learned dries up investments in research.

This will impact black Americans disproportionately because they have higher than average rates of chronic disease. They *were* poised to benefit the most from breakthrough treatments for conditions like diabetes, heart disease, and cancer that were in the research pipeline. Work on many of those drugs was ended because of Washington's threat of onerous price controls.

Members of Congress who care about patients more than politics should make it a priority to end these price controls that will undermine the vibrant U.S. biopharmaceutical industry.

Policymakers should focus instead on market-oriented reforms. To lower drug costs for consumers, Congress should, for example, allow rebates to go directly to consumers at the pharmacy counter rather than to the back pockets of Prescription Benefit Managers and provide new incentives for patients to adhere to their medication instructions. In addition, a key reason prices for medications are so high is because other developed countries do not pay their fair share of research and development costs. That's a trade issue that a new president should tackle.

Access to physicians: Medical professionals are experiencing significant burnout after COVID, and there are thousands of unfilled openings in hospitals and nursing homes throughout the country. But even without COVID, the paperwork burden can be crushing.

"In countless surveys and studies, and across specialties, physicians consistently cite the time and energy they must devote to filling out forms and other administrative tasks near or at the top of their list of grievances.," according to an editorial in the *Medical Economics Journal.* "The mantra repeatedly heard throughout the profession is, 'This isn't why I went into medicine.'"

"The problem is worsened by electronic health records (EHR), now used by close to 90% of office-based physicians," the editorial continued. "Once seen as a way to streamline documentation data sharing, EHRs instead have become enormous time-sucks. A December 2016 study in *Annals of Internal Medicine* found that physicians in outpatient settings spent about 27% of their day on direct clinical face time with patients, but 49% on EHRs and desk work. Many also worked up to two hours every evening on EHR-related tasks."[38]

Reducing that burden could allow doctors to spend more time with patients and see more patients, particularly those covered by programs like Medicaid, who must wait longer and have fewer options for care than those with private insurance. Reducing the administrative burden could be a way to effectively increase the supply of medical care and in the process give doctors more time to boost trust among patients, who have historically distrusted the medical establishment.

To achieve these goals, we would redirect resources to the states and give them more flexibility to approve health plans and coverage options that better meet the needs of their citizens who are empowered by having control over the resources that finance their care. This will lead to more flexible, affordable health care and coverage arrangements and to more focused assistance to those who most need help.

Health care is too local and personal for a one-size-fits-all approach to work. Washington has created hundreds of thousands of pages of rules and regulations in a clumsy and misguided effort to run our health care system. This has driven up costs, reduced choices, and made it harder for sick people to get care—all while giving a blank check from taxpayers to health insurers, hospitals, and other big health care businesses.

Health reform should be about your care and your coverage with you and your doctor in control of your health care decisions.

The consumer focus we see in other sectors of our economy also can work in health care to produce many more options for care and coverage. States should be free to approve plans that meet the needs of consumers, not just Washington's cookie-cutter policies.

The Left's proposals expand government power over health care and make doctors and patients pawns in the system. Instead, our ideas would expand access to better private coverage, with many more options of affordable plans that meet the needs of Americans.

We see some hopeful pockets of change:[39]

Patient-focused health reform is gaining momentum in the states.[40] For example, Texas enacted "Healthy Families, Healthy

Texas"[41] as an alternative to Medicaid expansion. This bipartisan package of reforms focuses on improving access, outcomes, and affordability of care and coverage.

Oklahoma also provides a friendly climate for the hugely successful Surgery Center of Oklahoma.[42] It is a state-of-the-art multispecialty facility in Oklahoma City, owned and operated by approximately forty of the top surgeons and anesthesiologists in the state. They offer surgery care at one competitively low price.[43] For example, the nearby Oklahoma University Medical Center billed $20,456 for the open repair of a fracture; the procedure costs an estimated $4,855 at Surgery Center of Oklahoma.

"We can offer these prices because we are completely physician-owned and managed. We control every aspect of the facility, from real estate costs to the most efficient use of staff, to the elimination of wasteful operating room practices that non-profit hospitals have no incentive to curb. We are truly committed to providing the best quality care at the lowest possible price," according to founders Dr. Keith Smith and Dr. Steven Lantier.

This surgery center was created before Washington imposed a ban on the creation of any new physician-owned hospitals. A 2018 White House Report on Choice and Competition[44] recommended that Congress lift the ban to allow the creation and expansion of these hospitals to give patients more choice and give big community hospitals much-needed competition.[45]

Dr. Brian Miller practices hospital medicine at the Johns Hopkins Hospital and also is an academic health policy researcher at the American Enterprise Institute. In 2021 testimony before the Senate Judiciary Committee, he reported that "Physician-owned hospitals (POHs) represent a powerful lever through which policymakers can promote market entry. Currently, new POHs are statutorily excluded from participation in the Medicare program, a policy with both a long history and recent legislative efforts aimed at its repeal in 2017 and 2019.[46]

Washington needs to shift its focus to proposals that will unleash this kind of innovation and energy that are pent up in our health sector. One way is to lift the ban Washington imposed on creation of new physician-owned hospitals like the Surgery Center of Oklahoma to put doctors rather than politicians in charge of health care.

Evidence the Consumer-Choice Model Works

My colleague Doug Badger and I described the Medicare Part D program's success:[47]

The federal government's largest prescription drug program is Medicare Part D. The program has made prescription medicines more affordable for millions of seniors, offering them broad coverage choices while holding down costs for taxpayers.

Part D, established in 2003 through the Medicare Modernization Act, has led to more than nine out of ten seniors having drug coverage, and they are paying less than predicted for their coverage. Their premiums averaged $33.50 in 2018, less than CBO said they would average in 2006, the program's first year.[48]

Part D has consistently come in under budget. Under the initial ten-year budget projections, Part D was expected to cost $770 billion. Actual cost after ten years: $421 billion. That's 45% less than expected.

That underestimates the value of Part D. Innovative new medicines reduce the need for hospital stays and physician visits. A 2016 study found that Part D actually resulted in net Medicare savings of $679 billion over its first nine years.

Instead of building on this island of success in the sea of red ink in other government programs, Congress has chipped away at the unique features that have produced Part D's success—a judicious use of regulation, genuine market competition, transparency, and consumer choice.

In the Medicare Prescription Drug Benefit Program, plans compete for enrollment based on the premiums and coverage design. Unlike Obamacare, which has caused insurers to abandon individual health insurance markets and leave consumers with few choices, Part D offers seniors a broad array of options. As a result, plans have a big incentive to negotiate the lowest price they can get to make their premiums attractive.

While Congress has made changes that have made the program less consumer-centric, the basic structure of the program should be a model for future reform.

Our Vision for the Right Kind of Health Reform

- Everyone who wants health coverage could get **a plan they can afford.**
- People would have **many more options** of coverage that fit their needs and pocketbooks.
- **Coverage would be secure** so people don't lose insurance if they lose or change jobs.
- For those with low incomes and the greatest health care needs, there is **a strong safety net.**

Americans are in no mood for another disruptive, massive overhaul of our health sector. We must begin with targeted reforms that empower patients, free doctors and nurses, and unleash entrepreneurial energy.

Here are some of the specific policy ideas to create more choices of health coverage in a market with genuine competition:

- **Health plans should be able to specialize** (instead of being required to be all things to all patients). Patients, especially those with chronic disease, should have a plan that provides continuity of care with medical professionals who specialize in their condition and disease.

- Allow **Medicaid recipients the dignity** of using the value of their subsidy to get private insurance. Most recipients find it extremely difficult to find physicians, especially specialists, who can afford to take the program's paltry payment rates. Recipients wind up in hospital emergency rooms to get even routine care—at a much higher cost to taxpayers, who foot the bill and at the expense of continuity of care for patients.

- Make **Health Savings Accounts** more flexible so anyone can use them in conjunction with more versatile plans, including plans that specialize in treating chronic conditions to help people like Janet that struggle to get the care they need in narrow-network plans.

- **Provide stronger consumer protections**. Advancing more patient-centered health care models will require additional tools and resources to support patients. For example, individuals need better information on prices, quality, and choices. Patients also should be able to reap the benefits from their cost-saving decisions and be protected from contract decisions outside of their control. Congress and the states should facilitate meaningful price transparency initiatives, permit patients to share in premium savings with insurance plans, and revisit flawed surprise-billing legislation.

- Give states the option of facilitating **private exchanges** in which health plans compete to offer affordable insurance rather than having only the ACA exchange monopoly that limits choices and inflates prices.[49]

- Codify the administrative rule that allows employers to offer, and employees to use, **tax-free dollars to buy insurance** they may prefer outside the workplace. This should be expanded to include allowing pooling of employer or other contributions from each spouse to buy one family policy.

- Give **small businesses** the option of joining together through Association Health Plans to get better prices on health insurance for their workers like larger companies do.
- Insist that hospitals and insurers follow the law in making their **prices transparent.**[50]
- Make **telehealth** a permanent option so patients have easier and better access to doctors.
- Provide incentives for states to **lift regulations** that restrict competition and increase costs, such as certificate-of-need laws.
- Repeal the moratorium on new or expanded **physician-owned hospitals** to broaden access to quality, innovative, patient-centered care.
- Crack down on **anti-competitive practices** in the health sector where excessive consolidation limits competition and increases prices. As a start, the Federal Trade Commission and Justice Department should routinely report to Congress the extent and effects of hospital consolidation on restraining competition.
- Clarify that the Stark law is **not intended to limit innovative** payment arrangements, care coordination, and patient engagement.
- **Remove restrictions** on physicians that discourage them from entering into private arrangements with their Medicare patients for direct primary care and other private options.
- Any reform plan must **protect life and protect the conscience rights of health care** providers to practice medicine without violating their values and beliefs. An

important guarantee is making sure that funding for health programs has Hyde Amendment protections to assure no federal dollars will be spent to fund abortions.

Drug Costs

- Don't buy the line that the government can "negotiate" lower drug cost in Medicare. Private plans compete fiercely in Part D to offer the lowest prices and the best selection of drugs. **Government "negotiation" is just a fancy word for price controls** that lead to shortages, drug rationing, and fewer new and better drugs. The Inflation 'Reduction' Act's price-control provisions should be repealed.
- Assure all **drug discounts and rebates** are passed along directly to consumers rather than to the middlemen.
- **Streamline and modernize the Food and Drug Administration (FDA)** drug approval processes so safe drugs can reach the market faster, reducing what is now an average of 12 years from design to market that costs billions of dollars—costs that get passed along in the price of the product.
- **Force others to pay their fair share of research costs.** Wealthy European countries piggy-back on U.S. consumers who pay more than their share of research costs. Rectifying this should be a top priority of the next administration negotiating trade deals.

Patients First

Just as physicians must always put their patients first, political leaders should do the same and stop catering to special interests. And stop promising "the government" can fix our health sector. Many of the problems with health care and costs are *because* of big government intervention, so we don't need *more* of it.

The solution lies in creating a truly competitive and transparent, patient-centered marketplace and getting rid of Washington's iron grip on health care.[51] The American people don't want another major overhaul of our health sector, but they do need targeted changes to create a patient-centered health sector that unleashes the innovation and energy pent up in our health sector to create a health sector that can be a model and a beacon for the rest of the world.

4

THE STATE OF BLACK HEALTH CARE IN AMERICA

Sally C. Pipes

The Two Americas?

The United States was founded on the principles of liberty and equality. We've sometimes failed to live up to those ideals. Nevertheless, Americans of all races today are freer, more prosperous, and more equal than they were even decades ago.

But the gap between blacks and Americans of other races on health measures remains wide. From access to insurance and prescription drugs to rates of chronic disease and mortality, black Americans fare worse than their peers.

To progressives, this is proof of systemic racism—and demonstrates that we need more government intervention in health care to equalize outcomes. But that will not solve black Americans' health problems. In fact, government programs deserve much of the blame for America's racial health divide.

If policymakers want to improve black Americans' health, they need to acknowledge that government intervention in the healthcare market is failing Americans of all races.

This chapter will begin by taking stock of health care in black America. From there, it will trace how federal welfare programs have failed black American enrollees by saddling them with subpar coverage and penalizing them for trying to climb the economic ladder. Finally, it will offer commonsense, market-based solutions that will benefit Americans of all races—black Americans in particular.

Taking Stock of Health Care in Black America

The most striking racial disparity in American health care is also one of the most basic: life expectancy. After all, what is the purpose of a healthcare system but to keep people alive and thriving?

The average life expectancy at birth for black Americans in 2021 was 70.8 years, compared with 76.4 years for white people and 77.7 years for Hispanic people.[1] Black males have the second-lowest life expectancy of any American subgroup—just 66.7 years.[2]

Things seem to be getting worse. White American life expectancy declined by 2.4 years between 2019 and 2021, while black American life expectancy declined by four years over the same period.[3]

Among whites, COVID-19 was responsible for 54.1% of the decline in life expectancy between 2020 and 2021, according to the Centers for Disease Control and Prevention (CDC). Unintentional injuries, which include drug overdoses, were responsible for 11.8% of the decline. Heart disease, liver disease, and stroke were collectively responsible for another 11.1%.[4]

Black life expectancy declined for different reasons. COVID-19 was responsible for 35% of the decline between 2020 and 2021—a lower share than for whites, even though COVID-19 was deadlier for black Americans.[5,6]

That's because "unintentional injuries"—a category mostly composed of car accidents and drug overdoses[7]—were responsible for 22.7% of the decline in black life expectancy. That's almost twice the share for white Americans.[8]

Deaths due to drug overdose have surged among black Americans in recent years. According to data from the CDC published in July

2022, overdose death rates jumped 44% for black people in 2020, compared to 2019. The corresponding figure for white Americans was 22%.[9]

In 2019, whites and blacks had similar overdose death rates. But one year later, the white overdose death rate was 31 per 100,000—compared with 39 per 100,000 for black Americans. That's the highest for any racial or ethnic group.[10]

This drug overdose crisis has afflicted both the young and the old. Black men over the age of 65 had an overdose death rate almost seven times that of white men in the same age group in 2020. Black people between the ages of 15 and 24 saw their overdose death rate leap 86% between 2019 and 2020—more than any other age-race group.[11]

Car accidents also take a disproportionate toll on blacks—a disparity that actually worsened during the pandemic. According to a report by the Governors Highway Safety Association, black Americans perished in vehicle accidents at a rate of 68.5 per 100,000 from 2015 through 2019. That was about 24% higher than the traffic fatality rate of 55.2 per 100,000 for white Americans.[12] And then in 2020, traffic fatalities increased by 23% for black Americans, while rising just 4% for whites, according to the National Highway Traffic Safety Administration.[13]

The longer-term gap in life expectancy is largely a function of chronic disease. In 2021, 16% of black Americans had diabetes, compared with 11% of white Americans.[14] Black Americans aged 35–64 are 50% more likely to have high blood pressure than whites.[15] As a result, black Americans aged 18–49 are twice as likely to die from heart disease as whites,[16] while black people are twice as likely to die of diabetes as white people.[17]

These higher rates of chronic disease can be explained in turn by overall population health. In 2021, two in ten black Americans reported "fair or poor health status," compared with just 14% of white Americans who self-reported the same thing.[18] According to research published in 2019 by the CDC, 80% of black American women are overweight or obese, compared to 67% of white women.[19]

The disparities start young. Nearly 13% of black children have asthma, compared to just under 8% of white children.[20]

But not all these disparities are the result of general health. Some are caused by disparities in care. A 2022 study found that black leukemia patients aged 18–29 were more likely to die or not go into complete remission when compared with white patients undergoing the same intensive therapy.[21] All told, black Americans have a higher rate of mortality for all types of cancer combined, compared to all other racial and ethnic groups.[22]

As of 2020, black Americans were nearly eight times more likely to be diagnosed with HIV than white Americans.[23] Black patients with HIV were nearly seven times more likely to die of the virus than white patients.[24]

What's Driving the Difference

A large portion of the healthcare discrepancies between black and white Americans coincides with income differences. The African American poverty rate in 2021—19.5%—was much higher than the national average of 11.6%.[25] That year, the average household income for non-Hispanic blacks was $48,297, compared to $77,999 for non-Hispanic whites.[26]

Poor adults of all races are five times as likely to report that they are in "fair or poor" health compared with those whose incomes are at or above 400% of the Federal Poverty Level.[27] In 2011, nearly 23% of adults with incomes below $35,000 reported poor health outcomes, while just over 5% of adults with incomes over $100,000 reported the same.[28] Poor Americans are at greater risk of mortality, as well as chronic conditions including heart disease, diabetes, obesity, and disability.[29]

But greater rates of poverty do not fully explain racial health disparities. One 2017 study compared health outcomes among people with incomes above $175,000 per year and found that black Americans still fared worse than their white counterparts.[30]

To really understand the issue, we must turn to social determinants of health—"conditions in the places where people live, learn, work, and play that affect a wide range of health and quality-of-life risks and outcomes," in the parlance of the CDC.[31]

Social determinants of health cover everything from neighborhood conditions and access to safe transportation to language and literacy skills and racial discrimination.[32]

In recent years, many people have zeroed in on just one of these social determinants of health—race and racism—to explain the disparate health outcomes between black and white Americans.

This argument's champions—as exemplified by an essay published in *Health Affairs* in February 2022—claim that "laws and policies...allocate resources in ways that disempower and devalue members of racial and ethnic minority groups, resulting in inequitable access to high-quality care."[33]

In this telling, "structural racism" explains just about all of the racial health gap. If we accept that argument, then addressing systemic prejudice is among the most crucial health policy tasks of our time.

But race is just one social determinant of health that negatively affects black Americans. And social determinants are part of a broader tableau of factors that determine racial health outcomes. To improve black American health outcomes, we must first dispel the notion that racism alone is the reason for these disparities.

Race is part of a broader determinant—socioeconomic status. As one review of the medical literature from 2007 put it, low socioeconomic status "is associated with more smoking, less physical activity, and poorer diets."[34] Together, these behavioral choices increase a person's risk of chronic disease and obesity, which in turn results in lower life expectancy.[35]

Nearly 12% of black American adults smoke cigarettes—a greater share than among Asian Americans or Hispanic Americans.[36] According to the CDC, black Americans have "the highest age-adjusted prevalence of obesity" of any racial or ethnic group.[37]

Lifestyle factors like these can help explain why black Americans are up to two times more likely than other racial groups to contract most major chronic conditions, according to a 2013 study.[38]

Insofar as race informs a person's socioeconomic status, it certainly affects a person's health outcomes. But individual lifestyle choices affect health just as much.

Breaking this cycle of poor lifestyle choices will largely depend on—and sometimes contribute to—breaking a cycle of poverty. Breaking that cycle, in turn, will require freeing black Americans from the ineffective, outdated government programs they largely rely on for health care.

Eleven percent of black Americans were uninsured as of 2021, compared to just 7% of white Americans.[39] Fifty-one percent of black Americans had private health insurance, and 38% were enrolled in Medicaid—the joint federal-state health insurance program for the poor—or some other kind of public insurance. Meanwhile, nearly three-quarters of white Americans had private insurance, while just 20% were on Medicaid.[40]

All told, more than half of Medicaid's beneficiaries are racial and ethnic minorities,[41] subject to the long waits, poor quality of care, and devastating outcomes endemic to government-run programs. If we want to improve health outcomes among black Americans, we'll have to start here.

The Perils of Government-Run Health Care

Medicaid is proof positive that access to coverage does not necessarily translate into access to care. Its beneficiaries wait and wait—and wait—for care.

One 2017 study found that Medicaid patients were more likely to wait 20 minutes or longer for previously scheduled appointments than privately insured patients.[42] Part of that difference can be attributed to the fact that Medicaid beneficiaries tend to visit understaffed clinics. But the study also found that Medicaid patients waited 5% longer to see the same doctor in the same practice.[43]

The only explanation for such a discrepancy, the study's authors concluded, is that physicians give preferential treatment to privately insured individuals over Medicaid beneficiaries.[44]

It's a prejudice that Medicaid beneficiaries face across the board. But that prejudice may largely be induced by the government. Medicaid pays providers just 62% of what they receive from private insurance, according to a 2017 study.[45] Due to this underpayment, 3 in 10 providers were unwilling to accept Medicaid beneficiaries as new patients, a 2019 report from the Medicaid and CHIP Access Commission found.[46]

By contrast, only 1 in 10 doctors is unwilling to take new patients on private insurance.[47]

Then there are the administrative hassles associated with collecting those below-market payments. Some 19% of Medicaid claims are not initially paid in full.[48]

The reticence to accept Medicaid extends across specialties, from general practitioners to pediatricians and psychiatrists.[49] One study looked at Medicaid patients in Colorado and found that they had to wait 1.4 times longer than privately insured patients to receive specialty care.[50] Colorado's Medicaid enrollees were also more likely to report that their insurance did not cover specialty care.[51]

A study of Virginia's Medicaid population found that primary care physicians in the state's urban areas were less likely to accept Medicaid than primary care physicians in rural areas. The study also found that physicians were less likely to accept Medicaid in areas with higher black and Hispanic populations.[52]

Contrary to what progressives claim, the Affordable Care Act's (ACA) Medicaid expansion did not make things better. The ACA (aka Obamacare) boosted the number of people enrolled in Medicaid. But it did nothing to improve the quality of that coverage—or to increase the supply of care available to beneficiaries.

In other words, Obamacare's Medicaid expansion funneled more people into queues.[53]

Several studies posit that Medicaid may be no better than going without insurance altogether. One landmark study of Oregon's Medicaid population found that "Medicaid coverage generated no significant improvements in measured physical health outcomes" compared with remaining uninsured.[54]

Another study, which looked at individuals with throat cancer, found that Medicaid patients and the uninsured were 50% more likely to die than those with private insurance, even after controlling for smoking, socioeconomic status, and other factors that increase cancer risk.[55]

The Welfare Trap, Part One

Despite the poor-quality care Medicaid offers, enrollees are not incentivized to leave the program. This is the result of a peculiar feature of welfare programs that penalizes beneficiaries for making money.

The "marginal tax rate" is the percentage of each additional dollar a person earns that they have to pay in taxes.[56] And the marginal tax rate implicit in earning your way out of Medicaid and other federal benefit programs is quite punishing.

One study found that for every $100 a poor person earns, they lose $50 in new taxes or benefits foregone.[57]

People who participate in multiple welfare programs—not just Medicaid but food stamps and subsidized housing programs—face the highest marginal tax rates.[58] In other words, the interplay of federal poverty programs and the tax system discourages people from earning more money.

The upshot is that a person could get a raise at work—and then lose public benefits whose value is almost as much as the value of that raise.

As we will see, black Americans fall disproportionately in this welfare trap, which not only keeps them in subpar government-run health insurance programs but also cuts them off from the myriad benefits of private health insurance.

I'm from the Government, and I'm Here to Help

Many black Americans not enrolled in Medicaid still feel the sting of government meddling in their health insurance. In 2022, nearly 13% of the ACA's enrollees were black, according to the Department of Health and Human Services' Assistant Secretary for Planning and Evaluation.[59]

While Obamacare is not a fully government-run program, enrollees in these plans face many of the same problems as Medicaid beneficiaries—and for many of the same reasons.

Nearly three-quarters of Obamacare plans have narrow networks, which force enrollees to choose from a limited number of covered hospitals and physicians—and could therefore make it difficult, if not impossible, to see their preferred provider.[60]

In theory, narrow networks are among the elements that allow health plans to keep the cost of coverage down. But in practice, the plans available on the ACA's exchanges are not "affordable" at all.

The average Obamacare deductible was $4,800 in 2023,[61] up from just under $2,000 in 2014.[62] Meanwhile, the average deductible for people with employer-sponsored insurance in 2022 was just over $1,700.[63] A year before the exchanges opened their doors, the average monthly individual market premium was $242. In 2019, the average monthly premium was $589.[64]

Even those premiums mask the true unaffordability of these plans. The government covers the entire premium for people who make between 100% and 150% of the federal poverty level[65]—between $30,000 and $45,000 for a family of four in 2023. People who make more than that pay a percentage of their incomes toward the premium that rises with income, up to a maximum of 8.5% at four times poverty, or $120,000 for a family of four.[66] And no one pays more than 8.5% of income in premiums.

As research from former Trump administration economic adviser Brian Blase has shown, subsidizing exchange plans for wealthy enrollees drives health care costs up and makes premiums more expensive without actually expanding coverage or making exchange plans more affordable.[67]

• • •

One government program is serving black Americans relatively well. Not coincidentally, it's privately administered—Medicare Advantage.

About 13% of Medicare Advantage enrollees are black, according to a 2020 report from Milliman, a consultancy. By comparison, 9% of enrollees in traditional Medicare are black.

Nearly half of black Medicare beneficiaries choose Advantage over traditional government-run Medicare.[68]

Medicare Advantage combines Medicare Parts A and B—which cover hospital and physician care, respectively—in a single, privately administered plan. Some Medicare Advantage plans also include Part D prescription drug coverage.[69]

The federal government pays private insurers a set amount for each Medicare Advantage enrollee and leaves it to insurers to determine how to pay for coverage—and what to cover, subject to some minimum standards.[70] Unlike the federal government, private insurers are capable of efficiently administering robust benefits at a reasonable cost.

Medicare Advantage beneficiaries spend about $1,640 less on health care each year than their counterparts in traditional Medicare, according to a 2021 study.[71] Advantage enrollees with "complex chronic conditions"—those "involving multiple morbidities that [require] the attention of multiple health care providers or facilities"—had a rate of avoidable hospitalization 57% lower than traditional Medicare enrollees.[72] [73]

Medicare Advantage plans also offer supplemental benefits not covered by traditional Medicare.[74] As of 2023, 99% of Medicare Advantage plans offered some kind of vision coverage, including eye exams and glasses. Ninety-nine percent offered hearing exams and hearing aids, and 98% provided dental benefits.[75]

On many metrics, Medicare Advantage offers superior care to the government-run alternative. One study found that minority enrollees in Medicare Advantage had greater access to primary care, flu vaccines, and colon cancer screenings than minority enrollees in traditional Medicare.[76]

Compared to other government health programs, Medicare Advantage is cheaper, more comprehensive, and higher quality. Black Americans in particular are better served by Medicare Advantage than by traditional Medicare or Medicaid. The reason is simple—private health insurance is better than public alternatives.

Shifting black Americans out of government-run healthcare programs and into private insurance plans is another key step toward boosting their health outcomes. This shift must proceed in two phases.

First, we must break the misconception that welfare programs are what's best for black Americans. That will require undoing decades of progressive policy malfeasance. And second, we must enact market-oriented reforms across the health sector to boost quality and cut costs across the board.

The Welfare Trap, Part Two

Medicaid is just one part of a broader landscape of federal welfare programs that do more harm than good for black Americans.

Since the 1960s, progressive activists and Democratic politicians have taken it as a foregone conclusion that perpetually expanding federal welfare programs is the best way to help poor Americans and minorities, including black Americans. But over the years, the social safety net has entangled more people than it has saved.

Broadly speaking, this is because welfare programs discourage people from working and improving their socioeconomic status. As renowned economist Thomas Sowell put it, "The political left's welfare state makes poverty more comfortable, while penalizing attempts to rise out of poverty."[77]

The Wall Street Journal's Jason Riley expanded upon Sowell's argument in his 2014 book *Please Stop Helping Us: How Liberals Make It Harder for Blacks to Succeed.*[78] Riley noted that between 1940 and 1960, well before any major civil rights or welfare programs took effect, the black poverty rate fell from 87% to 47%—gains attributable to African American migration to city centers and increased educational attainment.

Yet between 1972 and 2011, the black poverty rate stayed largely the same.[79]

Sowell put a finer point on it: "You cannot take any people, of any color, and exempt them from the requirements of civilization—including work, behavioral standards, personal responsibility and all the other basic things that the clever intelligentsia disdain—without ruinous consequences to them and to society at large."[80]

Indeed, a 2020 study from the National Bureau of Economic Research found that one-quarter of America's poorest households face *lifetime* marginal tax rates of 70% if they earn their way out of welfare programs.[81] Summarizing the study in *The Federalist*, policy analyst Chris Jacobs explained the welfare trap quite nicely: "Given the construct of the modern welfare state, it seems less logical to ask why poor people wouldn't work and instead to ask why they would."[82]

Unfortunately, health care is one policy area where, despite all evidence to the contrary, progressives think the solution is to continually expand the size and reach of government-run programs. But, in fact, the opposite is true.

Escaping the Welfare Trap

Market-oriented reforms can help black Americans secure better health care at lower cost—and ultimately realize better health outcomes.

For example, lawmakers could expand the use of health savings accounts, or HSAs. These accounts allow patients to set aside money pre-tax to use later for qualified medical expenses.

HSAs are a win-win. They empower patients to take control of their health spending and in so doing inject a degree of competition and transparency into an otherwise opaque healthcare sector. When consumers can shop for health care just as they do for other goods and services in our economy, costs decline and quality improves.

At the moment, only individuals enrolled in high-deductible health plans are allowed to make HSA contributions. This unnecessary rule penalizes low-income people in particular. Half of Americans have annual healthcare expenditures below $1,000.[83] Contributing just $83 per month to these accounts would allow low-income people to cover their expenses and save for the future.

Employers could further unleash the benefits of HSAs by making deposits to the accounts on employees' behalf. According to research from HSA provider Health Equity, employers can save 9.23% on Social Security, Medicare, and unemployment taxes, and even more on corporate taxes, by contributing to employee HSAs. A 1,000-person company that contributes $1,000 to each employee's account could save $300,000 in taxes each year, according to Health Equity's math.[84]

Lawmakers could also raise the contribution limits on HSAs, which were $3,850 for individuals and $7,750 for families in 2023.[85] The Cato Institute's Michael Cannon has suggested creating "large HSAs" by raising the contribution to the equivalent of what employers would otherwise spend on insurance, $8,000 for individuals and $16,000 for families.[86] Alternatively, lawmakers could raise the cap to match contribution limits for tax-advantaged individual retirement accounts—as of 2023, $6,500 for people under 50, and $7,500 for everyone 50 and older.[87]

In addition, Congress can consider allowing individuals to use HSA funds to pay insurance premiums, which is currently against the law.

Finally, to help the 11% of black Americans 65 and older, lawmakers could free Medicare beneficiaries to contribute to HSAs—something they cannot legally do at present.[88]

• • •

The government safety net could use a dose of market-oriented reform, too.

Lawmakers can help break the poverty cycle by changing how Medicaid is administered. Under the status quo, the federal government matches every dollar states spend on Medicaid beneficiaries. States with lower per capita income receive more than a dollar for each dollar they spend on the program.[89]

In other words, states can effectively double the impact of each additional state dollar they invest in Medicaid by attracting at least one federal dollar to match. And people in other states largely foot the bill for such expansions.

This structure encourages wasteful spending. Instead, Medicaid funds should be disbursed to states as block grants. Not only would that require states to manage their Medicaid programs in a more disciplined fashion—it would also allow them to tailor their programs to fit the unique characteristics of their populations.

Crucially, states could rework Medicaid to save beneficiaries from falling into the poverty trap. For instance, they could affix work requirements to benefits in order to keep beneficiaries from falling out of the workforce entirely.

Critics of block grants and work requirements often argue that they'll cut low-income Americans off from benefits. That's debatable.

More importantly, keeping people enrolled in Medicaid for long periods of time is not a public policy success. We should be working to help people improve their economic station—to create opportunities that can allow them to purchase private insurance on their own or to secure coverage through work. That's better for taxpayers—and individuals, too.

One way lawmakers can expand access to affordable insurance is by relaxing the rules that cover short-term and association health plans.

Federal rules promulgated during the Trump administration allow short-term plans to last up to a year, to be renewed for up to three years, and to be exempt from covering the costly "essential health benefits" mandated under the ACA.[90] The average short-term plan costs 70% less than an unsubsidized ACA plan.[91]

As of 2023, short-term plans were unavailable in fourteen states, including New York and California, which have the fourth- and fifth-largest black populations, respectively, in the country.[92] [93] These bans are largely driven by Democrats, who deride the plans as "junk insurance," in part because they present a viable alternative to Obamacare exchange plans.

In July 2023, the Biden administration proposed to roll back the Trump-era rules and set a maximum duration of three months for a short-term plan—four months, if extended.[94]

These bans do more harm than good. According to the Manhattan Institute's Chris Pope, short-term plans offer patients access to broader physician networks, and at a lower price, than similar Obamacare plans.[95] Because short-term plans increase competition in the insurance marketplace, they drive down premiums across the board. Premiums fell between 2018 and 2021 in states that allow the sale of short-term plans.[96]

Association health plans permit small businesses and self-employed workers within the same sector to band together to buy health insurance like a large employer. Association plans are also exempt from the ACA's coverage mandates, which allows them to cut costs and tailor benefits packages to fit individual beneficiaries' needs.

Access to Care, Not Coverage

Perhaps even more urgent than expanding access to health insurance for black Americans is expanding access to medical care itself.

One-fourth of black Americans live in primary care shortage areas, compared to just 13% of white Americans.[97] Black Americans are also more likely to live in "trauma deserts," where the nearest adult level I or II trauma center is more than five miles away.[98] And predominantly black neighborhoods tend to have fewer pharmacies than predominantly white neighborhoods.[99]

Lawmakers can do several things to boost access to affordable care. First and foremost, they can dismantle legal and regulatory barriers that limit the supply of medical care.

For example, certificate of need laws prohibit the building of new facilities—and in some cases, even the offering of new services—without government approval.[100] Thirty-five states have certificate of need laws on the books, including 8 of the 10 states with the highest black populations.[101] [102]

These laws are meant to keep costs down by stopping providers from building costly facilities or installing expensive equipment that communities don't need. The thinking is that providers will raise rates or order unnecessary procedures and tests to recoup and justify capital investments.

But in reality, certificate of need laws restrain competition and give incumbents the opportunity to effectively veto new entrants. These restrictions on supply yield higher costs. Indeed, research from the Kaiser Family Foundation shows that per-capita health expenditures are 11% higher in states with certificate-of-need laws than in states without them.[103]

Similarly, scope-of-practice laws restrict what types of services physician assistants and nurse practitioners can provide without a doctor's supervision. Those rules have the effect of limiting the supply of care.

There are 355,000 nurse practitioners (NPs) in the United States. Each has a graduate degree and advanced medical training, as well as prescriptive privileges in all fifty states and the District of Columbia.[104] But in nearly half of states, NPs are not allowed to treat or diagnose patients without a physician's green light.[105]

Physician assistants are bound by similar restrictions. In nine states, they lack full prescriptive authority.[106]

Scope-of-practice regulations are meant to protect patients. But studies of NPs show they perform just as well as doctors.[107] According to one, "Patients were more satisfied with consultations with nurse practitioners than those with doctors."[108]

Moreover, that additional oversight is expensive. A study from the Mercatus Center found that prohibiting physician assistants

(PAs) from prescribing drugs to Medicaid beneficiaries raises costs by more than 11%, on average. That's equivalent to $109 in additional expenses per beneficiary.[109]

Further, we do not have enough doctors to meet patient needs, especially in underserved areas where black Americans disproportionately live. The United States faces a shortage of up to 124,000 physicians by 2034, according to the Association of American Medical Colleges (AAMC).[110] The AAMC projects that this coming doctor shortage will hit low-income and rural areas particularly hard.[111]

Already, NPs are more likely than primary care doctors to work in federally designated healthcare deserts.[112] Freeing NPs and PAs to practice to the full extent of their education and skills could significantly improve access to care for the people who live in these deserts.

• • •

There are other ways to address the looming physician shortage and thereby increase the supply of care. States can relax their licensing requirements to allow physicians to travel more freely across state lines. They can make it easier for doctors trained abroad to practice in the United States.

They can also join the Interstate Medical Licensure Compact, which allows doctors to get licensed simultaneously in several states. As of 2023, 34 states had joined the compact.[113] If the rest follow suit, doctors could move more freely around the country to fill gaps.

To expand the pipeline of future doctors, we'll have to increase the number of residency spots. The number of students who graduated medical school rose 33% from 2002 to 2020, but the number of available residency spots remained the same. As long as the demand for residencies outpaces the supply of residency spots, boosting medical school enrollment will not address the physician shortage.[114]

It's particularly crucial to increase the number of residencies in underserved areas, since doctors tend to practice where they train.[115]

Public- and private-sector leaders can also expand integrated medical school programs, which allow students to begin training as doctors right out of high school. Many of these programs last about six years and bring doctors into residency and the workforce faster.[116]

Combining undergraduate education with medical school reduces the number of years a student spends in school. So, it can reduce the amount of debt an aspiring doctor must take on.

That should be particularly appealing to aspiring black doctors and their families. Black undergraduates have historically taken on more debt than their white classmates—about $25,000 more, according to the latest data.[117]

Training more black doctors is one way to potentially boost overall black American health. Black doctors are more likely than non-black doctors to work in underserved communities and conduct medical research into topics that are pertinent to the health of the black community.[118]

Some research also suggests that black patients experience better health outcomes when treated by black doctors[119][120]—although those studies' methodological rigor has been questioned, and other studies have found inconclusive evidence of such benefits.[121]

● ● ●

Perhaps the best way to improve access to affordable health care is to ensure that black Americans have ample economic opportunity. Prior to the COVID-19 pandemic, the American economy was roaring, especially for black Americans. As Jason Riley noted in a January 2022 column, "Between 2017 and 2019, median household incomes grew by 15.4% among blacks and only 11.5% among whites."[122]

Black Americans who are economically secure are Americans who can afford high-quality coverage, who can pay for timely care from high-quality providers, and who have the resources to score well on social determinants of health.

The way to rectify the health disparities between black and white Americans is not to focus on their differences but their similarities. Regardless of race, American patients benefit when they have ready access to efficient, high-quality care.

By understanding the limitations of federal welfare programs and encouraging regulatory strategies that stimulate the economy and encourage competition in the healthcare sector, policymakers can boost health outcomes for black and white Americans alike.

A rising tide truly lifts all boats.

5

HOW *BROWN V. BOARD OF EDUCATION* ERASED A BEACON OF BLACK EXCELLENCE

Ian V. Rowe

On May 17, 1954, the United States Supreme Court issued a landmark ruling that is considered by many civil rights activists to be the greatest judicial decision of the twentieth century. In *Brown v. Board of Education*,[1] the Court addressed the issue that "minors of the Negro race had been denied admission to [public] schools attended by white children under laws requiring or permitting segregation according to race." This momentous overturning thankfully nullified the precedent of *Plessy v. Ferguson*,[2] which in 1896 had established the "separate but equal" doctrine that allowed the government to legally sanction racial segregation in public schools.

Delivering the unanimous opinion of the nine-member court, Chief Justice Earl Warren wrote, "We conclude that in the field of public education the doctrine of 'separate but equal' has no place. . . . Separate but equal educational facilities for racial minorities is inherently unequal, violating the Equal Protection Clause of the Fourteenth Amendment."[3]

The landmark decision thus rightfully deemed schools that were racially segregated by *order of law*, were in fact unconstitutional. This meant *de jure* segregation—schools enforced by the government to exclusively educate white students only and *mandatorily* ban black students because of their race—could no longer exist and would be punished if they violated the new ruling. Yet this also meant *de facto* segregation—schools that had exclusively educated black students on a *voluntary basis* even though laws did not require it—could not exist because the interpretation of the term "inherently unequal."

Encapsulated in those two words—inherently unequal—is a noxious and racially reductionist principle that has for decades hindered America's quest for racial progress. The *Brown* ruling essentially said that even if all other factors were equal—funding, adequate facilities, high-quality teachers—all-black schools were nevertheless seen by the Court as inherently unequal, or more precisely, intrinsically deficient. Racially segregated schools—whether formed by legal mandate or community preference—were now treated with the same constitutional hostility by the Court and thus suffered the same fate of ultimate eradication.

When the Court ordered states to carry out the decision to end racial segregation with "all deliberate speed," *how* the remedy should have been administered was not clear. Rather than explicitly limit its scope to just prohibit legal segregation by race and rectify the resource disparities between black and white schools, the order in practice went further to coerce racial integration.

All white schools that heretofore had been segregated by *law* would now be forced to integrate by race, typically through bussing black students to white schools. All black schools that had been segregated by *choice* were eventually forced to close since they would now be deemed unconstitutional, even if those schools had superior academic outcomes. As we will learn later in this chapter, this underlying premise of inferiority of black-only institutions led to the demise of the Rosenwald Schools, one of the greatest examples of self-determination by the black community to pursue excellence.

Thus, while the *Brown* decision established an important precedent to end legal racial segregation, it ironically represents one of the most vibrant examples of the theme of *The State of Black Progress*—how the purge of American principles, sometimes by well-intended Supreme Court decisions—led to unintended and adverse consequences for segments of the black community.

Renowned economist Thomas Sowell observed this paradox on May 13, 2004, on the fiftieth anniversary of the Supreme Court's historic decision in *Brown*. In *The Wall Street Journal*, Sowell wrote "there has been remarkably little critical examination of the reasoning used in that decision. Indeed, much of what has been said about that decision over the past half-century has treated the result as paramount and the reasoning as incidental. But today, with 50 years of experience behind us, it is painfully clear that the educational results of *Brown* have been meager for black children. Meanwhile, the kind of reasoning used in *Brown* has had serious negative repercussions on our whole legal system, extending far beyond issues of race or education."[4]

How could a Supreme Court ruling so lauded for its impact on liberating black children from schools mired in the perception of segregated squalor, in reality, have undermined the very idea of black excellence in education and helped to erase one of the greatest feats of agency by the black community? Unraveling the answer to this question requires understanding more of the contemporaneous challenges regarding the legal framework around racial segregation in post–World War II America. Moreover, we must dissect the surprisingly complex motivations of Oliver Brown, the lead plaintiff in *Brown*, and the father of Linda Brown.

According to The African American Civil Rights Network,[5] by 1951, the country had "experienced tremendous change that brought the nation closer to ending legal segregation. As the Cold War ideologies of the Soviet Union and the United States emerged as global counterpoints, the practice of racial segregation became an international issue, rather than a domestic issue. While the United

States sought new allies to counter Soviet gains in Eastern Europe, it needed to shed the hypocrisy of advocating freedom and equality for all on the international stage while denying basic rights to its African American citizens at home."

In 1947, President Truman signed an executive order to desegregate the military. The Supreme Court declared unconstitutional the racially restrictive covenants that prevented African Americans and other minority groups from purchasing property in white neighborhoods. In 1947, Jackie Robinson integrated Major League Baseball by joining the Brooklyn Dodgers. And in 1955, Rosa Parks's refusal to give up her bus seat ignited a 381-day boycott, leading to the desegregation of transportation in Montgomery, Alabama.

Despite this progress, public school education still suffered from legally sanctioned racial division. There were huge disparities in funding between black and white schools, facilities, access to equipment, and the quality of education.

In 1954, seventeen states had laws requiring segregated schools (Alabama, Arkansas, Delaware, Florida, Georgia, Kentucky, Louisiana, Maryland, Mississippi, Missouri, Oklahoma, North Carolina, South Carolina, Tennessee, Texas, Virginia, and West Virginia), and four other states had laws permitting rather than requiring segregated schools (Arizona, Kansas, New Mexico, and Wyoming).

Throughout these states, school districts had the expensive burden of operating two racially divided school systems within one jurisdiction. In Topeka, Kansas, half-empty classrooms in segregated schools had to be maintained in order to keep the races separate.[6] Against this backdrop, the leading civil rights organization at the time, the NAACP, was seeking an end to legal segregation of black and white students in public schools, particularly in the American South, where most of the states legally segregating schools were based. In order to find strong plaintiffs, the NAACP encouraged black families to apply to all-white schools.

At the time, the young Linda Brown (who died in 2018[7]) was a third grader who attended the segregated, all-black Monroe Elementary School, a twenty-one-block walk from her home in Topeka, Kansas. The nearest school in her neighborhood, Sumner Elementary School, was only a few blocks away. But it was legally segregated for white students only.

As pictured in a 1952 photo (Figure 5.1),[8] Oliver Brown, an assistant pastor at St. John African Methodist Episcopal Church, applied for his daughter Linda (Figure 5.2) to attend Sumner Elementary. But the school board prohibited Linda from enrolling on the basis of her skin color.

That action allowed Brown to join twelve other plaintiffs who collectively formed the class-action case whose official full name was *Oliver L. Brown et al v. Board of Education of Topeka, Shawnee County, Kansas, et al.* (Brown's last name was alphabetically first.). Overall, thirteen plaintiffs represented twenty children.

Figure 5.1. Oliver Brown.   Figure 5.2. Linda Brown.

What is not well known is that Oliver Brown and some of the other plaintiffs were referred to as what *The New York Times* called "Reluctant Icons."[9] According to *The Washington Post*, Brown wanted his daughter to be allowed to enroll in the all-white elementary school—not because he felt the all-white school was superior to the all-black elementary school she attended two miles away—but because it was a matter of principle.[10] During a speech at the University of Michigan,[11] Linda Brown as an adult described her dad as a heavyset man who had once been a Golden Gloves champion boxer, and this was a fight that he was determined to win.

Ironically, Linda Brown's mother—Mrs. Leola Brown Montgomery —had attended Monroe Elementary School as a child beginning as a first grader in the fall of 1927, and graduating from eighth grade in 1935.[12] Monroe had been an institution in the community for decades, as the impressive structure shown in Figure 5.3 indicates.

Figure 5.4 is a picture of the third and fourth grades at Monroe Elementary School in Topeka, Kansas in 1892.[13]

Despite the fact that Oliver Brown applied for his daughter to attend the all-white Sumner school, there is much evidence that

Figure 5.3. Monroe Elementary School, Topeka, Kansas.

Figure 5.4. Third and fourth graders at Monroe Elementary School, Topeka, Kansas, in 1892.

many parents in the black Topeka community actually opposed the NAACP efforts to desegregate schools, which would mean the disbanding of their all-black schools. According to Charise Cheney, Associate Professor at the University of Oregon and author of the upcoming book *What Do We Have to Lose? School Desegregation in Topeka, Kansas After Brown v. Board*, a "primary reason that black Topekans fought the local NAACP's desegregation efforts is because they appreciated black educators' dedication to their students. Black residents who opposed school integration often spoke of the familial environment in all-black schools.[14]"

Such support of all-black schools by the black community contrasted with the rationale for the *Brown* decision, which actually rested far more on conjecture and social science than upon factual outcomes of schools at the time.

With sweeping certainty, Justice Warren argued that: "To separate [children in grade and high schools] from others of similar age and qualifications solely because of their race generates a feeling of inferiority as to their status in the community that may affect their hearts and minds in a way unlikely ever to be undone.[15]" The effect of this separation on their educational opportunities was well stated by a finding in the Kansas case by a court that nevertheless felt compelled to rule against the Negro plaintiffs:

> Segregation of white and colored children in public schools has a detrimental effect upon the colored children. The impact is greater when it has the sanction of the law, for the policy of separating the races is usually interpreted as denoting the inferiority of the negro group. A sense of inferiority affects the motivation of a child to learn. Segregation with the sanction of law, therefore, has a tendency to [retard] the educational and mental development of negro children and to deprive them of some of the benefits they would receive in a racial[ly] integrated school system.[16]

Such statements posited as fact that segregation inevitably led to a "sense of inferiority" among black children. This was the predominantly accepted social science at the time. The *Brown* team decided to use this conventional wisdom to their advantage by asking noted black psychologist Dr. Kenneth Clark to provide testimony and coauthor a summary endorsed by thirty-five leading social scientists on the prevalent conclusions of the impact of segregation. According to the NAACP Legal Defense and Educational Fund, in the 1940s, psychologists Kenneth and Mamie Clark designed and conducted a series of experiments known colloquially as "the doll tests" to study the psychological effects of segregation on black children.

> Drs. Clark used four dolls, identical except for color, to test children's racial perceptions. Their subjects, children between the ages of three to seven, were asked to identify both the race of the dolls and which color doll they prefer. A majority of the children

preferred the white doll and assigned positive characteristics to it. The Clarks concluded that "prejudice, discrimination, and segregation" created a feeling of inferiority among African-American children and damaged their self-esteem.[17]

According to the National Archives, this dependence on social science dominated the reasoning of the ultimate decision. In its Primary Sources,[18] the Archives describe Thurgood Marshall, one of the lead attorneys for the plaintiffs (later to become a Supreme Court justice himself), and his fellow lawyers as providing testimony from more than thirty social scientists affirming the deleterious effects of segregation on black children. These arguments were similar to those alluded to in the Dissenting Opinion of Judge Waites Waring in *Harry Briggs, Jr., et al. v. R. W. Elliott, Chairman, et al.*:

> These [social scientists] testified as to their study and researches and their actual tests with children of varying ages and they showed that the humiliation and disgrace of being set aside and segregated as unfit to associate with others of different color had an evil and ineradicable effect upon the mental processes of our young which would remain with them and deform their view on life until and throughout their maturity.... They showed beyond a doubt that the evils of segregation and color prejudice come from early training.... it is difficult and nearly impossible to change and eradicate these early prejudices however strong may be the appeal to reason.... if segregation is wrong then the place to stop it is in the first grade and not in graduate colleges.[19]

It is surprising that Thurgood Marshall so forcefully argued these views of the inherent inferiority of segregated, all-black institutions given that he himself attended the all-black Colored High and Training School (later Frederick Douglass High School) in Baltimore, graduating in 1925 with honors, and then enrolled at Lincoln University in Chester County, Pennsylvania, the oldest college for African Americans in the United States. Marshall certainly didn't evidence an "evil and ineradicable effect" upon his mental processes.

Nevertheless, Marshall and his colleagues were determined to address the reality that due to the legacy of slavery, in the mid-1800s, black people had very little access to high-quality education. In slave states, anti-literacy laws banned black people from accessing education on the premise that a tipping point of literate slaves might lead to insurrection and rebellion. For example, South Carolina had a law that would jail a person for six months and impose crippling fines if you even attempted to teach a slave to read and write. Things did not get much better during the Jim Crow era, which legally segregated schools.

• • •

Thirty years prior to *Brown*—when racial segregation was at its worst—an unlikely partnership formed that transformed education for two generations of black students in the rural South.

Educator, activist, public intellectual, and founder of the Tuskegee Institute, Booker T. Washington, had himself experienced firsthand the destitution and profound racial disparities in the rural South. Despite these obstacles, Washington's perseverance and disciplined upbringing eventually led to an education at what is now known as Hampton University. As an adult, he dreamed of a school-building project for black communities throughout the South that could help begin to lift black people out of poverty.

Washington presented his ambitious idea to build a network of schools to Julius Rosenwald, who at the time was the CEO of the nation's largest retailer, Sears Roebuck. Rosenwald was a board member of the Tuskegee Institute, so he had a deep, respectful relationship with Washington.

Moreover, Rosenwald's parents had emigrated from Germany in 1854 to the United States to escape anti-Jewish discrimination. So, he was empathetic to the black community that was facing state sanctioned oppression. With this mutual understanding, Washington collaborated with Rosenwald, and together they crafted a plan to make Washington's dream a reality.

In a region of the United States in which "Jim Crow" racial segregation was law, lynching was a common and brutal reality, and rural poverty was widespread on both sides of the color line, these Rosenwald facilities were typically constructed, maintained, and partially funded by the populations they served, becoming centers of local social life and sources of community pride. "The [Rosenwald] schools also were the most architecturally advanced school plans of that time. The initial designers for the Rosenwald program included architect Robert Taylor, the first black graduate of MIT, (who was) considered the first professional black architect in America. George Washington Carver was the landscape designer," says Brent Leggs, senior field officer at the National Trust for Historic Preservation.[20]

Over the years, to construct the buildings, Rosenwald contributed $4.4 million, or what would be nearly $80 million today. And, importantly, $4.7 million came from local blacks, in the form of cash, labor, land, and materials. Washington and Rosenwald had launched a challenge-grant program that led to the unprecedented construction of more than 5,000 school buildings—4,977 schools, 217 teachers' homes, and 163 shop buildings in 15 states, from Maryland to Texas—all dedicated to the education of black students. (See Figure 5.) Built between 1917 and 1932, the Rosenwald Schools educated more than 700,000 black children over four decades.[21]

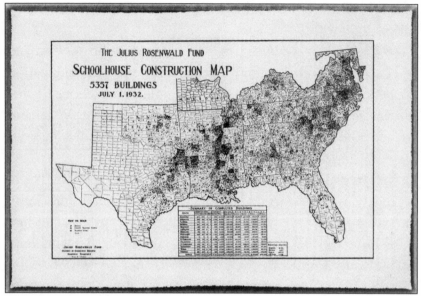

Figure 5.5. Julius Rosenwald Fund schoolhouse construction map (Fisk University Archives).

While the required donation from African American communities amounted to double taxation, their leaders nonetheless called on residents to organize fundraising drives to cover their share of a new school. "Get busy, Laurel, or hang your heads in shame," admonished the Prince George's Colored Public School Trustees in a 1924 report describing the existing pitiful buildings in the town of Laurel, Maryland.

The results were impressive. In one place, struggling sharecroppers set aside an area planted with cotton as the "Rosenwald Patch" and donated the profits from its sale to the school. Children saved pennies in snuff boxes, and at one fundraising rally, an old man who had been a slave offered his life savings of $38 "to see the children of my grandchildren have a chance."[22]

In the years between World War I and World War II, the Rosenwald schools helped close the gap between white and black academic achievement. Researchers at the Chicago Federal Reserve concluded that in the regions where "the Rosenwald Rural Schools Initiative built most of its 5,000 schools, the education gap between Southern-born Black and white males narrowed sharply in areas such as school attendance, literacy, and cognitive-test scores."[23] Using Census data and World War II records, the researchers found that Rosenwald's program explained a stunning 40% narrowing of the racial education gap. Many segregated schools, such as all-Black Dunbar High School in Washington, D.C., sent higher percentages of their students to college than comparable white schools did.[24]

Despite the proven track record of these all-black schools, when the U.S. Supreme Court ruled in *Brown* that legally enforced race-based segregation in schools was unconstitutional, exceptional all-black schools were impacted in different ways. According to economist Thomas Sowell, in Washington, D.C., "Dunbar [high school], which had been accepting outstanding black students from anywhere in the city, could now accept only students from the neighborhood in which it was located. Virtually overnight, Dunbar became a typical ghetto school. As unmotivated, unruly and disruptive students flooded in, Dunbar teachers began moving out and many retired. More than 80 years of academic excellence simply vanished into thin air."[25]

Throughout the American South, thousands of Rosenwald schools began to consolidate with white schools over time, and most of the structures were lost.[26] While there were student protests over their closing and demolition, most of the schools were gone by the 1970s. The Rosenwald Schools remain today one of the greatest examples of strong partnership across racial lines and black excellence, and they were ironically the victim of the unintended consequences of racial integration.

As a remembrance, in 2002, the National Trust[27] joined forces with grassroots activists, local officials, and preservationists to help raise awareness of this important but little-known segment of our nation's history, placing Rosenwald Schools on its 11 Most Endangered Historic Places list. Of the 5,357 schools, shops, and teacher homes constructed between 1917 and 1932, only 10–12% are estimated to survive today. The National Trust is providing technical assistance, grants, workshops, and conferences to help save these icons of progressive architecture for community use.

• • •

Fast forward to the present. What has the legacy of the *Brown* decision wrought for American public education overall, and in particular for the white and black students it was purported to serve and whose academic outcomes it was supposed to improve? According to the National Assessment for Educational Progress (NAEP)—also known as the Nation's Report Card—the percentage of fourth-grade public school students of all races performing at or above the NAEP Proficient level in reading was just 32% nationally in 2022.[28] It was only 29% for eighth-grade students in 2022.

NAEP results for the nation reflect the performance of students attending public schools, private schools, Bureau of Indian Education schools, and Department of Defense schools. Within the overall data, only 17% of black fourth-grade students and 42% of white fourth grade students performed at or above the NAEP Proficient level in reading in 2022. Indeed, in each year since the Nation's Report Card was first administered in 1992, less than half of the nation's white students in the fourth, eighth, and twelfth grades scored NAEP proficient in reading.[29] The sad irony is that closing the black-white achievement gap would mean black student outcomes would grow from sub-mediocrity to full-mediocrity. In 2022, NAEP also released its long-term trend reading and mathematics assessments, demonstrating that student achievement for nine-year-olds registered the largest average score decline in reading since 1990, and the first ever score decline in mathematics.[30]

As someone who has run public charter schools in low-income communities in the Bronx (borough of New York City) for over a decade, I know that the ultimate performance of any grouping of students has far less to do with their race than a range of factors such as quality of teaching instruction, high expectations, family structure and engagement, and the ability for parents and caregivers to choose the school they think is best for their child.

In places like the Decatur, Illinois, public school system, in 2019 only 2% of black third-graders were reading at grade level and only 1% were doing math at grade level. Is that absolutely dismal performance due to inferiority of skin color or systemic racism? As the reader ponders this question, it is instructive to note that in Decatur while single digit percentages of black students are reading at grade level, 97.3% of teachers were rated "excellent" or "proficient" in 2017, according to the Illinois State Board of Education. In 2018 that number was 99.7%. As *The Wall Street Journal* asks, "students are failing but the teachers are great?"[31] Perhaps an unaccountable and ineffective bureaucracy that leaves parents with no options is a more likely culprit, and not the racial composition of the students.

As evidence of how the ideology of *Brown* persists even in the present day—that an all-black education must be inherently bad—take, for example, the 2021 report from the UCLA Civil Rights Project.[32] The report outlined that "New York retains its place as the most segregated state for black students, and second most segregated for Latino students, trailing only California." The Civil Rights Project considers that "school segregation remains a vexing issue, with Black and Latino Students largely isolated from White and Asian peers." In an echo of Justice Warren's unanimous opinion in 1954, Gary Orfield, co-director of the Civil Rights Project said, "Racial segregation denies equal opportunity and creates a false path of inferior educational preparation that perpetuates inequality across generations."

What is so tragic about this misguided statement "of inferior educational preparation" solely due to race, is that in my ten-plus years running lotteries for public charter schools, I have never had a black nor Hispanic parent first ask if any white kids were enrolled at the school. Parents are desperate for high-quality options regardless of the racial makeup of the school, especially given the dismal choices currently available.

As another example, in District 12 of New York City (in the Bronx), of the nearly 2,000 public school students beginning high school in that district in 2015, only 7% graduated ready for college four years later. This means that a shocking 93% of students either dropped out of high school before completing their senior year, or if they did manage to graduate, they would still be required to take remedial classes in community college due to low math and reading scores on state exams. This district is composed of students who are predominantly black and Hispanic, and from low-income backgrounds. Yet there is currently a "cap" on public charter schools in New York City, banning the creation of new schools that could provide high-quality alternatives for parents desperate to send their kids to a great school. Without the ability to choose a good school, students from District 12 and many similar districts are almost guaranteed to require remedial classes in math and reading if they want to pursue a post-secondary degree.

This is why I founded Vertex Partnership Academies in the fall of 2022, the first-of-its-kind charter management organization that runs rigorous, character-based, International Baccalaureate public charter high schools, dedicated to equality of opportunity, individual dignity, and our common humanity. Vertex Student Scholars are immersed in a culture of democratic discourse guided by the four cardinal virtues of Courage, Justice, Temperance, and Wisdom. With the first campus now opened in the Bronx, the Vertex model requires and empowers all student scholars in grades nine and ten to take the International Baccalaureate Middle Years program. At the end of tenth grade, each student must choose either: (1) the International Baccalaureate *Diploma Program*, which prepares them to enroll and thrive in premier colleges and universities in the country or abroad; or (2) the International Baccalaureate *Careers Program*, which prepares them to graduate with a professional credential and directly enter the labor market with skills in a particular industry.[33]

These are the kinds of solutions that can actually unlock opportunities for millions of kids, not race reductionist ideas that unfortunately *Brown* set as a precedent.

• • •

As the Supreme Court put it in 1954's historic *Brown v. Board of Education* ruling: "It is doubtful that any child may reasonably be expected to succeed in life if he [or she] is denied the opportunity of an education." The Court described education as the "very foundation of good citizenship," and proclaimed that the "opportunity of an education . . . is a right which must be made available to all on equal terms." The lessons of *Brown* teach us that neither does the presence of white students guarantee a high-quality education, nor does the presence of all black students guarantee a substandard learning environment. Let us hope the promise of those powerful words can be achieved, regardless of the race of the students receiving that education.

6

K–12 EDUCATION: THE IMPERATIVE OF EMPOWERING PARENTS

Leslie Hiner

"Education…means emancipation. It means light and liberty."
— Frederick Douglass, 1894[1]

Parents today are demanding meaningful educational opportunities for their children in K–12 education. Parent groups advocating for the right to use education funding appropriated by legislators for their children's education are growing rapidly in numbers and influence. After experiencing inadequate learning support for their children, and closed schools, during the COVID epidemic, parents became painfully aware of what happens when their children do not receive a proper education: There is no light or liberty, as Frederick Douglass recognized well over 100 years ago.

In an interview with *The 74*, Sonya Thomas, executive director of Nashville PROPEL (Parents Requiring Our Public Education System to Lead), shared that many parents did not realize that their children's education was "so off track" until COVID revealed the truth. She furthermore exclaimed, "Nothing has changed. You would think that a pandemic would bring about a sense of urgency."[2] She has seen an increase in parents seeking educational choice, as many are feeling stuck, looking for help and answers.

Gwen Samuel, founder and president of the Connecticut Parents Union, voiced her demand for educational choice succinctly in a survey of parents published by the National Alliance for Public Charter Schools in 2022: "Our babies need schooling options now. Period. Education options help them move from surviving the pandemic to thriving despite the pandemic."[3]

Parents and grandparents expressing their frustrations about the weaknesses of the public education system they witnessed during COVID were vindicated by the National Assessment of Educational Progress (NAEP) scores, known as *The Nation's Report Card*. NAEP Long Term Trend (LTT) scores for nine-year-old children released in September 2022—the first assessment of academic achievement during COVID—revealed that children suffered unprecedented academic losses during COVID. The National Assessment Governing Board (NAGB) affirmed that reading scores revealed the largest decline since the 1990s and math scores declined for the first time in NAEP LTT testing history.[4]

A month after unveiling the LTT results, the NAGB released the NAEP results for fourth and eighth grade reading and math scores. The 2022 reports were consistent with findings from the LTT results. Achievement declines in fourth and eighth grade math scores were the largest reported "since initial assessments in 1990."[5]

The National Center for Education Statistics, a branch of the U.S. Department of Education, is concerned that this historic level of learning loss presents a serious and significant impact on educational achievement across the country. U.S. Secretary of Education Miguel Cardona stressed, "Let me be clear: these results are not acceptable."[6] Experts predict that the negative impact of learning losses for the current generation of children in K–12 education may last long into the future.

Furthermore, studies show that the level of learning loss varies according to a child's level of academic achievement at the beginning of COVID. A study of academic growth trends has revealed that achievement gaps between low-achieving and high-achieving children have widened.[7] Children who were struggling to achieve pre-COVID suffered more dramatic learning loss and lower improvement post-COVID than children who were in the higher level of academic achievement. This phenomenon has seen the greatest impact in areas with the greatest race and poverty disparities.

The widening gap between achievement levels will create hard-to-resolve challenges for teachers in diverse classrooms. Questions are emerging about how to provide additional support for children whose academic progress is slow to recover from COVID learning loss, while other questions are being considered about how to provide higher-achieving children the opportunities to excel at the same time.

Some education experts and public figures advocate helping the children quickly "catch up" academically. However, experts question whether children of the COVID generation will realistically be able to fully recoup their academic losses. Instead of placing the onus on public schools to magically fix dramatic educational losses from COVID, perhaps we should empower parents to stand up for their children and choose educational options that parents believe would best fit their children's crucial academic needs at this time. For example, tutoring, educational therapies, individual instruction, and more are all available to parents and children in states like Arizona and West Virginia that offer education savings account school choice programs. After all, it is reasonable to consider that a lack of accessible educational options during COVID may have contributed to the resulting learning loss problem.

Some foolishly doubt the motivation, perseverance, and knowledge of parents who are showing up at school board meetings complaining about curriculum and educational practices they witnessed during COVID. These practices failed to serve the educational needs of their children and disparaged values parents teach their children at home. Too many parents had a rude awakening to what their children were learning in school, and what they were not learning. Parental engagement at school district board meetings has become so active and contentious that one enterprising scholar has compiled a "Public Schooling Battle Map," listing parent complaints and demands as presented at school board meetings across the country. Concerns include sex education and sexually explicit learning materials, free speech restrictions, political bias in curriculum, gender identity confusion and pronouns, anti-Semitism and hostility toward religion, conflicting views on race relations and history, and even a question of whether the name of former President William McKinley is controversial, along with an extensive list of other grievances.[8]

Those looking to the future to find quick-fix answers for massive learning loss should understand that parents have played a central role in the development of education in this country and may be best suited to choose educational options that will be most advantageous for their children at this time. When education has gone off-course, or denied children basic human rights, throughout our nation's history parents and their supporters in the community have been the power behind forcing change, to right wrongs and get education on track.

Today, parents empowered with funding and knowledge about educational options play a key role in improving educational opportunities for children, and they fight for that opportunity.[9] Parents know that when they control how and where their children's state education funds are spent—at public or private schools or for other educational resources—education providers and policymakers have a compelling reason to listen to parents while working together to serve the needs of the children.

Parents are the first educators of their children and, in most cases, know the needs of their children better than anyone. Parents understand conditions where their children will be comfortable enough to relax, accept instruction, and engage in learning. This simple observation is normally disregarded as we focus on assigning children to schools to achieve policy goals such as maximizing financial benefit to public schools or creating a racial or income balance that fits broad societal goals. While these goals may have merit, if a child is failing to thrive because of the system established to accomplish those goals, that child's parents must have the option to find another way, another place, for their child to learn.

Government education systems are not worth much when they fail to help a child learn. At this time when children have lost so much learning in such a short period of time, we must refocus on providing parents the funded choice of educational opportunities most conducive for each child; our goal should not be to cram children *in general* into schools *in general* to fulfill a lofty government-mandated general policy. That's not working.

The most effective means to support each individual child is to empower parents to decide how and where a child is educated and to provide those parents with funding necessary to secure the educational resources their children need. This simple truth applies regardless of the nation's education challenges at any given time. Parents have a vested interest in seeing their children properly educated; if their children are failing to thrive, and if parents believe they can do something to improve their children's chances to succeed, they will stand up. Parents can be a powerful force for good.

In support of the proposition that parental control works, historical review will show that, whereas today's outspoken parents are often branded as political, bigots, not as smart as people with education degrees, or worse—domestic terrorists targeted by the FBI upon order of the U.S. attorney general as we witnessed in

2021—today's parents are well aligned with the parents and community leaders of our nation's founding period, who risked a great deal to make sure children received a proper education.[10]

The 1700s and Our Nation's Founding

The first public school, Boston Latin School, was established in 1635 by the Puritans, who recognized that knowledge of reading was necessary for their children to be able to understand the Bible. In 1647, the Massachusetts Bay Colony decreed that every town of fifty families should have a Latin school to also teach Puritan values and the Calvinist religion. [11] This edict was discretionary; taxation to pay for those schools was permissive, not compulsory, until 1827. Private schools thrived, while free public schools were largely regarded as places for pauper children.[12] When our nation's founders wrote the Constitution of the United States in 1787, they made no mention of education or schools. Education of children at the time of the founding was provided by parents, churches, towns, local women and tutors, and boarding schools (for wealthy families), while children participating in work apprenticeships typically learned basic reading and math skills on the job. There was no uniform method of providing education; it was handled locally, depending on the needs of individuals and their communities. Levels of learning, content of curriculum, and places of learning (in homes, churches, private or public schools, local gathering places) varied greatly.

Shortly after the end of the American Revolution in 1783, as the founders were designing a constitutional convention to revise the Articles of Confederation, they agreed that citizens should be educated with a common set of knowledge and ideals to be able to preserve freedom in this new nation. There was strong interest in unifying the country, in a manner that would set an example for new states to follow. To accomplish this goal, which included promotion of religious virtue and instruction in common values of morality and good character, states were *encouraged* to provide publicly funded schools open to all children.

Upon the initiative of Thomas Jefferson, this encouragement, which was not a government mandate, became attractive to those forming new states when federal land grants were offered to pay for establishing public schools in each township. This language was adopted in the Land Ordinance of 1785. Lands ceded to the country by "Indian inhabitants" would be surveyed and divided into 640-acre townships. The townships would then be divided into 36 sections, and the 16th section would be forever reserved for the maintenance of public schools. This language is still found in state constitutions today.[13]

The Northwest Ordinance of 1787, which was considered a counterpart to the Land Ordinance of 1785, created the Northwest Territory, and established a temporary government there, by which the territory could be divided into several states: Ohio, Indiana, Wisconsin, Illinois, Michigan, and the eastern part of Minnesota. This Ordinance contained a small bit of language encouraging the development of public schools.

The education clause in the Northwest Ordinance read:

> Religion, morality, and knowledge, being necessary to good government and the happiness of mankind, schools and the means of education shall forever be encouraged.[14]

This language adopted by Congress for the purpose of encouraging new states to create schools was simply encouragement; Congress did not mandate that states create and operate schools. However, Congress required the division of land granted to states to be done in a specific manner, which included setting aside the 16th section of each township as a method to raise revenue only for public schools. "Encouragement" was a way to compel states to create public schools without creating a federal mandate to do so.

The focus on morality and religion was reinforced by President George Washington when he stated in his 1789 inaugural address, "The foundation of our national policy will be laid in the pure and immutable principles of private morality." He and other founders perceived a need for citizens to be of good character with strong moral values so that policies adopted at the federal level—to reflect and serve the will of the people—would rest on a sure foundation.[15]

Several points merit attention: (1) A mix of individual morality and commonly held values was considered a preferred underlying foundation for education; (2) there was a general consensus that morality and values could not be learned or supported in the absence of religion; (3) education was considered a state, local, and personal issue (not federal except for land grants that offered funding for schools); and (4) although the federal government offered land grants to fund public schools, the requirement to create public schools was an encouragement, not a mandate.

Although parents who demand common morality, safety, and respect for God and country in public schools are considered radical today when they show up at school board meetings, at the time of our nation's founding, these principles were considered imperative to the future growth and success of the country.

Some call the land grant program an early federal-state partnership, while others view this as "carrot and stick" financial pressure that could not have been resisted by new territories requesting the right of statehood. Either way, the focus of education in our newly formed nation began with emphasis on families, communities, churches, personal morality, values, and religion—not government mandates or control.[16]

The Early- to Mid-1800s

Consistent with this focus on shared values, public schools taught a curriculum grounded in Protestant values. As states accepted land grants and made provision for trained teachers in the classroom (through the creation of what were called "normal" schools), teachers prepared to instruct children using the McGuffey Reader and the Old English Bible. Protestantism was considered an obvious and generally accepted way to teach good moral values and an understanding of God as a higher power. Protestantism was seen as divine truth, not a sect of a particular religion.

Horace Mann, a Unitarian, and secretary of the Massachusetts State Board of Education, is considered the father of public schools. He is largely credited for the rise of formalized public schools, the standardization of curriculum and testing, and the move to form American schools in the model of the Prussian factory schools where children would learn by rote while sitting in evenly spaced rows. In the early 1800s, Mann began the common school movement, which would be replicated in states across the country. He instituted statewide curricula and the funding of public schools using local property taxes. He also supported teaching Protestant values but rejected the Calvinist influence on discipline (which allowed physical punishment) and rejected the inclusion of any religious language or belief other than Protestant. At this point, the nation had shifted away from the Calvinism of the Puritans to Protestantism as a basis for instruction in schools.[17]

Prior to the imposition of compulsory education, attendance at any schools was inconsistent across the country. Parents did not jump at the option to send their children outside the home or church environment to be educated. The country was still largely rural and children were needed at home. In many areas, people objected to paying property taxes to support public schools and could not afford private school tuition.

A national compulsory education movement was created to require attendance at school; the nation's first compulsory education laws were passed in Massachusetts in 1852. Horace Mann's efforts to move the country into a full establishment of state-controlled Prussian-style public schools were the beginning of the highly regulated government-controlled K–12 education we have today. As the movement away from parent-controlled instruction to government prescribed instruction began, weaknesses in this system began to emerge.

One of the first challenges to government-controlled schools was the influx of immigrants into the country during the nineteenth century, many of whom were Catholic. Native-born Americans began to see public schools as a necessary means to imbue immigrants with American values and language. However, when Catholic children were required to read from and learn prayers from the Protestant Bible, conflict emerged. Those expecting to enjoy freedom of religion discovered that public schools only permitted freedom of one kind of religion, and that did not include Catholicism, practiced by most of the million-plus Irish immigrants who fled Ireland during the potato famine in the early to mid-1800s.

The Mid- to Late-1800s

Perhaps the most notorious conflict between Catholics and the public schools arose in 1854 in Ellsworth, Maine. When Catholic children objected to reading from the Protestant Bible, the town operating the public school did not accept their objection. When the children asked to read from their own Catholic Bibles because reading from the Protestant Bible and saying Protestant prayers was then considered an offense against their faith, the school expelled the children. In an angry public meeting, school leaders said, "We are determined to protestantize the Catholic children;

they shall read the Protestant Bible or be dismissed from the schools; and should we find them loafing around the wharves we will clap them into jail."[18]

The local Catholic priest, Father John Bapst, was then compelled to open a small school in the chapel of his church to educate the sixteen children who were expelled. As a result, the church was firebombed by those who believed that the children of immigrants must be compelled to attend public schools and accept the same common beliefs and values as everybody else. The public school was seen as a vehicle to force conformity of beliefs.

The father of Bridget Donahoe, one of the expelled students, billed the state for tuition at the new Catholic school his daughter attended due to being expelled. The state rejected his request, so he filed litigation against the town and the school.[19] At a public meeting discussing the lawsuit, town selectmen publicly threatened Father Bapst with harm and appropriated money to fight the lawsuit.

Local ruffians made good on the threat of the town selectmen, by kidnapping Father Bapst, stripping and denuding him, beating, and burning him, tarring and feathering him, running him out of town on a rail, and leaving him for dead—because he started a school for children after they were rejected by their public school.[20]

Father Bapst survived. He would not yield to the violence of those who would force so-called "common" values on others. With an unyielding will to survive notwithstanding harsh persecution for his faith, Father Bapst lived to become a founder and the first president of Boston College.

Parents of the Catholic students supported the Catholic Church in developing their own schools, which continue to this day.

While Father Bapst suffered horrible violence at the hands of those seeking to impose "common" values in 1854, he was not the only one who suffered for the sake of education in the nineteenth century when public schools began. The problem that emerged is that the focus on shared values began to shift; values supported by school and community leaders became limited in scope by the vested interests of some to exclude those who did not fit the interests of those in control of public schools.

Laws that forbade teaching slaves and free Negroes to read and write were prevalent in the South during the 1800s and continued in the form of Jim Crow laws in the early 1900s. In 1853 in Norfolk, Virginia, Margaret Crittenden Douglass learned from a local barber that there was nowhere for his children to receive instruction in reading and writing. Given that the barber and his children were free, not slaves, Margaret saw no reason why they should not receive such instruction. She believed strongly that every person should have religious and moral instruction, for which the ability to read was necessary. Ironically, her views were consistent with the intentions for public schools, that citizens share such common values. She offered to let her daughter instruct the children, and he accepted her offer. Sadly, Virginia had a law prohibiting "any white person" from assembling with slaves or free Negroes for the purpose of teaching them to read and write. Mrs. Douglass was sentenced to one month in jail for instructing free Negro children to read and write and was forbidden to continue offering instruction. [21]

These prohibitions and cultural discomfort with the education of black children emphasized the compelling necessity of reading and education to many who suffered under bondage. For example, the wife of Frederick Douglass's owner in Maryland secretly taught Frederick his ABCs. When her husband discovered his wife's deception, he angrily told her, "If you teach that nig— . . . how to read, there [will be] no keeping him. It [will] forever unfit him to be a slave." At that moment, Frederick Douglass learned that reading would unfit him for slavery; thus, he was determined to learn to read so that he could be unfit.[22]

In 1856, only two years after Father Bapst's terror in Maine, the infamous *Dred Scott* decision of the U.S. Supreme Court justified these anti-education laws by declaring that black people, whether enslaved or free, could not be citizens. The Court reasoned that, because the founders considered black people to be subordinate and inferior to whites, the Constitution could not have been intended to confer rights on black people as whites did not recognize blacks as peers at the time the nation was founded.[23]

Common prohibitions against educating black children and allowing black children to attend schools with white children were cruel vestiges of slavery. Unsurprisingly, these prohibitions persisted in most of the Southern states that fought to preserve slavery during the Civil War of 1861–1865. States that opposed slavery were more likely to permit the education of black children and some states allowed integrated public schools. Massachusetts outlawed segregated public schools in 1855, before the Civil War, which was unusual yet understandable given the long-standing respect for education in that state.

History is replete with stories about children denied the right to be educated, or the opportunity to be well educated, either by law or by culture. When this occurs, there is usually a parent, community of parents, or someone in a position to take action to help the children—individuals like Father Bapst, Bridget Donahoe's father, Margaret Douglass, and the wife of Frederick Douglass's slave owner.

Sometimes courts were useful, at least in the North. In April 1868, before ratification of the Fourteenth Amendment, granting her citizenship, Susan Clark, of Muscatine, Iowa, sued the board of directors of the local white school for denying her admission to the school. The board's defense was that Susan was of the "colored race" and that they had a separate school for children of her race. The Iowa Supreme Court held that the board had no such discretion. Under the laws of 1868 in Iowa, all children between five and twenty-one years of age had an equality of right to attend common schools, and that meant that the board had no discretion to tell Susan that she could only attend a separate school. The Court opined that "all youths are equal before the law." Susan was admitted to the white school.[24]

Notwithstanding adoption of the Fourteenth Amendment to the U.S. Constitution in July 1868, which granted citizenship to formerly enslaved people, in years following the Civil War, *separate but equal* became the new cultural standard. This standard was memorialized by the U.S. Supreme Court in *Plessy v. Ferguson*.[25] The problem was that "equal" did not carry its usual meaning. Public schools for black children that were deemed "equal" were *good enough* according to some, but severely lacking in quality. They were in no way comparable to white schools; they received only a small fraction of the funding received by white schools.

Once again, parents and people in a position to help stepped up.

The Early to Mid-1900s

Booker T. Washington of the Tuskegee Institute and Julius Rosenwald, a Jewish philanthropist and president of Sears Roebuck, stepped up to help black children in the South who were failing to learn at barely funded, segregated public schools or who were unable to access any school. Between 1917 and 1932, 5,000 Rosenwald Schools were built in the South and served more than 700,000 black children over a forty-year period.[26] The need was great; these schools were built during the zenith of the Ku Klux Klan (KKK) in America. The rebirth of the KKK began in 1915 and soared to a membership of several million before collapsing under the weight of its own corrupt leadership in the late 1920s. That Washington and Rosenwald were so successful at educating largely poor black children in the South during this time of the KKK's greatest strength is truly a story of courage and perseverance.[27]

By 1918, all children were required to attend school because of the successful compulsory education campaign begun by Horace Mann in the late nineteenth century. Oregon went too far and required attendance at public schools only, effectively eliminating private schools. Nuns operating a private Catholic school sued, and the U.S. Supreme Court in 1925 held that, "The fundamental liberty upon which all governments in this Union repose excludes any general power of the State to standardize its children by forcing them to accept instruction from public teachers only. The child is not the mere creature of the state; those who nurture him and direct his destiny have the right, coupled with the high duty, to recognize and prepare him for additional obligations."[28] This ruling remains good law today.

This ruling by the U.S. Supreme Court clearly upheld the original intent of our nation's founders. The obligation for children to learn was clearly presented as a duty, as the founders intended, yet the high court preserved the right of parents to determine how and where their children would receive an education. The founders "encouraged" but did not mandate public schools; their focus rested on lifting education as a priority to establish a focus on shared values in our new nation yet left the method of education discretionary.

Rosenwald schools began to close after the National Association for the Advancement of Colored People (NAACP) Legal Defense and Educational Fund won a decisive victory against segregated schools in *Brown v. Board of Education*.[29] The battle to desegregate public schools was hard-fought and took years of work by smart, dedicated lawyers and black parents whose strength of conviction could withstand ongoing persecution. *Brown v. Board* was decided in 1954, with a second opinion issued in 1955 designed to compel implementation of their decision without delay. Reaction to *Brown v. Board* was a mix of acquiescence and violent objection; courage was necessary by all those involved in the legal case and subsequent desegregation of schools.

Parents stood strong as they sent their children into schools where white adults lined the path into the building, hurling obscenities. Parents stood strong as their children were escorted into school by armed members of the military. Parents stood strong as friends and neighbors chastised them for raising the ire of white government officials and unknown ruffians who would make life more painful for blacks because of parents standing up for the right of their children to receive a proper education.

Desegregation to Resegregation

Busing black children to white schools was part of desegregation. It did not last. Busing was extremely controversial, as it uprooted children from the safety and comfort of learning in an environment familiar to them. Busing began in 1971, when North Carolina was sued for continuing to maintain segregated schools well over ten years past *Brown v. Board*. Although busing was seen as a way to implement and enforce the U.S. Supreme Court's order to desegregate the schools, it worked fairly well in some areas, but was a disaster in others.

In 1965, the Massachusetts state legislature enacted the Racial Imbalance Act, which outlawed schools with a student body of over 50% minority. However, for nine years the Boston School Committee paid no attention to the Racial Imbalance Act, which led to the NAACP suing to enforce the Act. They alleged Boston had an intent to segregate the children by creating a dual education system that separated black and white students and underfunded black schools.

Boston's busing system began in 1974 by federal court order. The court's remedy was to invoke a plan of extreme busing whereby white children would be bused to black schools on the opposite side of town and vice versa. This plan took children from Irish

Catholic neighborhoods with a strong sense of identity and bused them to black ghettos with their own very different sense of identity and culture.

In 1975, hundreds of mothers reciting "Hail Marys" marched to the Bunker Hill Monument to protest forced busing. A skirmish broke out between the mothers and police. These protestors were largely working-class mothers who opposed sending their children across a very large city to attend school, which had the effect of disrupting the continuity of both white and black neighborhoods. There was regular unrest.

Parents asked the court to allow open enrollment, a form of school choice that was available for the court to use as one option to desegregate the schools. That request was denied.

Parents had lost the right to decide where to send their children to school, had lost their natural choice. A leader of mostly stay-at-home moms in Charlestown said, "I want my freedom back. They took my freedom. They tell me where my kids have to go to school. This is like living in Russia. Next they'll tell you where to shop."[30]

Thomas Sowell opined that "the black family—which survived slavery, discrimination, poverty, wars, and depressions—began to come apart as the federal government moved in with its well-financed programs to 'help.'" A Roxbury mother in Boston said, "Busing took away the community feeling we had for our neighborhood schools," she says, "the feeling of 'It's our school and we love it.'"[31]

Busing ended in Boston in 1988. The public school district had declined from 100,000 to 57,000 students. Parents spoke with their feet.

Resegregation

Elsewhere across the country, racial achievement gaps of the 1960s and 1970s were substantially narrowed by the 1980s. It appeared at the time that desegregation was working to reduce racial inequality in educational achievement. The outcome of desegregation appeared positive for black students academically, and no negative impacts were found for white students.[32]

However, public schools today are segregated once again by race and income inequality; levels of academic achievement are dismal. Yet there is little urgency in public policy or from parents to integrate the schools, as occurred in the 1950s. Indeed, many parents in the black community seek schools that are predominantly black, particularly when this includes a majority-black teaching staff.

Ongoing long-term studies at Stanford University's Center for Education Policy Analysis reveal that racial segregation is not the lone driver of achievement gaps between black and Hispanic students and white and Asian students. Racial segregation's impact on achievement gaps is related to racial *economic* segregation. When a school's racial segregation of black and Hispanic children creates racial economic segregation, i.e., if the black and Hispanic children being racially segregated are, along with their peers, living in high poverty, it is the racial economic segregation that drives continuing achievement gaps. Whereas low-funded schools may have difficulties delivering education, the funding of the school is just one of many variables that may explain growing achievement gaps.[33]

Strategies to reduce racial segregation alone will not be enough to achieve racial equality of educational opportunity. As racial income and wealth disparities fall away, racial segregation may also decline. However, it is inconceivable that government mandates or more public school regulations or programs will create wealth in high-poverty racial minority communities; also, direct aid is not a long-term sustainable solution.

Frederick Douglass was right: Education is emancipation. The most direct way to facilitate educational opportunity that leads to personal freedom, for any child, is to empower parents with the freedom and funding to choose whatever educational option will best serve that child. This will not create wealth and income equality overnight, but it will open the path toward income equality, success, financial reward, and happiness for this generation and future generations.

Conclusion

The focus on shared values (based on virtue, not government fiat), which has been an underlying theme of education in this country since the founding, continues to enjoy support today. School parents were asked recently in a national poll whether they believe it is important for students in grades 9 through 12 to learn "values, moral character, or religious virtues." By a wide margin, black parents more than any other demographic said this is extremely important (56% of black parents versus 34% average of other demographic groups). Also, 78% of black parents said it is very or extremely important.[34]

Two years after busing ended in Boston, the nation's first modern-day voucher—giving parents the funded option to access schools for their children that shared their values—was advocated by a strong parent-led coalition in Milwaukee, then signed into law in 1990. Today, parents in thirty-two states, plus the District of Columbia and Puerto Rico, have the funded opportunity to choose private schools and other educational options for their children's K–12 education. Parents may access state funding or private scholarships funded by private donors incentivized with state tax credits. State legislators have enacted a total of seventy-seven educational choice programs; twenty states offer multiple programs to help parents fund education. West Virginia offers one program, the Hope Scholarship education savings account, but nearly every parent in the state has access to this funding. Arizona's education savings account is also now open to all children in the state. Eight more states—Arkansas, Florida, Indiana, Iowa, North Carolina, Ohio, Oklahoma, and Utah—passed similar programs.[35]

States commonly expand educational choice programs because they work. Parents in states without educational freedom continue to demand the right to have school choice. As evidenced here, the system of public education in our country is not infallible and cannot serve every child because children and families have diverse needs and values that may not be achievable or shared by the government-operated education system. Nonetheless, all children and families have value in the eyes of God and deserve equality of educational opportunity. Parents will stand up and fight for their children to have access to education that works for them. All parents should be empowered with educational choice, providing the vehicle for their children to access the light and liberty of education.

7

HOW PUBLIC HOUSING HAS HARMED BLACK AMERICA— AND STILL DOES

Howard Husock

The very names of the housing projects tell a story about Black America. In New York, there are the Langston Hughes and James Weldon Johnson Houses, named for the Harlem Renaissance poet and the composer of "Lift Every Voice and Sing" (the "Negro National Anthem"), respectively. In Detroit, there were the Frederick Douglass Houses, until they were demolished. In Chicago, the Robert Taylor Homes were named for a pioneering black banker and Chicago Housing Authority member. They were also declared "severely distressed" and demolished. But there can still be found in Chicago the Ida B. Wells Homes, named for the courageous anti-lynching journalist—and later the subject of a searing documentary film by famed director Frederick Wiseman.[1]

That so many of the projects were named for African-Americans provides a lesson about both history and the present. Public housing, championed by progressives including Eleanor Roosevelt, was meant as a particular benefit for blacks. Indeed, Roosevelt herself attended the ribbon cutting for Detroit's Brewster Houses. The prevailing idea was clear: This was to be housing for African-Americans—replacing the "slums" they were said to have lived in and, as implied by the project names, slated to continue to be housing for blacks—a benefit for a minority facing both poverty and discrimination in the private housing market. Public housing would not only be for blacks—but they were not to be excluded and, because of their concentration in neighborhoods denigrated as slums, were effectively designated as beneficiaries.

The benefits, both of public housing and successor forms of subsidized housing, have proved illusory, to say the least. The "projects," far from replacing slums, instead required the demolition of important, self-reliant black communities across the United States—replete with homeowners; small, black-owned businesses; churches; and mutual aid groups. Viewed from the outside, they were slums; experienced from the inside, they were communities. The belief that the government could manage and maintain housing better than "slumlords" would be tragically contradicted by the combination of public housing's rapid physical decline, an environment without local owners that fostered crime, and policies that encouraged single parenthood.

It is only slightly hyperbolic to characterize a great many public housing projects—named, ironically, for successful black Americans and overwhelmingly black residentially—as de facto reservations, versions of South Africa's apartheid-era townships. One cannot but conclude otherwise when visiting the East New York section of Brooklyn, where the Brownsville Houses, the Langston Hughes Houses, and the Marcus Garvey Houses all loom, framing canyon-type streets without stores or street life, in keeping with the modernist vision of those who planned them. Predominantly black Brownsville has the highest concentration of public housing in the nation. Within one square mile, the community comprises more than 873 stories in more than 100 different buildings.[2] Some 65% of Brownsville Houses residents are black; the remaining residents are virtually all Hispanic, many of whom are also people of color.[3]

The numbers are sobering. In a nation in which 13% of the population is African-American, 47% of those who live in public housing overall are black.[4] Blacks similarly comprise 40% of "beneficiaries" of the program meant to improve on public housing— "housing choice vouchers" (a.k.a. "Section 8," named for a section of the National Housing Act), which subsidizes private apartment rentals. (It's common for residents of housing projects that have been demolished to be given such vouchers.) What's more, 44% of the nearly 1 million public housing apartments still standing are 80% or more "minority," as per federal data. What was conceived as a benefit has, for many, become a dead end of poverty for many.

The average time lived in a New York City public housing project is more than twenty years. They live in buildings that a federal monitor of that system described this way:

> Mold grows unchecked at many NYCHA developments, often on a large scale. Across the city, residents are provided inadequate heat in winter, leading to frigid apartment temperatures. Pests and vermin infestations are common, and as senior New York City officials have acknowledged, NYCHA "has no idea how to handle rats." Elevators often fail, leaving elderly or disabled residents trapped in their apartments or sleeping in building lobbies because they cannot return to their homes. Leaks, peeling paint, and other deterioration are commonplace, but go unaddressed.[5]

It is well worth reviewing how all this happened—the neighborhoods Black America lost, how blacks were steered into public housing, its disincentives to self-improvement—and the steps that should be taken to extricate blacks from housing that invites dependency and discourages upward mobility.

That black neighborhoods were leveled to make way for public housing is undeniable. Public housing and its close and enabling cousin, urban renewal, had twin goals: to clear away "slums" and to replace such neighborhoods with "safe and sanitary" government-owned-and-operated housing. It was considered a mark of progressive thinking to be willing to include black neighborhoods among those that would benefit. It was entirely fitting that Roosevelt, the quintessential patrician progressive First Lady, herself cut the ribbon in 1935 on one of the nation's first public housing projects, the Brewster Houses in Detroit.

The Brewster project literally replaced a portion of the Detroit neighborhood of Black Bottom (not a racial term originally), where, no doubt, some residents lived in difficult conditions— including a lack of indoor plumbing. But Black Bottom was also a neighborhood where black Southern immigrants were flocking for freedom and opportunity and where black property and business ownership was common. The Urban League and other black mutual aid groups were active, as was religious life.

The 1930 Census captures the specifics of what actually stood on Brewster Street before it faced the wrecking ball. On this one short street alone, there were thirteen businesses, including a tire "recliner," a store fixtures manufacturer, a lumber business, and one simply described as a "factory." One cannot know how many were owned by blacks—but they were places that offered employment. In addition, this one neighborhood street had two churches, including one almost certainly a black congregation (Antioch Baptist), a grocery, a restaurant, a city recreation center and playground, a lawyer's office, a contractor, and a taxi and livery service. (Think here of August Wilson's brilliant play *Jitney* to ponder how a simple taxi business could be a key part of local life.) Brewster Street was, in other words, the site of urban dynamism—even more so because it intersected Hastings Street, black Detroit's commercial and entertainment heart, where the blues was being played at Porter Reed's Music Bar, Blue Haven, the Silver Grill, Joe's Tap Room, and countless other small businesses.[6]

A varied supply of residential property on Brewster Street, too, offered a chance to own small homes, many with rental units offering the chance for owners to begin to accumulate wealth. On one relatively short block, there were no fewer than 34 two-to-four-family homes, the majority of them two-family structures whose rental income could help make ownership possible. Others had ground-floor retail space and residential apartments above them—again offering a combination of residential and income-producing property. This was, in other words, city life in what could well be called an immigrant neighborhood, a destination of the fabled Great Migration from the Deep South. The local owners of such housing faced economic competition for tenants from public housing—which, at least when it opened, featured more modern housing at artificially low rent. From the start, public housing, then, was a threat to black property values and gradual wealth accumulation.

It would all be swept away by a combination of highway construction (the Chrysler Freeway) and public housing—"projects" in which ownership was a contradiction in terms, in which there were no stores, restaurants, blues joints, or grocery stores. Its modernist designers—influenced by world-famous architects including Le Corbusier and Philip Johnson—believed commercial and residential uses should be kept separate—and public housing set into campuses with "towers in the park." It was the government endorsement of this vision—notably through its implementation by city planning czars such as New York's Robert Moses—that allowed it to take physical form.

The story of Brewster Street, moreover, was the story of Chicago's Bronzeville, Pittsburgh's Hill District, central Harlem in New York, Desoto-Carr in St. Louis, Central Avenue on Cleveland's East Side—black neighborhoods all of which faced the wrecker's ball, to be replaced by the alleged benevolence of public housing.

Not only couldn't residents own their own housing in the "projects," but they were denied the potential appreciation in value of the properties they had owned in historically black neighborhoods. Property ownership would have offered a chance to accumulate wealth. There is no doubt that black wealth growth was deeply harmed prior to the 1968 Fair Housing Act by notorious policies such as "redlining"—the approach used by the Federal Housing Administration to designate newly developing suburban neighborhoods as off-limits to blacks because of government fears that black presence would cause whites to leave and undermine home values that government was insuring. So, too, was it held back by outright discrimination and racial covenants (which, it's worth noting, also targeted "Hebrews").[7] But the substitute—public and other forms of subsidized housing—would cause their own substantial damage. Worse still, that damage is still ongoing.

One must acknowledge, to be sure, that moving out of black neighborhoods, for those who would have liked to do so, was not easy in 1935, when the Brewster Homes were opened. That had been the "up and out" path of European immigrants. It was not illogical, in the face of racial covenants and white hostility, for progressives such as Eleanor Roosevelt to conclude that government provision of better residences was the right approach. That far less would have been required to make modest physical improvements in Black Bottom or other thriving black neighborhoods was not considered, however. Think here of parks, pools, and playgrounds, even public baths, as had once been built to ameliorate conditions in the cold water flats of New York's Lower East Side. Improved "public goods"—including good local schools—complementing neighborhoods replete with dispersed ownership, businesses, and churches would have been a far better approach than demolition.

Instead, blacks were steered into public housing.

Blacks had the misfortune of arriving in the Northern cities at the same time the public housing movement and its close cousin and enabler, urban renewal (first authorized through federal funding in 1949), reached policy fruition. Instead of property ownership, blacks would disproportionately become tenants of government. The implications of that are many and subtle—not just for accumulating wealth but for community life and behavioral norms. When one is a small, owner-occupant landlord—of, say, a two-family home—one is a kind of small businessperson, mindful of expenses but also keeping the customer (the tenant) satisfied. Leaky roofs will not do.

Tenants cannot afford to be blasé about potential eviction—and thus have good reason to keep their children in line. So, too, did they have the example of property ownership before them, in the person of neighborhood landlords, a status to which they might aspire. By contrast, in public housing, inviting extended family members or others to share one's apartment violates the rules, limiting occupancy to those on the lease. In a private dwelling, one may choose to take in lodgers or voluntarily accept crowding with extended family members as a way to accumulate savings.

Immigrant groups today continue that approach, in part because "overcrowding" can be a considered way to save for eventual home purchase. Foreign-born Asians and Hispanics are both more than twice as likely[8] to live in a technically overcrowded residence than U.S.-born blacks. It might seem counterintuitive to view crowding as a rational choice—but it can be, and it's one that accepting public or subsidized housing forecloses.

When one owns property, one must learn to maintain and repair—often through do-it-yourself techniques designed to minimize costs. In public housing—or later versions of subsidized housing—one lives what amounts to an institutionalized life, in which one appeals to a faceless management for repairs or improvements. Together, all these factors lay the groundwork not for self-improvement and upward mobility but for dependency.

The sheer numbers are important. Blacks comprise some 13% of the overall U.S. population—but 48% of public housing households.

Not coincidentally, blacks lag whites in homeownership—43% compared to 71%.[9] Received wisdom may implicate racism and poverty—but public and subsidized housing must share the blame. So must the 1949 amendments to the National Housing Act, which funded "urban renewal"—providing funds for cities that took it upon themselves to clear cut black neighborhoods.

Absent federal funding to demolish it, Black Bottom might still be standing. Sales of property there might have financed improved financial standing for residents. Instead, Washington made possible what Aretha Franklin—in her version of B. B. King's "Why I Sing the Blues"—called "Negro removal," the phrase that began at the grassroots and was popularized by James Baldwin. Aretha knew firsthand. Her father's church was originally in Black Bottom. Again, keep in mind that there were decades following the demolition of Black Bottom during which Detroit was not yet in its Rust Belt configuration but was prosperous.

To be sure, physical conditions in the early days of public housing were generally an improvement over the older homes where blacks had become the latest immigrant wave to live. (Indeed, in and around Brewster Street, Jews and Jewish-owned businesses remained in 1930). But conditions in high-profile projects quickly deteriorated—as questionable design combined with decreasing revenues from tenant rents. Public housing policy had originally assumed that those rents would support the operations and maintenance of the buildings. But that was not to be.

Catherine Bauer, the early public housing advocate whose 1934 book *Modern Housing* was the movement's blueprint, would note by 1957 that households with a choice of where to live were choosing to leave public housing, leaving behind only the poorest.[10] Those households balked at the rent levels that would have been required for adequate maintenance. So it was that, in 1969, tenants, in what would become the signature project for public housing's ills—the thirty-three high-rise buildings that comprised the Pruitt-Igoe complex in St. Louis—staged a well-publicized rent strike.[11]

The tenants were overwhelmingly black, and their concerns were heard by Massachusetts Senator Edward Brooke, the first black senator elected since Reconstruction. He introduced the so-called Brooke Amendment to the National Housing Act—which, by law, limited public housing rents to 25% (later 30%) of household income.[12] In one stroke, public housing authorities would be starved of maintenance funds—and resident households would face a profound disincentive to increase their earnings.

When one's rent increases with income, that disincentive is very real. No private tenant would ever sign such a lease—but millions of black Americans remain saddled with one. Economists call this a high marginal tax rate—33 cents on every additional dollar one earns must go to the government landlord.

Notably, the same income rule applies to those receiving housing vouchers—the program of rent subsidies that began in 1973, as the physical problems of public housing became well known—especially through the dramatic demolition of the entire Pruitt-Igor complex. As with public housing, black Americans would "benefit" disproportionately from what are now called Housing Choice Vouchers, which subsidize rentals in privately owned apartments. Blacks comprise 40% of housing voucher recipients. [13]

The lure of dependency takes further forms. Households get priority for public or other subsided housing based on income—those in most need, that is, the poorest, go to the head of the line.

Such households, not surprisingly, tend to be single-parent, female-headed families.

Only 6% of public housing households, and 8% of voucher households, are married couples raising children.[14] The remainder are single parents or the low-income elderly, many of whom were once raising children by themselves but whose own kids have moved out, in some cases to their own subsidized unit. That can be the case because—in contrast to cash public assistance—there is no limit to the time one can stay in public or subsidized housing. In New York City—with some 180,000 public housing apartments—the average "tenure" is more than twenty years.

So it is that public and subsidized housing must be implicated in the increase in black, single-parent households. Their poverty helps them qualify for assistance, by enabling them to get priority on waiting lists. Indeed, young mothers of new babies who are doubled up with their own mothers are technically considered "homeless"—that is, they lack their own homes—and go to the head of the housing help line.

The effects of the rise in single parenthood among blacks cannot be overlooked when considering the racial gap in homeownership rates. The Urban Institute has found that "if black households were married at the same rate as white households, the black-white homeownership rate gap would decrease by 27 percent."[15] The same research finds that the racial homeownership gap is greater today than when housing discrimination was legal—and, of course, when urban renewal had yet to demolish communities in which black owner-occupancy and owner-presence had yet to be replaced by public housing.

Tragically, we cannot undo the mistakes and damage of the housing policy past—with which millions of Americans, including a disproportionate number of black Americans, continue to live. We can, however, take steps to ameliorate the damage.

That means changing the rules that govern public and other subsidized housing. Those living in such apartments must be free to sign the same type of rental leases as nonsubsidized households enjoy: a flat rent for a fixed period. As it stands, as voucher or public housing tenants earn more income, they pay more rent—34 cents on each new dollar (30% of income). This has all sorts of ill effects: discouraging finding a higher-paying job, forming two-income families that would face higher rents, and discouraging savings. We should follow the example of the Delaware State Housing Authority, which, as part of its Moving to Work program, combines capped rent and savings account escrows with a seven-year ceiling on assistance.[16] Rents saved by the option of a fixed-rate lease are placed into an escrow savings account. A similar program has been adopted by the housing authority of San Bernadino, California, which specifically sets out as a key goal the encouragement of tenants' economic independence, including what it calls a shift from "entitlement to empowerment." Longitudinal studies out of San Bernadino report the positive results:

- Earned income for families in the program increased by an average 31.4% during their five-year term of assistance.
- Full-time employment increased by 20%.
- Unemployment decreased by 26.5%.

Of course, as households move out and up, vouchers become available for other needy families.[17] This healthy turnover should be a core part of public and subsidized housing. Poverty should not be viewed as inevitable, nor should support continue without limit.

These findings point to practical ways to move toward a less dependency-inducing system. The U.S. Department of Housing and Urban Development (HUD) reports an 8% turnover rate annually among housing voucher units; it has risen to as high as 15% in some years. That suggests that as new tenants enter the system, new rules could be applied—gradually shifting the program from an unlimited safety net to a transitional form of support. Increasing turnover while improving the situation of vouchered households should be key goals of the program.

Nor should more imaginative approaches be ruled out. The Atlanta Housing Authority (AHA), after demolishing virtually all its public housing projects, provided housing vouchers for the former tenants—but linked that support to work (or ongoing education or training) requirements. In 1994, Renée Glover, a child of Jim Crow–era Jacksonville, Florida, took the reins of the AHA—then the nation's fifth-largest public-housing system, with 50,000 tenants and voucher recipients, 99% of them, like her, African-American.

When Glover took charge of the AHA, just 18.5% of household heads in the city's bleak projects held jobs. At a time when Atlanta had the nation's highest murder rate, crime was six times higher in the projects than the city average.

Lawlessness prevailed in these campus-style complexes. Drug gangs had their own apartments for conducting business, such as grisly initiation ceremonies (in one, teenagers performed oral sex on a six-year-old boy to prove that no act was too horrible to commit). Calls to 911 were so numerous, Atlanta police said that reports of anything but the worst violent crime had to wait, sometimes for more than eight hours.

"It was very common to start the night shift with 50 or 60 calls pending," said one official.[18] In part, that's because the projects came alive at night, especially during the summer. With so few residents working, most slept during the heat of the day and came out after dark. "You'd think it was midday at midnight," observed Glover. "Everyone was out barbecuing, partying on the porches. And you were always hearing gunfire."

For Glover, the projects were clearly a "toxic environment" to be leveled—and she proceeded to do it. Starting with grants from the Clinton-era HUD, and then using private financing, she reduced the city's 14,000 public-housing units to 2,000, most of them in complexes for the elderly.

Gone were troubled projects like Bowen Homes—immortalized in a rap lyric by the Shop Boyz: "My hood I love them ladies, / My hood I love them babies, / I can't forget my niggas, / Bowen Homes we love you baby!"

Glover then leased the land to private developers, who built apartment and townhouse complexes there; in return, the developers agreed to dedicate 40% of the new units to tenants who qualified for public housing. Two-fifths of the projects' residents relocated to these "mixed- income" complexes. The remaining three-fifths received housing vouchers and used them to move into other private apartment buildings.

These may or may not be the best uses for those sites—and the verdict is pending on how well these replacements will be maintained over time. But they were the political price of a greater good—getting rid of the projects. By 2021,[19] only two "family" projects and seven buildings for the elderly poor remained AHA properties.

Such Atlanta-style "vouchering-out" has happened elsewhere—notably in Chicago, after the infamous Robert Taylor Homes and other South Side high-rises were knocked down. But Atlanta, using special autonomy that the George W. Bush–era HUD granted it under a program called Moving to Work, imposed a unique requirement on both the voucher recipients and the tenants of the new mixed-income complexes: They had to work (or be enrolled in a genuine limited-time training program).

The AHA would require its beneficiaries, like recipients of cash welfare, to work. Those not working risk losing their right to a subsidized apartment. Further, the management of both the mixed-income complexes and the ordinary apartment buildings where vouchers are used have broad discretion to kick out tenants for not working or misbehavior. Over a two-year period, the AHA evicted 109 tenants for failing to comply with the work requirement and another 67 for criminal activity.

During Renée Glover's tenure, the employment rate for subsidized tenants reached 70%. A team of financial counselors regularly visited tenants to help them develop a "wealth accumulation" plan. This is what it looks like to begin to wean households from a culture of dependency.

Even more imaginative plans should be permitted for local housing authorities, which need federal discretion to adopt approaches like Atlanta's. Local housing authorities should have the discretion to give priority to married couples—or to encourage marriage by not increasing rent when a household has two earners. New development could break up towers in the park-style campuses with new streets, where small owner-occupied homes could be built, along with places for small businesses.

Across the country, much high-value real estate is locked up by public housing. Surprisingly, some cities and housing authorities actually assign values to their properties, despite the fact that they are tax-exempt. Some of the figures are eye-popping. In New York, the city's housing authority estimates the value of the Baruch Houses site on the Lower East Side at $111 million. That's an outlier nationally, but there are valuable public housing sites in Philadelphia and Savannah, in the booming Vanderbilt University area of Nashville and on the potentially lucrative Lake Erie shore in Buffalo. Those potential sale values could be used to address the obvious problem of the potential plight of tenants in projects that face the wrecker's ball.

The proceeds of a sale should be used to buy out tenants, rather than relocating them to yet another project. Call these reparations perhaps—not for racism but for hubristic progressivism, which was premised on the belief that government could be a good landlord.

Divvying up the proceeds of a Baruch Houses sale could come to a dizzying $564,000 for each of its 197 households. Even some smaller, less valuable projects could lead to substantial buyout totals. Cities could likely offer far less and still convince tenants to take the buyout and start over, with a substantial nest egg. Funds could also become available to repair the remaining public housing.

There's an additional benefit: Cities would have fewer public housing projects to manage and a means to reduce bloated housing authority bureaucracies.

Figure 7.1. New York City, New York

Development Name	Assessed Total Value (2020)	Number of Units	Buyout Per Unit ($)
Baruch Houses Addition	$111,251,700	197	$564,729
Vladeck	$61,189,200	250	$244,757
Chelsea	$67,097,700	426	$157,506
Elliott	$77,460,750	608	$127,403
Fulton	$101,625,300	945	$107,540

Source: Assessed total value is publicly available here: https://www1.nyc.gov/site/finance/taxes/property-assessments.page. Number of units in public housing complex have been compiled by the author.

Figure 7.2. Philadelphia, Pennsylvania

Development Name	Assessed Total Value (2022)	Number of Units	Buyout per Unit ($)
Parkview	$2,729,500	19	$143,658
Cecil B. Moore Homes	$2,729,500	29	$94,121
Martin Luther King Plaza IV (LP)	$3,928,000	42	$93,524
Sen. Herbert Arlene Homes	$2,729,500	32	$85,297
Ludlow Scattered Sites (LP)	$3,928,000	75	$52,373

Even as approaches to disentangle blacks from subsidized housing dependency and its legacy are pursued, there are new mistakes to avoid. It is no favor to lower-income minority households, for instance, to relax credit standards to make it easier for them to buy homes. That's the risk of the Community Reinvestment Act (CRA) bank regulations, which incentivize banks to invest in so-called "underserved communities." Some, including Federal Reserve Board of Governors member Lael Brainerd, have called for taking race specifically into account to assess CRA compliance. Like public housing before it, this is misplaced benevolence.

Granting loans to those who do not meet traditional down payment or underwriting criteria, such as those with marginal credit scores, will do more harm than good to "underserved" neighborhoods. There is little worse for the lower-income homeowner who "works hard and plays by the rules" (a phrase often invoked by President Bill Clinton) and makes regular home mortgage payments than to have a neighbor who defaults on a loan and leaves behind a vacant structure. But therein lies the risk of extending credit to the marginal borrower.

It's important to keep in mind that the 2008 financial crisis and its resulting widespread mortgage foreclosures disproportionately affected blacks. Indeed, some 240,000 black homeowners lost their houses.[20] A combination of factors undoubtedly contributed to those losses. But as Edward Pinto of the American Enterprise Institute and former chief economist at Fannie Mae (the key entity in creating bond markets based on home mortgages), has written,[21] "The financial crisis had a single major cause: the accumulation of an unprecedented number of weak mortgages in the U.S. financial system." Pinto links the proliferation of such mortgages, whose foreclosures would undermine home values broadly, to federal "affordable housing goals" that encouraged lenders to extend credits to those who might not have adequate down payments or the financial capacity to make monthly payments.

To be sure, blacks were not the only "subprime" borrowers harmed when the U.S. housing market came crashing down. But any regulation that creates a lending standard meant to extend credit to the "underserved" (often a euphemism for race) creates the risk of harming those meant to be helped—in the public housing tradition.

The same culture of relaxed mortgage underwriting plagues the Federal Housing Administration (FHA), which extends low down-payment, highly leveraged loans to low-income borrowers.

Such lending is perennially plagued by high default rates, reaching 17.5% in early 2022.[22] As one industry newsletter observed: "Homeowners who live in these markets of higher-risk mortgages tend to have a lower-income and are largely members of minority groups."

There is a broader point here. The very process of striving and saving is an end in itself—one that requires steady employment and that rewards two-earner households and frugality. Those traits lay the groundwork for the good credit scores, which are rewarded by affordable mortgage loans—and should be valued for their own sake. They are and have always been the key to upward mobility for any group, including black Americans.

The same risk—that of sending the message that striving and saving are not required—is implicit in another federal policy: the Obama-era initiative entitled Affirmatively Furthering Fair Housing (AFFH). Halted by the Trump Administration but revived by the Biden Administration, this policy is premised on the idea that relocating low-income households to higher-income zip codes will improve their socioeconomic prospects. Obama-era Deputy HUD Secretary Ronald Sims captured the essence of the idea when he asserted, "Your zip code should not determine your future." Sims, himself black, emphasized that the idea of "moving to opportunity" would not only assist those being relocated from disadvantaged neighborhoods but would correct for what he viewed as ongoing racial segregation, based on residential patterns if no longer by law.

But the idea of "moving to opportunity" as an approach to uplifting the prospects of blacks poses yet another example of government harming by trying to help. The idea sends an unhelpful message: One can move to a better neighborhood by, in effect, hitting the housing lottery, rather than taking the incremental steps—striving, saving, marrying, deferring children until after marriage—that enable one to move to that "better" neighborhood. Moreover, it is impractical, to say the least, to aim to relocate poor, minority families en masse to affluent zip codes—and assume that there will be enough places for them to live, as well as that those zip codes will not be changed by the newcomers. We should also be concerned about middle-class black families that have scrimped and saved to move to those same neighborhoods, only to find they now have neighbors who have been rewarded without doing the same. This is a recipe for resentment among people of all races. AFFH is an ineffective tool for ameliorating the segregation that is alleged to be a problem. As the sociologist Herbert Gans long ago observed,[23] race ceases to be a source of tension when social class is similar among the races. Importing those of a different socioeconomic status thus becomes a recipe for tension.

The same risk accrues to another new federal housing program in which blacks disproportionately participate. The Low-Income Housing Tax Credit program provides financial incentives for private developers to set aside a percentage of housing units as income restricted.

Blacks comprise 33% of these households, nearly three times their representation in the overall population. Some 25% of those households are located in neighborhoods (as defined by census tracts) that are 80% or more minority. As with public housing, the program steers blacks with housing vouchers into rental units where they face the same earnings disincentives as in public housing.

Efforts to disperse these subsidies into areas of lower minority concentration led to litigation before the U.S. Supreme Court. In *Texas Department of Community Affairs v. Inclusive Communities Project Inc.*,[24] the Court ruled that Texas could be subject to a "disparate impact" judgment for failing to deconcentrate new tax credit development into non-poor areas.

As with AFFH, the case transcends the commonsense meaning of fair housing—that no one should be denied the chance to
own or rent based on race—and permits government to take race
into account in its decisions about where to locate new, subsidized
housing. As the Court ruled:

> While the automatic or pervasive injection of race into public
> and private transactions covered by the FHA has special dangers,
> race may be considered in certain circumstances and in a proper
> fashion. This Court does not impugn local housing authorities'
> race-neutral efforts to encourage revitalization of communities
> that have long suffered the harsh consequences of segregated
> housing patterns. These authorities may choose to foster diversity
> and combat racial isolation with race-neutral tools, and mere
> awareness of race in attempting to solve the problems facing inner
> cities does not doom that endeavor at the outset.

Ignored here is the possibility that government intervention has
helped create the "problems facing inner cities" and that steering
blacks into subsidized housing exacerbates those problems—whether
the new housing is built on inexpensive, inner-city lots or in more
costly suburban areas (where expenses will mean that fewer units
will be built). Broadly, then, it is far better for government to do
what it is meant to do: to take the steps required to ensure that
poor neighborhoods are good neighborhoods and can serve as the
launching pads for upward mobility. Those steps include safe and
clean streets, good schools, and available parks and recreation. These
are the purposes on which government should always focus—and
doing them well will benefit poor blacks and other low-income
Americans. Would that Eleanor Roosevelt and her many heirs had
understood that long ago.

8

FEDERAL HOUSING PROGRAMS AND THEIR UNINTENDED CONSEQUENCES

Edward J. Pinto

The nine most terrifying words in the English language are: "I'm from the government and I'm here to help."[1] This statement is especially true when applied to black households and housing policy. The federal government has a sordid role that began in the 1920s.

First, it undertook actions to preserve and perpetuate racially segregated neighborhoods through zoning. By the 1930s and 1940s, these actions became much more explicit with the establishment of the Federal Housing Administration (FHA). Beginning in the late-1940s, the federal government undertook a series of housing, urban renewal, and highway building programs that would have deleterious effects on both black households and neighborhoods.

From the late 1960s through the late 1980s, these programs designed to "help minorities" would multiply and expand, along with the expansion of federal loan guarantee programs. These loan guarantee programs (predominantly through the FHA) were increasingly targeted to "help" black borrowers.

Beginning in 1992, Congress mandated Fannie Mae and Freddie Mac, under the regulatory supervision of the U.S. Department of Housing and Urban Development (HUD), to undertake a massive expansion of "affordable housing programs," again targeted to "help" black households and neighborhoods.

After spending incalculable sums of money, after many millions of foreclosures, and after the destruction of large areas of our cities, the federal government has little positive to show for its attempts to help black households and neighborhoods:

- In 1920, the white homeownership rate was 48% and the black rate was 24%, with the black rate at 50% of the white rate.
- In 1970, the white homeownership rate was 66% and the black rate was 42%, with the black rate at 64% of the white rate.
- Through the second quarter of 2022, the white homeownership rate was 74% and the black rate was 45%, with the black rate at 61% of the white rate.

As Figure 8.1 illustrates, up until 1970, blacks saw substantial progress in both the increase in the black homeownership rate (from 24% in 1920 to 42% in 1970) and in the ratio of the black homeownership rate to the rate for whites (from 50% in 1920 to 64% in 1970). Progress by blacks since 1970 for the homeownership trend has been minimal, while the ratio of black homeownership to that of whites has actually declined. In 2022, the black homeownership rate stood at 45%, up only marginally from 42% in 1970. In 2022, the ratio of the black homeownership rate to the white rate stood at 61%, down from 64% in 1970.

Since Congress mandated "affordable housing programs" in 1992 and the Federal Reserve adopted quantitative easing in 2008, the median home inflation-adjusted price has nearly doubled. Affordable housing programs and lower interest rates haven't helped as these actions were quickly capitalized into higher home prices. (See Figure 8.2.)

Figure 8.1 Black Homeownership Rate, 1920–2022

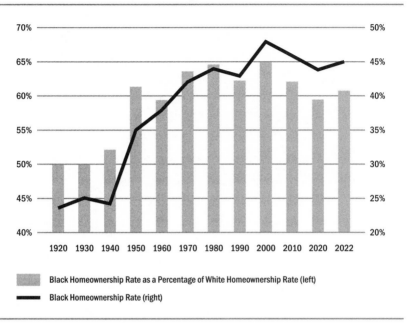

Black Homeownership Rate as a Percentage of White Homeownership Rate (left)

Black Homeownership Rate (right)

Source: U.S. Census Bureau

Figure 8.2 Median Home Price in the United States (DQYDJ)

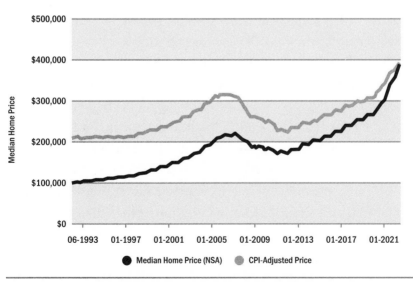

Source: PK. "Historical US Home Prices: Monthly Median Value from 1953–2022."
Don't Quit Your Day Job. Accessed October 2, 2022. https://dqydj.com/historical-home-prices/.

Figure 8.3   Median Wealth by Household Characteristics: 2019 (In 2019 dollars)

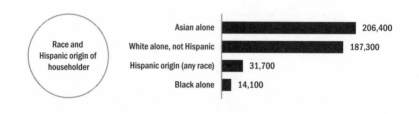

Source: Neil Bennett, Donald Hays, and Briana Sullivan. "Wealth Inequality in the U.S. by Household Type: 2019 Data Shows Baby Boomers Nearly 9 Times Wealthier than Millennials." *U.S. Census Bureau. August 1,* 2022. https://www.census.gov/library/stories/2022/08/wealth-inequality-by-household-type.html.

These policies have contributed to black households having only $14,100 in median wealth, compared to $187,300 for white households. (See Figure 8.3.)

For blacks, "I'm from the government and I'm here to help" have been truly terrifying words.

Zoning and Land Use[2]

From its initial use in the United States, zoning has been as much a tool for segregating people as for separating land uses.

Single-family zoning, minimum lot size requirements, and other land use restrictions, along with extended and complex approval processes that favor deep-pocketed developers of higher-end properties are restricting housing supply and driving up its cost in large swathes of the U.S. Despite serious housing affordability challenges in many regions, particularly in and around highly productive urban centers, it is currently "illegal on 75 percent of the residential land in many American cities to build anything other than a detached single-family home."[3]

The federal government had a central role, starting in 1921, in encouraging states and localities across the country to adopt low-density, one-unit zoning. By the 1950s, local policymakers also began to implement discretionary approval processes. Government bodies and neighborhood interest groups increasingly began determining what could be built on a site-by-site basis in what would become a lengthy and expensive approval process for many areas of the country.

Prior to the 1920s, development in the U.S. was not generally restrained by zoning. Until that point, different types of small residential and small commercial development were interspersed. They included single-family houses, accessory dwelling units, small lot detached single-family houses, attached single-family houses, two- and three-family homes, duplexes, triplexes, quadplexes, town or row houses, small multifamily buildings, with some commercial uses interspersed. This varied residential stock created opportunities for people of different income levels to live in the same neighborhoods, with some being renters, others owners. In many cases, related family members lived together in structures with two-to-four residential units. Today we call this approach light touch density (LTD).

In 1921, the federal government undertook the first efforts to encourage state and local governments to adopt standardized zoning ordinances that would achieve the goal of segregating land uses economically—larger single-family detached homes would be sited in zones that excluded smaller, less expensive structures. Given the prevailing racial income disparities, this would have the effect of indirectly segregating people by race.

Then Secretary of Commerce Herbert Hoover assembled what he considered to be the country's best and brightest experts in zoning and planning into the Advisory Committee on Zoning in 1921.[4] In 1922, the Commerce Department published a Zoning Primer, stating:

> For several years there had been developing a feeling that some agency of the Federal government should interest itself in building and housing. The Congress of the United States made an appropriation for such activities for the year 1921-1922. The department was to "collect and disseminate such scientific, practical, and

statistical information as may be procured, showing or tending to show approved methods in building, planning, and construction.[5]

That same year, the Commerce Department published its first Standard State Zoning Enabling Act, which state legislators could adopt as a means of granting zoning authority to their localities.[6] The Primer and Standard State Zoning Enabling Act were a how-to guide for implementing district-based zoning. Both encouraged state and local policymakers to adopt zoning that established detached single-family zoning districts that excluded other, more affordable structure types, including attached single-family development and two- to four-unit structures along with larger apartment buildings.

The 1922 primer focused on the perceived evils of residential density:

> A zoning law, if enacted in time, prevents an apartment house from becoming a giant airless hive, housing human beings like crowded bees. It provides that buildings may not be so high and so close that men and women must work in rooms never freshened by sunshine or lighted from the open sky.[7]

And it spoke favorably of a 1920 Ohio court case which held that "[o]ne and two-family houses were less subject to noise, litter, danger of contagion, and fire risk than multi-family houses, and that they could be placed in different districts under the police power."[8] Similarly, the Commerce Department's Standard State Zoning Enabling Act noted that the grant of zoning power under the state's police power is "for the purpose of promoting health, safety, morals, or the general welfare."[9] But the Act went beyond addressing health and safety or nuisance concerns. It contradicted the Primer's favorable view of placing one- and two-family houses in the same district by explicitly stating the ultimate, desired result:

"With proper restrictions, [limiting population density] will make possible the creation of one-family residence districts."[10] Thus, the goal right from the start was to create zones where all structure types but one-family homes were outlawed and two-plus family structures were excluded and relegated to other zones.

The enabling act established the legal basis for one-family [detached] residence districts, and it went on to argue: The "essence of zoning" is the ability to have "regulations [on the use of buildings and structures] in one district…differ from this in other districts."[11] These regulations would include limitations on minimum lot size; building size; front, back, and side setbacks; and maximum building height and number of stories; all of which tended to drive up the cost of such homes.

In the first comprehensive book on zoning and planning in the United States, published in 1922, lawyer Frank Williams argued that the "invasion of the inferior [races] produces more or less discomfort and disorder, and has a distinct tendency to lower property values. As a result, zoning along race lines has been attempted in various parts of our Southern States, where [N]egroes are most numerous. Such zoning in this country, however, is illegal, and has never been attempted as a part of zoning of any other country."[12]

Like the federal enabling act, Williams advocated for zoning districts and land use restrictions that could be used to separate higher-cost neighborhoods, consisting of single-family detached dwellings, from lower-cost neighborhoods with lots of rental units. Because the legacy of slavery and discrimination meant that African Americans had much lower incomes and wealth than white Americans, economic zoning further entrenched racial segregation from the time these rules were implemented.

The federal government's promotion of the Primer and Standard State Zoning Enabling Act ushered in a rapid adoption of zoning by localities across the country. As of September 1921, only 48 cities and towns with a total of fewer than 11,000,000 inhabitants had adopted zoning ordinances. By 1931, a total of 46,000,000 U.S. inhabitants lived under zoning, comprising 67% of the urban U.S. population.[13]

In his book on the early days of American zoning, historian Seymour Toll argued "[that] such a swift spread of law could occur despite the intricate processes of many state legislatures and hundreds of local governments is at least statistically extraordinary."[14] As local zoning ordinances spread rapidly during the 1920s, most municipalities began dividing residential districts into sub-districts; one district limited to single-unit detached housing, separated from all other, more affordable, types of housing.

Over time, supporters of zoning openly described this economic segregation as a means of achieving racial segregation. Stanley McMichael and Robert Bingham, leading observers of real estate markets and the growth of cites, made only two observations about racial and national groupings in the 1923 edition of their treatise on zoning:

> Zoning by race or color is invalid under the United States Constitution. [15]
>
> [...]
>
> In some allotments, attempts have been made to prevent [by private deed restrictions] the sales of lots to so-called undesirable people. Courts, however, have refused to enforce restrictions of this nature.[16]

However, by the time McMichael and Bingham came out with a new edition in 1928, a new chapter had been added, entitled "Racial and National Settlements and Groupings":

> Immigrants entering the country in such large numbers, many being unable to speak English, caused the growth of many racial

and national settlements in American cities. While settlements of foreign-born residents or colored people sometimes have the effect of making cities grow rapidly, it is significant that in some instances, notably where Negroes congregate, land values in the locality occupied by them are depressed.... [While welfare workers often disapprove of the geographic congregation of foreign-born into settlements,] if the population should spread throughout a city, it might have a decidedly depressing influence over a wide range of residential territory.[17]

[...]

Attempts to pass laws segregating the colored people to a given district have not been successful from a legal standpoint, on account of the fourteenth amendment to the constitution of the United States.[18]

They also expanded the title "Zoning" in the first edition to one titled "Zoning and Private Restrictions." It echoed Williams's language portraying African Americans as "invaders":

The steady flow of the Negro into the middle and northern states and cities has made the racial problem national in importance. Neighborhoods populated by white persons have been invaded by colored families, and often aristocratic residential districts have suffered tremendous lessening of property values because of the appearance of a Negro resident.[19]

In 1926, a pivotal Supreme Court decision, *The Village of Euclid v. Ambler Realty Co.*, gave the federal-led zoning wave an important legal victory. Ambler Realty sued the village of Euclid, Ohio, arguing that the town's zoning ordinance on 68 acres of Ambler's land that limited its use, in part through one-unit zoning, had reduced the value of its property without compensation.[20] However, the

Supreme Court ruled on the side of Euclid, finding that local land use restrictions, including single-family zoning, were a valid use of police powers.

One initial justification for zoning was that it protected property values by excluding specific nuisances in residential areas—"an odious factory invading a high-class residential district, or a ubiquitous grocery store appearing on a corner opposite an aristocratic residence."[21] The Supreme Court echoed this argument, describing apartments as "very often...a mere parasite" and "very near to being nuisances." The lower court's trial record noted that the commission that drafted Euclid's zoning ordinance relied on "the primer that is issued by Mr. Hoover's department in Washington."[22]

In the following year, the Supreme Court granted zoning another legal victory in *Berry v. Houghton*, finding that Minneapolis could exclude a four-unit apartment house in a one-unit residential district.[23] Recall that the Commerce Department's very first Standard State Zoning Enabling Act published in 1922 set as a goal "the creation of one-family residential [zoning] districts."[24] With these two decisions, the U.S. Supreme Court validated the constitutionality of this objective and exclusionary zoning became the standard throughout nearly the entire country.

FHA Makes Segregation Explicit

In 1934, Congress and the Roosevelt administration established the FHA to expand access to mortgage credit. The FHA insured private mortgages, reducing risk to lenders and homebuilders and also expanding access to credit by encouraging lending with longer terms, lower interest rates, and lower down payment requirements. But the FHA insured loans primarily for white Americans, discriminating against African Americans and other minorities.

The agency created underwriting manuals for participating lenders, limiting federal underwriting to only those "areas surrounding the location to determine whether or not incompatible racial and social groups are present, to that end an intelligent prediction may be made regarding the possibility or probability of the location being invaded by such groups."[25] The FHA made the tie to and purpose of zoning and segregation explicit:

> The best artificial means of providing protection from adverse influences is through the medium of appropriate and well drawn zoning ordinances. If the framers of the zoning ordinance have used excellent judgment in establishing areas, and if the provisions of the ordinance itself have been well worded and drawn from a thorough knowledge of conditions existing in the city and those which will most probably exist in the future, and if the zoning ordinance receives the backing of public approval, an excellent basis for protection against adverse influences exists.[26]

Words were not minced in describing adverse influences and the goal of segregation. The FHA's underwriting standards provided:

- The [FHA] Valuator should investigate areas surrounding the location to determine whether or not incompatible racial and social groups are present, to that end an intelligent prediction may be made regarding the possibility or probability of the locations being invaded by such groups....A change in social or racial occupancy leads to instability and reduction in values....Once the character of a neighborhood has been established it is usually impossible to induce a higher social class than those already in the neighborhood to purchase and occupy properties in its various locations.[27]

- [I]f the children of people living [in a pleasant area] are compelled to attend school where the majority or a goodly number of the pupils represent a far lower level of society or an
  incompatible racial element, the neighborhood will prove far
  less stable and desirable than if this condition did not exist.[28]
- Recommended [deed] restrictions include: prohibition of the
  occupancy of properties except by the race for which they were
  intended.[29]

From 1935 onward, the FHA was a significant force in real
estate finance, and its underwriting standards were widely adopted,
cementing existing patterns of segregation in place by encouraging
investment in exclusively white neighborhoods and discouraging it
in predominantly African-American or integrated neighborhoods
as a result.[30]

The FHA's practices built on the Hoover administration's efforts
to promote low-density, single-family zoning across U.S. localities. By 1940, 80% of the subdivisions built to FHA underwriting
standards were exclusively single-family construction, at an average
density of 3.26 houses per acre.[31] Developments in localities from Los
Angeles to Upstate New York were denied FHA financing because
their zoning ordinances did not confine development to low-density
single-family strictly enough.[32]

From the late-1940s through the 1970s, the federal government
undertook a litany of housing and urban renewal programs that
would target black neighborhoods. These programs had lasting
deleterious effects on both black households and the neighborhoods themselves. Here are just a few of the more than two dozen
congressional enactments:[33]

- The 1949 Housing Act authorized Slum Clearance and Urban Redevelopment, including a major expansion of public housing programs and a shift to high-rise buildings. New Haven became a model for slum clearance. "In order to rehabilitate, however, entire neighborhoods were decimated, displacing thousands. In the 14 years of renewal efforts almost 8,000 people (predominately poor and minority residents) living in 11 downtown neighborhoods lost their homes."[34]
- The 1966 Demonstration Cities and Metropolitan Development Act authorized the Model Cities Program, modeled after New Haven's neighborhood-clearing efforts.
- The 1968 Housing and Urban Development Act created the Urban Renewal Neighborhood Development Program and a 10-year plan for the elimination of all substandard housing in the United States. The resulting destruction of a multitude of neighborhoods in American cities, especially black ones, is documented in *Cities Destroyed Cash: The FHA Scandal at HUD.*[35]
- In 1974, the Housing and Community Development Act created the Community Development Block Grant program.
- In 1977, the Housing and Community Development Act created the Urban Development Action Grant Program.

The federal government's exclusionary zoning paradigm facilitated a shift from by-right zoning to discretionary zoning, giving rise to "Not in My Backyard" advocacy (NIMBYism).

While the zoning laws implemented under the model of the Commerce Department's Enabling Act limited development rights substantially and were deleterious to lower income, especially black households, owners still generally retained the right to build what was legally permitted within a zone (by-right zoning). However, by the 1950s, some state and local policymakers substantially eroded this principle as they adopted increasingly discretionary approval processes. This ended up granting increasing power to neighborhood groups that often sought to limit development, especially smaller and less expensive single-family and multi-family units.

Policymakers in San Francisco and other California localities were early adopters in the curtailment of by-right zoning, as they gave birth to discretionary review. In 1954, the San Francisco City Attorney determined that "the city had 'supreme control' to issue building permits and could use its own discretion to decide whether projects were compliant."[36] Following this decision, city policymakers adopted a policy of holding discretionary review hearings for many proposed developments, providing a platform for anyone with the resources to attend these hearings to delay or prevent building permits.

The move to discretionary approval was not limited to urban jurisdictions. Critics of suburbia as it developed after World War II played an important role in the evolution of land use restrictions to becoming a growth control regime. As a 2011 report by the California Department of Transportation explains:

> The postwar suburban boom fascinated but also appalled many urban theorists, reform advocates, planners, architects, and others. Both the landscape and the society of suburbia have been critiqued, and often condemned, by a succession of commentators, beginning in the immediate postwar years and continuing to the present. The critics have reacted to the scale of postwar tract construction, the rapid loss of farmland and other open space, the lack of architectural variety, and the perceived (or imagined) social ills of the new suburbs. Some predicted that the new tracts of inexpensive houses built shortly after World War II would become the slums of the future.[37]

Zoning and attendant land use regulations had changed from a means to regulate development types and drive up costs to a means to limit growth of any sort. California led the way by enacting growth control regulations beginning in the 1960s.[38] Notwithstanding this shift, the use of zoning to regulate and limit development types continued. For example, San Francisco's Residential Rezoning of 1978 eliminated about 180,000 legally buildable housing units.[39] The result was entirely foreseeable. Housing in California went from being about as affordable as the rest of the United States to the least affordable.[40] Over time, lack of supply and decreasing affordability spread to much of the nation.

The legacy of the zoning and land use regime encouraged by the Department of Commerce and expanded by the FHA continues today in the form of thousands of state and local zoning and land use codes, the vast majority of which continue to reserve large areas zoned exclusively for single-unit homes. These codes, by increasing the cost of building housing, were successful in pricing racial and ethnic groups out of newly built neighborhoods. These same policies were designed to keep multi-family housing in zones away from neighborhoods consisting of one-unit, detached structures.

In the 1980s and 1990s additional programs designed to "help minorities" would be enacted, accompanied by a massive expansion of federal loan guarantee programs. These loan guarantee programs (predominantly through the FHA) were now increasingly targeted to "help" black borrowers.

- The Tax Reform Act of 1986, which created the Low Income Housing Tax Credit, has perpetuated racial segregation (e.g., Chicago tax credit program mostly

produces affordable housing in poor black areas[41]). This
was a continuation of the many other subsidized housing
programs that added supply in a manner that perpetuated
segregation.

- The Federal Housing Enterprises Financial Safety and
  Soundness Act of 1992, which granted HUD the authority
  to set affordable housing mandates for Fannie Mae and
  Freddie Mac.
- HUD's 1995 National Homeownership Strategy: Partners
  in the American Dream, which led to more than 10 million
  foreclosures and did much to create the wealth disparities
  blacks now face.

For a time, these programs gave the illusion of progress for the
black homeowners, as the home ownership rate jumped from 43%
in 1990 to 50% in 2004. But this increase would end in disaster as
it was fueled by foreclosure-prone lending. By 2022, the rate had
fallen back to 45%, only 1 percentage point above the 1970 rate of
44%. The federal government's efforts to "help" black households
once again had disastrous consequences.

**The path forward to building sustainable intergenerational wealth
for lower-income and minority Americans.**

There is a growing consensus that to make housing more affordable is to increase supply, not to ease credit, increase government
subsidies, or suppress interest rates. Even a few progressive think
tanks and cities have come around to this view.[42] In order to stop
the price spiral that is pricing lower-income Americans out of the
housing market and driving up rents, we must address the following issues:

More supply:

Federal mandates are not the answer. They have crashed and burned time after time.

Zoning and land use policies are fundamentally a state and local issue and should be addressed at those levels. Fortunately, many cities and states are already experimenting with increasing housing supply. California's accessory dwelling unit (ADU) law and SB-9, for example, relax single-family zoning by restoring property rights and relying on private enterprise. If California can pass this, then it should be the blueprint for other jurisdictions. These and other efforts to restore LTD will result in a more varied residential stock and create opportunities for people of different income levels to live in the same neighborhoods, with some being renters, others owners. In many cases related family members will be able to live together in structures with two-to-four residential units. LTD also expands the supply of naturally affordable housing, thereby reducing the reliance on site-based subsidized housing and its segregationist past. However, one needs to be both patient and careful, as reversing the effects of 100-year-old policies on zoning will take decades.

Eliminate demand boosters as they create unaffordability when there is an imbalance between supply and demand:

Congress should task FHA, not the government-sponsored enterprises (GSEs), with guaranteeing loans for high-risk, low-income borrowers. These should be sustainable and wealth building by limiting mortgage default risk at loan origination through the use of 15- and 20-year loan terms.

HUD should study how to increase borrower resiliency by examining the effectiveness of the residual income test, month's reserves at closing, the Massachusetts Housing Finance Agency unemployment program, and a loan with a reserve accumulation component. In all cases, the data should be made available to private researchers for independent study and evaluation.

The Federal Housing Finance Agency, as regulator of Fannie Mae and Freddie Mac, should set a limit on mortgage default risk (MDR) at loan origination. The MDR is a comprehensive stressed default rate, which represents the worst-case scenario stress test similar to a car crash test or a hurricane safety rating. The National Mortgage Default Rate has been shown to be highly predictive of loan defaults even during an event such as the COVID-19 pandemic.[43]

The MDR would also help end policies, especially risk layering, that have saddled low-income households, especially ones of color, with default-prone loans.

Shrink the government's footprint in the housing market:

The rationale for doing so is clear:

Not in spite of, but because of the government's efforts over the last 60 years, black homeownership today stands at about the same level as in 1964. The GSEs (e.g., Fannie Mae, Freddie Mac) continue to dominate lending with about 50% market share, with total government involvement at about 80%. GSE subsidies are not well targeted to helping low- and moderate-income, first-time buyers. The lion's share of the benefit is going to existing middle- and increasingly upper-income homeowners.

Build resiliency in neighborhoods and borrowers by reducing the loan term on high-risk loans to 20 or 15 years on high-risk loans.

The FHA should implement LIFT Home loans for low-income, first-time, first-generation home buyers.[44]

GSEs should implement the Wealth Building Home Loan to reduce risk to taxpayers and to encourage borrowers to build equity.[45]

The advantages are that a shorter-term loan builds equity much faster than a traditional 30-year loan, the earlier pay-off date provides access to additional cash flow to pay children's post–high school education, and fund retirement. A 20-year term loan reduces default risk by about 50%, which allows for lower Fair Isaac Corporation (FICO) score loans to be made more safely and thereby provide a big boost to expanding black and Hispanic home ownership, as a low credit score is a major impediment to loan approval. The 20-year term has better default mitigation and remediation options compared to a 30-year loan.

Policies such as these will help address long-standing and worsening homeownership and intergenerational wealth disparities. This could be particularly beneficial to low-income blacks as they have been lagging behind in these crucial categories for far too long.

9

THE IMPACT OF ECONOMIC STABILITY IN MARGINALIZED ZIP CODES

Craig Scheef

Disclaimer: The views and opinions in this article are those of the author. They do not purport to represent the views or opinions of his employer.

Introduction

In this essay, we examine:

- The competing economic systems (free enterprise capitalism vs. socialism) and their associated merits and deficiencies that contribute to *economic stability* (prosperity and in-migration) or economic decay (poverty and out-migration).
- The stakeholders of the free enterprise system.
- Marginalized zip codes of an otherwise prosperous and growing city and state to determine what economic policies contribute to these areas' lack of participation.
- The policies leading to the Great Black Migration (1910–1970) and the subsequent reversal (1970–present), and which gainers and losers (state and city) through their policies are business friendly or depart from the principles of free enterprise.

The American Free Enterprise System vs. Socialism

A vast amount has been written concerning the differences (pros and cons) between the two primary economic systems in developed countries. Given our topic is migration, specifically black migration, we must compare the two opposing economic models through the lens of people relocating to improve their quality of life. This is informative when considering the policies of the United States, as well as any of her states, cities, or communities.

Data presented in this section represent excerpts from the April 30, 2019, Special Report of David R. Burton, "Comparing Free Enterprise and Socialism."[1] David Burton is Senior Fellow of Economic Policy in the Thomas A. Roe Institute for Economic Policy Studies at the Heritage Foundation. In this writer's opinion, this report is the latest, the most robust, and the best available data-supported information on the topic.

What Is Socialism?

Government ownership of the means of production is the central principle of traditional socialists. Traditional socialists' and communists' economic policies involve state-owned enterprises and a high degree of government control over all aspects of economic life. However, over time, policymakers came to understand that they did not need to have legal ownership of, or legal title to, businesses or other property to manage them by regulation, administrative actions, or taxation—a brand of socialism we see in America.

Moreover, not having legal title means they can refute responsibility when government control does not work out well. Thus, the meaning of the term "socialist" evolved considerably during the last half of the twentieth century to mean a *strong government role* in the economy, the pursuit of aggressive redistribution-ist policies, high levels of taxation and regulation, and a large welfare state—but not necessarily government ownership of the means of production. In this sense, many twenty-first-century proponents of "socialism" promote policies designed to promote greater economic equality and to protect workers that are often indistinguishable from those of modern progressives, social democrats, or labor parties.[2]

Socialism's Record

Today many believe "it is time to give socialism a try."[3] The truth is socialism has been "tried" many dozens of times. Everywhere it has been seriously tried, it has led to mass poverty and despair. Socialism's record is unblemished by success. It is an old, tried, failed ideology. To deny this evident historical fact requires a willing blindness or an extraordinary degree of historical igno-rance.[4] The adoption of *any* set of policies that achieved anything approaching actual economic equality (socialism) would so alter incentives, destroy productivity, and impede the ability of soci-ety to develop the information and vitality necessary to meet the needs and wants of its people, that general impoverishment—and, if possible, migration—is the known result.[5] Moreover, it is naïve to believe that people in politics or government are somehow dif-ferent from, more special than, or better than others.

Like most, they generally act in their own interest and are no more or less charitable or selfless than those outside government. Socialism amounts to the politicization of nearly all aspects of our lives. Recent examples of socialist failure include Venezuela, North Korea, Greece, Cuba, and Brazil. Dramatic examples of past socialist failures include the Maoist People's Republic of China, the Union of Soviet Socialist Republics, and the other Council for Mutual Economic Assistance (COMECON) countries (including the People's Republic of Bulgaria, the Republic of Cuba, the Czechoslovak Socialist Republic, the German Democratic Republic [East Germany], the Hungarian People's Republic, the Mongolian People's Republic, the Polish People's Republic, the Socialist Republic of Romania, the Socialist Republic of Vietnam, and the People's Socialist Republic of Albania), the Khmer Rouge in Cambodia, and several dozen developing countries.[6] Not to be missed, most democratically run U.S. cities and states.

Socialism has often led to mass murder. Socialist regimes have killed 100 million to 110 million people (not counting national socialist Germany).[7] Where less extreme versions of socialism have been tried, usually in democratic societies, it has led to a pronounced slowdown in growth and usually a decline in the standard of living. Even more moderate steps to reduce economic inequality—such as those associated with modern welfare-state progressivism or mixed economy social democracy—have a significant cost in terms of reduced incomes and social welfare. In other words, economic equality would dramatically reduce the size of the economic pie that progressives seek to divide equally. Winston Churchill famously stated, "Socialism is a philosophy of failure, the creed of ignorance, and the gospel of envy, its inherent virtue is the equal sharing of misery."

Burton asserts, a relatively simple way to determine whether ordinary people find socialist countries, states, cities, or zip codes to be superior or inferior to their relatively economically free counterparts is to observe relative immigration and emigration. People *"vote with their feet."* Socialist countries, states, counties, and cities typically either have significant out-migration or must build walls and use coercion to keep people within their jurisdictions. Relatively economically free jurisdictions have high levels of immigration and/or have border enforcement designed to limit the number of people coming in.

Is Socialism Ethical?

Burton provides nine reasons socialism is unethical.

1. In seeking to achieve equality of outcomes by some measure or some other government-dictated allocation of income or wealth, it seeks to treat unequal circumstances equally.[8] Those who work, study, take risks, defer consumption, or undertake unpleasant tasks would be provided equal incomes to those who do not.

2. Socialism systematically tramples on our liberty and involves the systematic application of coercion.[9] Politicians and bureaucrats—not the people themselves—would make many of the most important decisions in our lives and severely restrict our choices.

3. Socialism necessarily involves denigrating our humanity, dignity, and ability to flourish. It would radically curtail the ability to choose one's calling, to chart our own course in life, to excel, to be creative or innovative, to dissent, and to raise our families as we decide to be best.[10]

4. Mild socialism harms the public's standard of living. To the extent that socialism is seriously implemented, it demonstrably leads to mass poverty and deprivation. There are no counterexamples. Knowingly adopting a set of policies that will lead to mass deprivation or even a markedly lower standard of living is unethical.[11]

5. Socialism is a poor steward of scarce resources. It encourages overuse and over-consumption of underpriced resources and makes achieving any economic end more costly in terms of resources used.[12] Moreover, it typically increases externalities, such as pollution, imposed on society.[13]

6. Taking another's money for yourself or to give to someone else—whether using government as an intermediary or not—is

not morally praiseworthy. Having George "rob Peter to pay Paul" or allowing Paul to take from Peter does not rise to the level of virtue or have moral merit. Voluntarily using your own time and money to help another is a different matter. Beneficence, charity, and compassion are virtues.[14] But charitable acts involve voluntarily giving of yourself to another—not compliance with state coercion.

7. By placing most power in society in the state and removing power and resources from the private sector, socialism harms voluntary associations, civil society, and the communities and the web of relationships that they constitute. Socialism impedes and often seeks to suppress relationships fostered by non-governmental institutions and centers of power and influence not controlled by the state.[15]

8. Socialism stifles dissent and free speech and promotes a deadening, bureaucratic uniformity.[16] Government control or regulation of the media, political speech, and elections is the norm in socialist countries.

9. Socialism endorses and formalizes counterproductive envy, resentment, and hostility toward achievement and accomplishment.[17] It seeks to tear down and diminish those who excel or succeed.[18]

What Is Free Enterprise?

Free enterprise or a free-market system is an economic system based on voluntary exchange in which entrepreneurs and businesses compete by offering goods and services to other businesses or consumers. Firms successfully compete by offering better and less expensive products or by offering innovative new products. Firms that make poor investments or fail to innovate by improving products or reducing prices typically become unprofitable and ultimately fail. Workers and employers reach mutually agreeable terms of employment and are typically free to end the employer–employee relationship when they want to do so.

Markets and, critically, the price mechanism can operate with little government interference. A free-enterprise system: (1) provides robust private property rights[19]; (2) enforces contracts[20]; (3) provides rules against fraud; (4) maintains rules against imposing substantial negative externalities (pollution, for example)[21]; and (5) entails government provision of true public goods.[22] Free enterprise is sometimes called capitalism, although free enterprise is about much more than the accumulation or use of capital.

The Record of Free Enterprise

Free enterprise caused a 30-fold improvement in the well-being of ordinary people over two centuries.[23] There is a strong correlation between economic freedom and material well-being.[24] Economic growth and living standards improve when societies increase economic freedom (reduce regulation). The move toward greater economic freedom has lifted billions of people out of socialist-caused poverty, most notably in China and India.[25] In the developing world, free-enterprise policies can lift a country from poverty to a Southern European standard of living over a few decades.[26]

Free markets are much better at providing low-cost, high-quality goods and services that people want than a government-controlled economy. To the extent that government interferes with market processes and substitutes political control for unimpeded markets, economic performance will decline. There are six primary (and inter-related) reasons for the superior efficacy of markets over politics as the regulator of economic life.[27]

- Competition increases choice and promotes efficiency.
- Markets provide better incentives.

- The price mechanism better allocates scarce resources to meet consumer wants than bureaucracy or politics.
- Markets and private enterprises better develop and use information.
- Markets and private enterprises provide greater and more rapid innovation and discovery.
- Markets employ distributed planning rather than central planning.

Is Free Enterprise Moral?

Free enterprise does not endure socialism's moral failings. The moral advantages of free enterprise can be summarized as follows:

1. It rests on voluntary cooperation among free people whether as workers, managers, investors, or consumers and rejects coercion.
2. It empowers ordinary people rather than politicians, bureaucrats, and the politically well-connected.
3. It allows people to author their own lives, to choose their own calling, to innovate, to create, to be different, and to flourish.
4. It leads to dynamism and an improved standard of living and has lifted more people *out of poverty* than any other system.
5. It encourages the sound stewardship of scarce resources.
6. It affords the dignity of self-sufficiency rather than offering the corrosive lethargy of dependence.
7. It rewards work, prudence, thrift, diligence, creativity, and innovation.[28]
8. It leaves room for, and does not seek to control, voluntary associations, civil society, charity, and families.
9. It leaves room for people to dissent, and to speak freely.

The central economic question facing any society, community, or marginalized zip code is the degree to which economic life should be organized or controlled by government entities or based on a spontaneous order arising from the voluntary actions of individuals and civil society.[29] Should economic cooperation be voluntary, as it is in free markets, or based on government coercion, as it is with socialism? In other words, who should control the economy—politicians (democratically elected or otherwise) and bureaucrats or the people?

Communists, socialists, social democrats, liberals, and progressives support an economy largely planned, controlled (regulated) by government. Conservatives, classical liberals, and libertarians support an economy governed by the rule of law where people interact and cooperate largely free of government interference.

The Stakeholders in the Free Enterprise Economic System

In this next section, we review six stakeholders of the free enterprise system. During which, we take a brief detour, to evaluate a real-life case study—an examination of Southern Dallas (and the associated stakeholders) through the lens of free enterprise. These stakeholders must be considered both beneficiaries and stewards of this ecosystem. For zip codes to flourish and poverty to abate, each participant must appreciate their respective role, responsibility, and interdependency with their fellow stakeholders. Disregard for this important detail is itself an impediment to the free enterprise system operating optimally.

The Nuclear Family

Families are the building blocks of society. As the family goes, so goes the community. The decline of intact families, since and because of the War on Poverty (1964), contributes significantly to a decline in educational performance, a dramatic increase in crime, and a dramatic increase in poverty. Arguably, the decline of intact families is the largest impediment to our goal of a robust free enterprise ecosystem. Consider the impact the family has on all stakeholders. Government is shaped by voters (families). Healthy intact families pay taxes that fund public education, law enforcement, government, and social programs. Business owners and investors require a sound, well-educated, and productive workforce. The educational system needs healthy and safe children and parental support to operate optimally. The burden on government and law enforcement resulting from increased crime rates and economic dependency, associated with broken nuclear families, is undisputable.[30]

First, The War on Poverty (welfare system) is an example of a socialist government policy that creates, not abates, poverty. Whether or not this legislation was well-intended or politically self-serving can be debated. What cannot be debated is welfare's abysmal results.

As shown in Figure 9.1, after World War II, the United States enjoyed a dramatic *decrease in poverty*, resulting from the longest and strongest economic expansion in its history. This period is known as The Golden Age of Free Enterprise Capitalism.[31] Previously mentioned, in 1964, President Lyndon B. Johnson introduced a colossal socialist welfare system that promised to eradicate poverty. In reviewing the chart, one must wonder, how much longer the 20-year decrease in poverty, created by free enterprise, would have continued, if not for the War on Poverty.

According to the Cato Institute, a libertarian think tank, since the Johnson Administration, almost $19 trillion has been spent on welfare, with poverty rates being about the same as during the Johnson Administration.[32] This number does not begin to fully count the cost of this destructive socialist program. In addition to breathtaking economic cost, this failed but ongoing socialist initiative decimates the family, as shown in Figure 9.2.

Figure 9.1 Self-Sufficiency: Percentage of Individuals Who Live in Poverty
(Excluding Welfare Benefits)

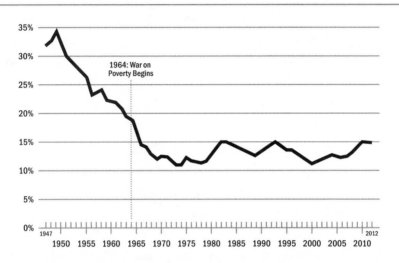

Sources: Figures for 1950–1958: Gordon Fisher, "Estimates of the Poverty Population Under the Current Official Definition for Years Before 1959," U.S. Department of Health and Human Services, Office of the Assistant Secretary for Planning and Evaluation, 1986. Figures for 1959–2012: U.S. Census Bureau, Current Population Survey, Annual Social and Economic Supplements, "Historical Poverty Tables—People," Table 2, https://www.census.gov/hhes/www/poverty/data/historical/people.html (accessed September 10, 2014).

Figure 9.2 Percentage of Births to Unmarried Women

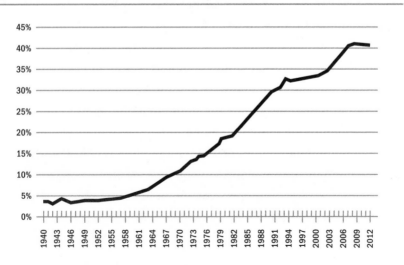

Source: Institute for Research on Poverty, University of Wisconsin

The growth of the poverty-ridden family today is linked directly with the growth of the family headed by the single mother. Children living in female-headed families with no spouse present have a poverty rate of 45.8%, over four times the rate for children in married-couple families (9.5%).[33] From the time our social welfare programs started in the mid-to-late 1960s, to the year 2000, the number of births by women who were not married and living in a committed relationship—the foundation behind a nuclear family structure—went up by a staggering 400%.[34]

In 2014, drawing heavily from government data and peer reviewed sociological and economic research, Robert I. Lerman and William Bradford Wilcox published an extensive research article in *The Economist* confirming the fundamental role the intact nuclear family has on society. Lerman is a Professor of Economics at American University and a Senior Fellow at the Urban Institute in Washington, DC, and Wilcox is a professor of sociology at the University of Virginia.[35]

Their executive summary states, "All the latest evidence confirms that the institution of marriage is a key to productive adulthood, the cornerstone of a stable family, and the basic unit of a healthy community. Its effects go well beyond the married couple. It shapes our whole society, from workforce participation to economic inequality to the effectiveness of education. Children raised by married parents have better odds of succeeding in school, excelling at work, and building a stable relationship of their own."[36]

Drawing from Department of Labor data, they showed how American families experienced an average 80% increase in their real income from 1950–1979. Family income inequality was relatively low, and more than 89% of prime working-age men were employed. All those trends have reversed, and are accelerating to the downside, with the composition and structure of the family playing the most crucial role in this reversal.[37]

In 1980, married parents headed 78% of households with children. By 2012, that had dropped nearly 20%. The researchers, again relying on hard primary data, showed why that was significant. "Married families enjoy greater economies of scale and receive more economic support from kin, and married men work harder and earn more money than their peers, all factors that give them an economic advantage over cohabiting and single-parent families."

The economic impact on individual family units, as well as society, cannot be overstated. Even adjusting for race, education, and other factors, if the share of married parents remained at 78% through 2012, "the rise in the overall median income of parents would have been about 22%, substantially more than the actual growth of 14%." And if the post-1979 immigrants, coming mostly from low-income countries, are adjusted for, the "growth in median family income would have been 44% higher than 1980 levels." They conclude that the decline in the share of "married-parent families with children largely explains the stagnancy in median family incomes since the late 1970s."[38]

Traditional nuclear family units, including a mother, father, and children, have been proven to be more viable in almost every facet of sociological construct. As the researchers explain, "Family structure appears to matter for children's well-being because, on average, children growing up without both parents are exposed to: More instability in housing and primary caretakers, which is stressful for children; Less parental affection and involvement; Less consistent discipline and oversight; and Fewer economic resources."

Sociologists Sara McLanahan and Gary Sandefur, in summarizing their research on family structure, put it this way: "If we were asked to design a system for making sure that children's basic needs were met, we would come up with something quite like the two-parent ideal. Such a design, in theory, would not only ensure that children had access to the time and money of two adults; it also would provide a system of checks and balances that promoted quality parenting."[39]

Lerman and Wilcox summarize, "The research to date leads us to hypothesize that children from intact, married families headed by biological or adoptive parents are more likely to enjoy stability, engaged parenting, and economic resources and to gain the education, life experiences, and motivation needed to flourish in the contemporary economy—and to avoid the detours that can put their adult futures at risk."

Many of the forces negatively affecting the family are cultural and can be attributed to the gradual, yet accelerated, erosion of social mores. But many of the destructive contributors are driven by governmental policy, statute, and legal code, like the IRS "marriage penalty," and welfare programs that facilitate the absolution of parental responsibilities. And some are couched in principles espoused by political correctness that defy empirical data, the most egregious of the latter represented by the redefinition of marriage, the cornerstone to the family unit, which only further dilutes and weakens the building block of society.

Next, because of the War on Poverty's destructive effect on family structure, children and teenagers' academic achievement and overall achievement is greatly worsened. Elementary school children from intact biological families earn higher reading and math test scores than children in cohabiting, divorced-single, and always-single parent families.[40] Adolescents from non-intact families have lower scores than their counterparts in intact married families on math, science, history, and reading tests.[41] Adolescents living in intact married families or married stepfamilies (with stepfathers) performed similarly on the Peabody Vocabulary Test, but adolescents living in single-mother families or in cohabiting stepfamilies (with their biological mother) did worse than those in intact families.[42]

Adolescents from single-parent families and cohabiting families are more likely to have low achievement scores, lower expectations for college, lower grades, and higher dropout rates than children from intact biological families (after controlling for other family socioeconomic factors).[43]

Over 57% of children who live in intact biological families enter college, compared to 32.5% of children in stepfamilies, 47.5% of children in single-parent families, and 31.8% of children who live in families with neither parent present.[44] Students from disrupted families are less likely to complete four-year college than their peers from intact biological families.[45]

Finally, President Johnson's social experiment failed to consider the effect of fatherless families on crime rates. Today, nearly 25 million children have an absentee father.[46] According to the professional literature, the absence of the father is the single most important cause of poverty.[47] The same is true for crime. Of all adolescents, those in intact married families are the least likely to commit delinquent acts.[48] Children of single-parent homes are more likely to be abused, have emotional problems, engage in questionable behavior, struggle academically, and become delinquent.[49] Problems with children from fatherless families can continue into adulthood. These children are three times more likely to end up in jail by the time they reach age 30 than are children raised in intact families and have the highest rates of incarceration in the United States.[50]

This modern form of family disintegration—or more accurately non-formation—has its consequences for criminal behavior. The growth in crime is paralleled by the growth in families abandoned by fathers.[51] States with a lower percentage of single-parent families, on average, will have lower rates of juvenile crime. State-by-state analysis indicates that, in general, a 10% increase in the number of children living in single-parent homes (including divorces) accompanies a 17% increase in juvenile crime.[52] Conversely, children of intact married families are the least likely to engage in serious violent delinquency compared to children of single-mother, single-father, and mother-stepfather families.[53]

Along with the increased probability of family poverty and heightened risk of delinquency, a father's absence is associated with a host of other social problems. The three most prominent effects are lower intellectual development, higher levels of out-of-wedlock parenting in the teenage years, and higher levels of welfare dependency.[54] According to a 1990 report from the Department of Justice, more often than not, missing and abandoned children come from single-parent families, families with stepparents, and cohabiting-adult families.

Worth noting, according to the Aspen Foundation, structural or systemic racism represents a system in which public policies, institutional practices, cultural representations, and other norms work in various, often reinforcing ways to perpetuate racial group inequity.[55] Given that President Johnson's "War on Poverty" disproportionately damages families of color, it is likely Johnson's ongoing failed (or successful depending on your motives) socialist welfare experiment is the epitome and the poster child of systemic racism.

President Johnson's War on Poverty and the "Social Justice" movement known as Black Lives Matter (BLM) have the destruction and disruption of the nuclear family and systemic racism in common. Like most socialist legislation monikers (e.g., War on Poverty, Affordable Care Act), the name creates a forcefield against anyone who dares disagree with it. Who can argue against a name/slogan like Black Lives Matter? Of course, they do. However, the agenda of BLM is far different from the slogan.[56] When we dig deeper, we see the mission of BLM is a socialist, Marxist, fascist playbook wrapped in a noble and virtuous name.[57] The Founders of BLM boast "We are Trained Marxists."[58] The BLM website previously had a "What We Believe" page that has been taken down (previously found at https://blacklivesmatter.com/what-we-believe/) because of understandable outrage.[59] On that page it stated:

We disrupt the Western-prescribed nuclear family structure requirement by supporting each other as extended families and 'villages' that collectively care for one another, especially our children, to the degree that mothers, parents, and children are comfortable.

The idea BLM is trying to suggest is that the traditional nuclear family itself is a "Western-prescribed...structure." This idea is fiction.[60] Clearly, BLM does not see strengthening the nuclear family structure as good for the black community, but bad for it, which is why they seek to "disrupt the Western-prescribed nuclear family structure requirement." They seek this objective even though strengthening the nuclear family would improve the well-being of the members of the black community, and work to reduce, and eventually eliminate, all the disparities that are found within the label of systemic racism.

Tragically, BLM does not stop there. They seek to offset the damage caused by disrupting and NOT supporting and strengthening the nuclear family structure in the black community *"by supporting each other as extended families and 'villages' that collectively care for one another, especially our children, to the degree that mothers, parents, and children are comfortable."* This type of wording is eerily like the wording of Giovanni Gentile, the father of fascism, back in the 1920s and '30s.[61] What does this phrase mean? If you ask BLM to explain themselves on this matter, they basically go the route of socialism with massive social welfare programs. They believe that these kinds of programs, this type of government, are how communities support and care for one another. In other words—and this is how the writer sees it as someone outside the black community—they want to take our social welfare programs, as terrible as we've clearly explained them to be, and *double down* on them, as if taking something that's been bad for all communities will suddenly become good for them if we do it even more.[62]

If BLM really believes that black lives *truly* matter, then why wouldn't they want to strengthen the black nuclear family? Seeking to "disrupt" it will only make things worse. The poverty too prevalent in the black community today can substantially be attributed to our social welfare programs and their negative effects in destroying the nuclear family structure among blacks. If we do not stop our welfare programs soon, but *double down* on them, the state of the black community will become much, much worse—it will not just be a tragedy but a calamity of unprecedented proportions in the annals of human history and civilization.[63]

The Educational System

As examined previously, two-parent families benefit the educational system by supplying safe and supported students. Public schools are part of the government. It should neither be schools' nor government's role to raise or indoctrinate our children on the imaginary virtues of socialism.[64] Neither is it the government's role to indoctrinate our children to hate their country and hate the color of their skin.[65] The business owner, entrepreneur, and other employers benefit from well-educated and well-adjusted team members.

Government, too, benefits from fully functioning adults that do not burden the criminal justice or welfare system.

The role of the school or university is to educate students in a broad range of areas. They provide a host of experiences that ought to prepare students to become contributing members of society that are able to support themselves and pay their share of taxes. Historically, places of education provided a venue for civil debate about diverse ideas and solutions. Ideas such as free enterprise capitalism vs. socialism. Solutions to problems like poverty. Traditionally, centers of education are places to seek truth and innovation.

Just as choice, liberty, and free enterprise produce the most productive economic system, choice and liberty provide the answer for our broken educational system. In an ideal world, every child would have access to the education that is right for him or her. All parents would be able to choose from a diversity of high-quality options regardless of their means. Parents and educators would harmoniously spend their time and energy on providing the best possible education. Educators would be responsive to parents and employ sound pedagogical practices. Over time, innovations would expand the diversity and improve the quality of the educational options available. Our education system would produce literate and informed citizens, well-prepared for adult life.[66]

Sadly, the state of our education system is as disturbing as the current state of the nuclear family. As discussed, one begets the other. To a large extent our schools and universities have become mainstays of socialism and antagonists of American values such as faith, family, and free enterprise.[67] Most students are assigned to their school based on the location of their parent's home. Children from low-income families that cannot afford private schooling or homes in wealthier districts are too often trapped in underperforming schools. Given their captive audiences, these schools are more responsive to bureaucrats and special interests than to students and their parents.

Our education system's troubles are not confined to low-income districts—America's students as a whole lag many other industrialized nations on international tests. Government expenditures on K–12 education have more than doubled over the last 40 years (adjusted for inflation), and yet U.S. students' academic performance at the end of high school is flat.[68] Top-down regulations intended to improve quality instead stifle diversity and innovation. And rather than fostering harmony, too often government schools force citizens into social conflict.[69]

Generally, the only way parents have retained control over their children's education in the long run has been for them to assume, as much as possible, the direct financial responsibility for it. The research suggests that even modest parental co-payments significantly increase the efficiency of schools and their responsiveness to parents' demands.[70]

America needs more free enterprise in education. Parents must be free to choose the education that is best for their children, no matter where they live or how much they earn. Educators should be permitted to determine their own curricula and approaches and be free to set their own prices and compensation. Schools must be free to innovate and compete to attract and retain students. And they must be both free to profit from their successes and compelled to suffer losses for their failures, because the profit-and-loss system (free enterprise) spurs innovation, efficiency, and the spreading of best practices. Likewise, educators must be free to compete in the labor market for positions that give them the greatest professional freedom and compensation.

These components of educational freedom are interdependent. For example, parental choice is only meaningful if schools have the freedom and autonomy to differentiate themselves. Policy-makers who might consider regulating or constraining one of these factors—educational choice and financial responsibility for parents; freedom, competition, and the profit/loss system for schools—must consider the impact that such a policy would have on the other factors and the system in general.[71]

The Business Owner/Entrepreneur

In addition to their critical role in a free enterprise ecosystem, business owners and capitalists have responsibilities. In this writer's opinion, business ownership is a sacred stewardship. The best business owners approach leadership with a selfless attitude towards the organization's stakeholders (e.g., team members, community, vendors, customers, shareholders) and must filter decision making and guide strategic planning with these stakeholders' best interests in mind. A significant portion of today's government regulation has been created due to corrupt greed-driven behavior of bad actors. There must be no place for such people in our free enterprise system.

Entrepreneurs are the catalyst to the free enterprise economy. These courageous individuals are important because they are willing to invest and take risks to start a new enterprise. According to data from the Bureau of Labor Statistics, approximately 20% of small businesses fail within the first year. By the end of the second year, 30% of businesses will have failed. By the end of the fifth year, about half will have failed. And by the end of the decade, only 30% of businesses will remain—a 70% failure rate.

Free enterprise encourages entrepreneurs to invent, create, and innovate. The industry of the entrepreneur profits its community's citizens. Small businesses generate most jobs in the United States. That common concept has been fueled for years by policymakers, both Republicans and Democrats, U.S. presidents included. Small businesses drive the economy's engine and do more than any other sector to spur jobs and growth.[72]

The U.S. Small Business Administration supports these claims, citing internal reports that show, for example, that small companies accounted for 64% of new jobs created in the U.S. between 1993 and 2011.[73] Small businesses, representing roughly 95% of all U.S. companies, are certainly important to the nation's economic growth, providing employment for roughly half of U.S. employees. Worth noting, new businesses, not necessarily small ones, account for virtually all new job creation in the U.S. and nearly 20% of gross job creation, according to a 2015 study by the Kauffman Foundation, a research nonprofit. In the last three decades, the study adds, firms under a year old have created 1.5 million jobs annually.[74]

According to the Office of Management and Budget, 50% of federal income tax is paid by individuals, 7% from corporate income tax, 36% from payroll tax, and 8% from excise and other taxes. The taxes paid by individuals are a result of that individual having a job created by an entrepreneur. Therefore, 92% of federal income taxes are a result of some courageous entrepreneur deciding to exercise their right to free enterprise. Winston Churchill was correct when he stated, "Some regard private enterprise as if it were a predatory tiger to be shot. Others look upon it as a cow that they can milk. Only a handful see it for what it really is—the strong horse that pulls the whole cart."

Finally, as mentioned, most entrepreneurs fail. Some survive. And a few become wealthy. We must ask ourselves, given the value entrepreneurs create, is the coveting socialist's demonization of the few that become wealthy justified?

The Investor/Capitalist

The investor, also known as a free enterprise capitalist, plays a critical role in the free enterprise system. Investors, like entrepreneurs, operate, in part, with a profit motive. Capitalists survey the market for equity investment opportunities that meet their criteria. They look for entrepreneurs to bet on and provide capital for profitable growth and potential acquisitions. Equity capital takes the first risk of loss and therefore seeks the highest rate of return in the capital stack of an enterprise. The capital stack represents the funding side of a business's balance sheet and may consist of numerous other forms of capital (common equity, preferred stock, subordinated debt, and senior debt). Each form of capital provides the capitalist with varying rights in the event of liquidation and varying expected returns based on these liquidation rights and the unique inherent risks of the enterprise being funded.

Capitalists may work in venture capital, private equity, investment banks, hedge funds, family offices, and Small Business Investment

Corporations (SBIC). Tens of thousands of these various investment firms exist within the U.S. and much more worldwide, each with its own investment strategies, industry expertise, investment product specialty, risk tolerance, investment horizon and expected rate of return. These investors seek rates of return of 20–30% to compensate them for their risk. They often experience a full loss on one or more investments, expecting other investments to make up for the loss and be a "home run."

We must emphasize, capitalists are exceptionally considerate of the economic, political, and business environments of the businesses in which they invest. A state, city, or community with business-friendly economic policies, effective law enforcement, minimal crime, unspoiled politicians (or at least minimally so), excellent schools, an educated work force, and healthy family formation is a magnet for investment capital. Consequently, small businesses have a much higher likelihood of success, long-term growth, and additional job creation.

Figure 9.3   The U.S. Cities With The Most Homeless People
CoCs with the largest number of people experiencing homelessness in 2020*

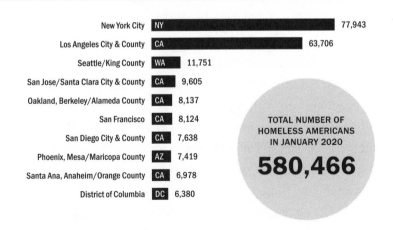

New York City	NY	77,943
Los Angeles City & County	CA	63,706
Seattle/King County	WA	11,751
San Jose/Santa Clara City & County	CA	9,605
Oakland, Berkeley/Alameda County	CA	8,137
San Francisco	CA	8,124
San Diego City & County	CA	7,638
Phoenix, Mesa/Maricopa County	AZ	7,419
Santa Ana, Anaheim/Orange County	CA	6,978
District of Columbia	DC	6,380

TOTAL NUMBER OF HOMELESS AMERICANS IN JANUARY 2020

580,466

*CoC – Continuums of Care that are local planning bodies who coordinate homelessness services in certain areas

Source: U.S. Department of Housing and Urban Development

Conversely, a state, city, or community with crippling regulations, under siege and facing ineffective law enforcement, high crime rates, corrupt and business-hostile politicians, poor schools, and poverty creating single-parent households sees investment capital reject and avoid its economy. These conditions represent impediments to free enterprise and consequently represent the impediments to poverty abatement.

Additionally, existing businesses in the dysfunctional community must flee to survive and have a chance to flourish. Often a capitalist investment strategy includes relocating a good company to a healthier environment, to optimize their investment.

Take, for example, the state of California compared to the state of Texas. A record number of companies are leaving California for states with a better business climate. Reports show that Texas remains their number one destination. One study estimates that 1,800 California relocation or "disinvestment events" occurred in 2016, the most recent year available, setting a record yearly high going back to 2008. About 13,000 companies left the state during that nine-year period. Of the 1,800 events in 2016, 299 of those departures landed in Texas.

Texas's rank as the top destination for California companies is especially significant considering that the large majority of corporate relocations cross only one state line, according to Joseph Vranich, president of Pennsylvania-based Spectrum Location Solutions LLC.[75] "A lot of people don't want to be more than one hour from other members of their family they might be leaving behind, or their good friends or their favorite country club—whatever it is," Vranich said in an interview with the *Dallas Business Journal*. "For Texas to do as well as it does to attract California companies is really remarkable in and of itself."

North Texas has enjoyed a wave of California company headquarters relocations. In the past few years, health care giant McKesson (NYSE: MCK), convenience store distributor Core-Mark (Nasdaq:

CORE), and medical technologies company DJO announced moves from the Golden State to Dallas–Fort Worth (DFW). In addition, California companies—like Toyota Motor North America (NYSE: TM), Kubota Tractor Corporation, Charles Schwab Corp. (NYSE: SCHW) and Jamba Juice, among others—have announced corporate moves or regional hub launches in North Texas. Forty-three of the 123 corporate headquarters that have relocated to DFW since 2010 came from California, according to the Dallas Regional Chamber of Commerce.

"Departures are understandable when year after year CEOs nationwide surveyed by Chief Executive Magazine declared California the worst state in which to do business," said Vranich, who jokes that he loves California's weather, but not its business climate. Until recently, Spectrum and Vranich were based in Irvine, California. Texas, on the other hand, consistently ranks as one of the best states to do business in, he said.[76]

The top reason to leave California is no longer high taxes, although that still ranks highly, Vranich said. "The legal climate has become so difficult that companies should consider locating in jurisdictions where they will be treated fairly." Hostility toward businesses, high utility and labor costs, punitive regulations and worrisome housing affordability for employees are among California's other negatives. "Signs are that California politicians' contempt for business will persist," he said.

During the study period, 275,000 jobs and $76.7 billion in capital funds were diverted out of California. The departing companies acquired at least 133 million square feet elsewhere—and probably much more because such information often went unreported in source materials, Vranich said.[77]

Lest we North Texans become too full of ourselves, we ought to acknowledge certain areas of North Texas are suffering from similar free enterprise impediments as those in California.

As a useful case study, let us take a brief diversion from our free enterprise stakeholder analysis and inspect the critically important area in North Texas known as Southern Dallas. The 13 zip codes in the southern half of the loop (bisected by Interstate 30) includes Southern Dallas. This area represents approximately 200 square miles.

Why has this area not benefitted from the same (or any) relocation wave as other areas of North Texas? Why have we not enjoyed the same business formation and lure of investment capital in this trade area?

This writer's original desire was to avoid the topic of racism, in our conversation regarding poverty. Yet when we investigate the history of Dallas, as well as most major metropolitan cities in the United States, it is impossible to deny the racism of the 1940s, '50s, '60s, and '70s played a major role in muting the economic growth of Southern Dallas. Prospering minority communities were left out of planning decisions, highways divided the city and destroyed neighborhoods.[78] Racism has been our first impediment to free enterprise.

One example, Tenth Street is one of Dallas's oldest neighborhoods, and it is deeply important to the history of African-American culture and life in the city. It is one of the city's Freedman's towns, established after the Civil War when freed slaves founded their own neighborhoods. The nucleus of the Tenth Street neighborhood formed in the 1880s and 1890s south of the floodplains of the Trinity River and on the eastern side of Oak Cliff—a place where the black community could own property during Reconstruction and its aftermath.

Across generations, the neighborhood grew and nurtured business leaders, artists, and families. There was free enterprise, and there was prosperity.

What happened to the neighborhood?

The story is the construction of R. L. Thornton Freeway (Interstate 35) directly through the middle of the neighborhood in the early 1950s.

The highway construction did several things. First, it demolished thriving businesses, undercutting its economic heart. Second, it cut Oak Cliff in half, destroying homes and separating neighbors from each other, disrupting the social networks that make neighborhoods thrive. Third, those who lost businesses and homes scattered to new neighborhoods, further destabilizing the community.

In an era in Dallas history with a huge shortage of housing for African Americans who were unwelcome in white neighborhoods, these forced moves magnified the detrimental effects of segregation and midcentury racism. As the city's black population grew and homes were lost to freeway construction in the 1940s, a series of bombings targeted black families that moved to traditionally white neighborhoods. In 1950 and 1951, at least 12 new bombings again targeted the homes of black families in South Dallas who had moved into formerly white blocks. No one was killed and no one was ever convicted for the crimes. These bombings sowed fear and amplified mistrust, leaving African Americans with extremely limited choices about where they could safely live in the city. All these actions together created a massive disinvestment in Tenth Street that went, and remains, un-redressed. There are many people alive today in Southern Dallas that remember these events that are not easily forgotten. Distrust is understandable.

Tenth Street is only one of many Dallas neighborhoods eviscerated by highway and infrastructure construction in the 1950s and 1960s. The Freedman's town of North Dallas—of which only St. Paul United Methodist Church, Moorland YMCA/Dallas Black Dance, and remnants of Booker T. Washington High School remain today—was bulldozed during the construction of Central Expressway in the 1940s, Woodall Rodgers Freeway beginning in the 1960s, and I-345 in the 1970s. The construction of the southern portions of Central Expressway and C.F. Hawn Freeway bisected Lincoln Manor and Bonton, leaving the neighborhoods, which had been contiguous, connected only by Bexar Street. Hundreds of families lost homes, and businesses and churches closed. Listings in the 1956 edition of the *Negro Traveler's Green Book* for Dallas businesses hospitable to traveling African Americans show clusters of properties that were all in the shadows of this urban surgery: the Howard, Lewis, and Powell Hotels; the Palm Café; and the Shalimar Restaurant all disappeared.[79]

For three decades, Dallas City planners focused infrastructure investment on North Dallas. Being nowhere close to the investment in North Dallas, the highway system in Southern Dallas was inadequate to attract business investment. South of the Dallas Central Business District, Interstate 35 was nearly devoid of exit ramps and access roads. Interstate 20 is the same. Prior racism has come back to haunt the city as investment and development grew north into Collin, Denton, and now Grayson Counties. Surely, this represents billions of dollars in lost tax revenue for Dallas County, annually.

In addition to racism, let us examine the four additional impediments to free enterprise's ability to thrive:

1. Family formation
2. Education
3. Crime
4. Political climate (government)

1. Family Formation

Figure 9.4 Percentage of Single-Parent Households in Southern Dallas Trade Area Zip Codes

Zip Code	% Of Single-Parent HHs	Zip Code	% Of Single-Parent HHs
75211	32	75149	36
75227	36	75203	32
75210	47	75208	26
75215	63	75216	50
75241	58	75233	46
75217	35	75237	70
		75232	43

Source: DFWHC Foundation—Healthy North Texas

The single-parent households average of all zip codes within Dallas County is 30.5%. As shown in Figure 9.4, all zip codes in South Dallas, except one, is above the Dallas County average. Two are at least twice the Dallas County average. the Dallas County average. When examining the 16 competing North Texas counties our report is more disheartening. North Texas counties with the lowest percentage of single-parent households benefit most from in-migration and relocations from other states and business formation.

Figure 9.5 Single-Parent Households by County in North Texas

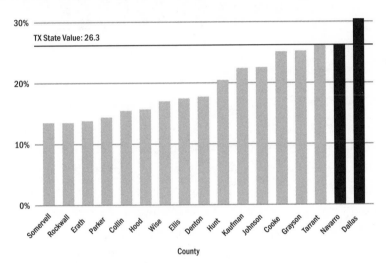

Source: DFWHC Foundation – Healthy North Texas

2. Education

Figure 9.6 Average High School Drop-Out Percentages in Southern Dallas Trade Area Zip Codes

75211	45	75149	24
75227	34	75203	34
75210	38	75208	29
75215	26	75216	33
75241	21	75233	29
75217	44	75237	20
		75232	25

Source: Texas Education Agency

Figure 9.7   Average High School Drop-Out Rate by County in Texas

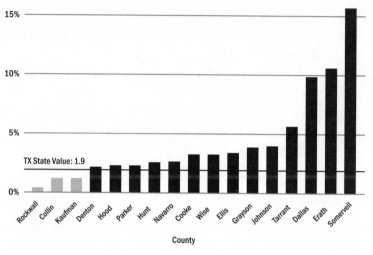

Source: Texas Education Agency

Reviewing the same 13-zip-code Southern Dallas trade area, we see the average high school drop-out rate is 31%, or 1,500% higher than the Texas average of 1.9%. The high school drop-out rate for all zip codes in Dallas County is 10%, or 500% higher than the state average.

The drop-out rate of Dallas County and our Southern Dallas group compared to competing North Texas counties is alarming. However, it provides a credible explanation as to why this area of North Texas may not receive its share of corporate relocations, in-migration, and business formation.

3. Crime

Figure 9.8 Crime Rates in Southern Dallas Trade Area Zip Codes

Zip Code	Property Crimes/1000	Violent Crimes/1000	Zip Code	Property Crimes/1000	Violent Crimes/1000
75211	54	17	75149	36	6
75227	35	10	75203	72	20
75210	79	17	75208	15	3
75215	58	17	75216	64	17
75241	66	23	75233	35	10
75217	46	16	75237	53	17
			75232	49	14

Source: Neighbohoodscout.com

To provide perspective, the property crime per 1,000 citizens and violent crime per 1,000 citizens for the city of Dallas are 34 and 9, respectively. For the state of Texas, the property crime per 1,000 and violent crime per 1,000 is 24 and four, respectively. According to neighborhoodscout.com, the average Total Crime index for the 13 zip codes in the Southern Dallas trade area ranges from 1–10 (100 is the safest). Meaning, 90-99% of the neighborhoods in the United States are safer than our 13-zip-code Southern Dallas trade area.

Unfortunately, neighborhoodscout.com does not provide data on a county-level basis. However, the database does provide similar crime statistics on a city basis. We consider the crime statistics for the major cities in the 16 competing counties a fair barometer of crime, instead.

Figure 9.9 Crime Rates in North Texas Cities

City	Property Crimes/ 1000	Violent Crimes/ 1000	Crime Index	City	Property Crimes/ 1000	Violent	Crime Crimes/ 1000
Rockwall	16	1	35	Granbury	42	2	6
Plano	17	2	32	Decatur	35	1	10
Allen	11	1	53	Sherman	26	4	15
McKinney	10	1	54	Denison	18	4	25
Kaufman	19	2	26	Frisco	12	1	49
Denton	20	2	24	Southlake	12	.3	50
Glen Rose	9	.4	90	Grapevine	28	2	15
Ft. Worth	27	4	23	Cleburne	19	3	25
Gainesville	22	5	18				

Source: Neighborhoodscout.com

So much unnecessary suffering. Place yourself in the shoes of an entrepreneur, a business owner, or family seeking to relocate. What would your criteria be for the trade area, city, or state you would consider? North Texas counties with the lowest crime rates benefit most from family and corporate relocations from other states, as well as new business formation.

4. Political Climate

The final free enterprise impediment of our Southern Dallas case study is the political climate. Do our elected officials champion the free enterprise system, or do they promote and legislate socialist policies shrewdly labeled as liberal or progressive? Also, is the perception of these elected officials amongst entrepreneurs, business owners, investors, and the electorate that they are of high (or at least acceptable) moral character, or is the perception that these elected officials are self-dealing and corrupt? If it is the latter, on these two questions, free enterprise will not prosper.

Annually, with each legislative session, the Texas Association of Business (TAB) publishes a voting scorecard, which reports how each state legislator voted on business legislation during the current and historical legislative sessions. Legislators with scores of 90 or above receive the highest distinction as the TAB "Champions of Free Enterprise." Legislators with scores of 80–89 receive the distinction of "Fighters for Free Enterprise." The table below reflects the TAB Scorecard for the four state house seats and one state senator representing our 13-zip-code area.[80]

Figure 9.10 TAB Scores for Southern Dallas Representatives

Southern Dallas Representatives	TAB Score
House District 100	60
House District 104	56
House District 110	58
House District 111	38
Senate District 23	56
Average	54

Source: "Scorecard." Texas Association of Business. Accessed December 29, 2022. https://www.txbiz.org/scorecard.

We can confidently assume, other elected representatives (school board, county commissioners, city council, etc.) in this trade area share similar views regarding free enterprise, business, and socialism.

For comparison purposes, we provide the Texas House and Senate average TAB Scorecard for legislators representing the 16 competing North Texas counties.

Figure 9.11 TAB Scores for Legislators in North Texas Counties

County	Average TAB Score	County	Average TAB Score
Rockwall	77	Navarro	92
Collin	83	Cooke	84
Kaufman	77	Wise	87
Denton	79	Ellis	89
Hood	83	Grayson	89
Parker	87	Johnson	89
Hunt	80	Tarrant	76
Erath	85	Somervell	88
Average TAB Score of 16 Competing Counties			84

Source: "Scorecard." Texas Association of Business. Accessed December 29, 2022. https://www.txbiz.org/scorecard.

As this analysis shows, the pro–free enterprise voting record of the 16 competing counties is significantly better than our 13-zip-code trade area representing Southern Dallas. We need keep in mind, the Economic Development Departments of these 16 counties utilize this information to compete against one another (including Dallas County) for new residents and business relocation from other states. In this regard, there is much work to be done.

Next, we evaluate the degree to which prospective families, business owners, entrepreneurs, and corporations seeking to relocate view the moral character, extent of self-dealing, and perceived corruption of political figures in our 13-zip-code trade area. Almost without exception, where there is poverty there is political corruption and vice versa. The end notes to this paper provide a list of articles written, over recent history, regarding Southern Dallas corruption among its political figures.[81] The reader is encouraged to review each of these articles. Note, this is not an exhaustive list. Alternatively, merely Google "South Dallas Corruption." By any measure, the answer to this query is sad news for Southern Dallas. Business owners and companies view this as a "hidden cost" to doing business. This is not to say political corruption does not exist elsewhere. We know it does. However, to the degree that perceived self-dealing, bribery, and shakedowns may exist, we acknowledge its destructive impact on family formation, free enterprise, business formation, prosperity, and the pursuit of happiness. Consequently, we are obligated to recognize its contribution to poverty.

Financial Institutions

Now, we return to our review of the critical stakeholders of the free enterprise economic system.

Financial institutions ("commercial banks") are financial intermediaries and play an important role in the financial system and the free enterprise economy. As a key component of the financial system, banks allocate funds from savers to borrowers in an efficient manner. Banks are financial intermediaries. They provide specialized financial services, which reduce the cost of obtaining information about both savings and borrowing opportunities. These financial services help to make the overall economy more efficient. Because commercial banks represent such a crucial role in the economy, they are heavily regulated by both federal and state governments.

Commercial and consumer banks follow the homeowner, entrepreneur, investor capitalist, and business owner into a trade area—not the reverse. Businesses form through capital being placed at risk. As businesses become profitable and grow, jobs are created. These job holders and businesses need banks to safely hold their cash. Banks come into the market or investors/capitalists form new banks to serve this need and to provide additional low-cost non-dilutive capital for growth. If a community or trade area lacks business formation, investment capital, an educated work force, or safe and stable neighborhoods, banks struggle to operate.

Commercial banks make money, primarily, on the spread between the rate they pay on deposits (liabilities) and the loans they make. Currently, the spread for most commercial banks is approximately 3.5–4.0%—a very thin margin. Banks obtain this spread by borrowing on short term rates (deposits) and lending out the money over a longer term. Depending on how management has positioned the balance sheet, an unexpected swing in interest rates can have a dramatic impact on earnings. To make an acceptable return for investors (10–12%), banks operate with significant balance sheet leverage. They have a typical debt-to-equity ratio of 10–12x. To protect earnings and equity capital from potential loan losses banks normally reserve 1.00–1.50% of commercial loans, which produces an allowance for potential loan losses. Think about this. For a commercial bank to remain profitable it must be precise on its loan decisions 98.5–99.0% of the time! All these attributes add up to the fact that a commercial bank is a fragile enterprise that is unsustainable if "equity" investment risk is accepted.

Compared to our Investor/Capitalist stakeholder, commercial banks cannot tolerate nor survive a high level of risk. Commercial banks reside in a safer position on the aforementioned capital stack, or at least they should. Commercial banks mitigate these risks by:

- Preventing being the source of first loss.
- Basing the commercial loan approval on proven, existing, and sustainable cash flow from operations. Cash flow should cover required loan payments with an acceptable margin.
- Securing a secondary source of repayment (collateral) where the verified collateral value exceeds the loan amount by an acceptable margin.
- Including a personal guaranty and verifying the financial wherewithal of the business owner(s).
- Approving borrowers with a strong character and history of handling borrowing arrangements in a satisfactory manner.
- Approving borrowers with proven operating competency.

The perspective provided above makes the point that commercial banks are not sources of common equity, venture capital, preferred stock, or venture debt. Commercial banks' operating margin, funding structure, and financial leverage are not built for these types of risks. Furthermore, in this writer's opinion, making loans to borrowers with insufficient ability to repay is immoral and represents lending malpractice. No banker enjoys foreclosing on borrowers. Foreclosure and/or bankruptcy can ruin a life and the ability to borrow from banks or other creditors in the future.

Strangely, misled public representatives seek to make banks a scapegoat for a community's poverty and a lack of economic prosperity.[82] Regrettably, they have lost their way. These consist of legislators unaware about basic economics and the power of the free enterprise system and legislators unwilling to take responsibility for their failures. Pending our readiness to recognize the true causes of poverty—detailed in this essay—we have little prospect of moving from poverty to free enterprise prosperity.

Government

Government is an essential stakeholder in the free enterprise economy. A key idea underlying a free enterprise system is that we, as individuals, know best how to pursue our own well-being. A free enterprise system is largely self-regulating. Therefore, government should play a limited, but important, role, allowing individuals to make most of the economic decisions. Also, government is a key beneficiary of the free enterprise system. As any government jurisdiction's gross domestic product increases, so does its tax revenue.

Specifically, government has two roles: rule maker and umpire. In its role as rule maker, government makes and enforces laws governing the conditions under which voluntary transactions are made. These laws are designed to protect the rights to private property and individual freedom and to preserve and promote competition. As an umpire, government acts to settle disputes resulting from conflicting interpretations of the rules. Beyond this, government has no other major economic responsibilities. Indeed, in a pure free enterprise system the governmental role is clearly and specifically limited to keeping the system free and competitive. Government participation in day-to-day economic decision making is not a part of a free enterprise system.

This is like the structure of organized sports today. In football, for example, the rules committee determines the rules of the game. The officials enforce them. The commissioner settles disputes over conflicting interpretations of the rules. This provides a framework that allows the teams to compete on an equal footing. What would our reaction be if an official intercepted a pass, made a tackle, or kicked a field goal? Similarly, the government in a free enterprise system provides a framework that allows individuals an equal opportunity to compete in the marketplace. It may not participate in answering the "what to produce," "how to produce," and "how to divide" questions.[83]

Nonetheless, Americans' belief in free enterprise does not and has not precluded a major role for government. Many times, Americans have depended on the government to break up or regulate companies that appeared to be developing so much power that they could defy market forces. In general, government grew larger and intervened more aggressively in the economy from the 1930s until the 1970s. But economic hardships in the 1960s and 1970s left Americans skeptical about the ability of government to address many social and economic issues. Major social programs (including Social Security and Medicare, which provide retirement income and health insurance for the elderly) survived this period of reconsideration. But the overall growth of the federal government slowed in the 1980s. The pragmatism and flexibility of Americans resulted in an unusually dynamic economy. Change has been a constant in American economic history.[84]

Citizens rely on the government to address matters the private economy overlooks in sectors ranging from education to protecting the environment. Despite their advocacy of market principles, Americans have used government at times in history to nurture new industries or even to protect American companies from competition.[85]

Government has responsibilities, as well. Just as business ownership is a sacred stewardship, so are public service and political offices. Elected officials are representatives serving the people. They are civil servants who work for us—not vice versa. Elected officials who believe they are the "leaders" of given jurisdictions have lost their way. We, the electorate, must push back on politicians who perceive themselves as our leaders. They serve us. Period.

The Great Black Migration and Reversal

From 1910 to 1970, black Americans took part in a "Great Black Migration," which saw approximately 6 million move out of the South and into other parts of the country. The movement was of such magnitude that, by 1970, the South retained only a little more than half of the nation's black population. As we'll see, however, Census Data over the past 50 years clearly show the Great Black Migration reversed, as many returned to the South in a "New Great Black Migration."[86]

Prior to the Great Migration, the South was the main regional home for black Americans. Beginning with American Independence, until the start of the twentieth century, at least nine in ten black Americans lived in the South, mainly in rural areas. Even though the Thirteenth Amendment gave black residents new freedoms, black migration from the South was minimal because of farm tenancy arrangements, poverty, high levels of illiteracy, and the lack of opportunities in the North.[87]

The Great Migration took place in two separate phases: The first, between 1910 and 1930, was started by the mixture of newly available factory jobs in Northern cities (which were further increased by U.S. involvement in World War I) and the slowdown and eventual government restriction of immigration. Jointly, these events caused anxious employers in cities such as New York, Philadelphia, Chicago, and Detroit to look to Southern black workers to fill their largely unskilled jobs. Although the tug of Northern jobs was a major impetus for migration, there were also strong Southern "forces," including poor working conditions, Jim Crow segregation laws, political disenfranchisement, and racial violence. Perhaps just as important was the drying up of agricultural employment following farm mechanization and the boll weevil's damage to cotton crops.

The second phase of the Great Migration took place after a national migration pause during the Great Depression. Significant increases in manufacturing during World War II offered even greater employment opportunities to Northern cities as well as to Western coastal cities such as Los Angeles and San Francisco. The postwar period found many returning black military veterans settle in these Northern and Western destinations. Even as the South became more urbanized and economically vibrant in the 1950s and 1960s, it continued to go through black out-migration.

From 1940 to 1970, nearly 80% of all increases in the black population took place outside of the South. In contrast to their largely rural settlement patterns at the beginning of the Great Migration, in 1970, eight in 10 black residents lived in metropolitan areas, with one in four living in New York, Chicago, Philadelphia, Los Angeles, or Detroit. Similarly, in 1910, the largest black populations resided in Georgia, Mississippi, and Alabama; in 1970, the states with the highest number of black residents were New York, Illinois, and California.

The Great Migration reversal began gradually, in the 1970s, steadily increased in the 1990s, and became an exodus in subsequent decades. The reversal was triggered by numerous factors. First, by the 1970s, national deindustrialization was happening and conditions in the North shifted, adversely affecting black workers.

Deindustrialization led to the ruin or relocation of large numbers of blue-collar jobs, many of which black urban residents had occupied. Simultaneously, the "promise" of Northern cities was quickly declining, with many black residents residing in less advantaged, segregated city neighborhoods. Widespread "white flight" to the suburbs further isolated these neighborhoods from communities where employment opportunities and tax bases were growing.[88]

Black dissatisfaction over declining employment opportunities, discrimination, and de facto segregation in Northern and Western cities led to a series of well-publicized urban race riots in the 1960s. Meanwhile, a favorable business climate coupled with new infrastructure (such as interstate highways) and other improvements (such as the widespread availability of air-conditioning) paved the way for industries and employers to head to Southern states, giving rise to the "New South."

Careers in thriving parts of the South are not the only reason that black Americans have been moving there. Social ties and large black populations are powerful draws as well. The cultural and family ties associated with residence within the black community were evident in the past; although the black Americans who took part in the Great Migration were less likely to return to the South than white Southern out-migrants were during in the same period, they kept in contact with family and maintained kinship networks that promoted further migration. Black Americans' ties to the region, whether personal or cultural, have also been evident in the Southern return, especially among Northern city residents who did not fare well during the deindustrialization period and found a familiar and welcoming environment among family and friends in the South. But there are ties to the region for a broad spectrum of black residents, including retirees with family histories in the South and young professionals who want to join areas with growing middle-class black populations.

Figure 9.12 States with Greatest Black Net Migration Gains and Losses

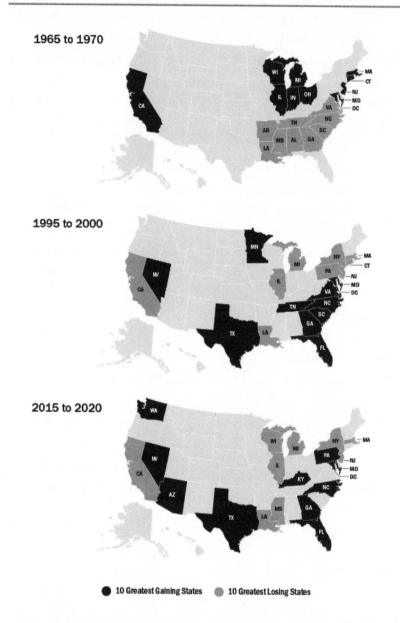

Source: William H. Frey analysis of Decennial US Censuses, 1970 and 2000; Census Bureau American Community Survey 2016–2020

Figure 9.13 Black net migration: Metro areas with largest gains and losses, 1965–1970, 1995–2000, and 2015–2020

Southern metro areas are in italics

1965–1970		1995–2000		2015–2020*	
Greatest Gains					
Los Angeles	55,943	*Atlanta*	*114,478*	*Atlanta*	*68,835*
Detroit	54,766	*Dallas*	*39,360*	*Dallas*	*32,895*
Washington, D.C.	*34,365*	*Charlotte, N.C.*	*23,313*	Phoenix	31,355
San Francisco	24,699	*Orlando, Fla.*	*20,222*	Las Vegas	30,180
Philadelphia	24,601	Las Vegas	18,912	*Houston*	*27,165*
Greatest Losses					
Birmingham, Ala.	*-12,177*	New York	-193,063	New York	-301,430
Memphis, Tenn.	*-8,498*	Chicago	-59,282	Chicago	-114,890
Mobile, Ala.	*-8,017*	Los Angeles	-38,833	Los Angeles	-60,505
Pittsburgh	-5,003	San Francisco	-30,613	*Miami*	*-59,190*
New Orleans	*-4886*	Detroit	-15,095	*Washington, D.C.*	*-35,565*

*2015–2020 Net Migration represents 5x the annual estimated net migration for the 2015–2020 period based on the 2016–2020 American Community Survey

Source: Analysis of Net Migration, 2015 and 2020, Census Bureau American Community Survey 2016–2020

The 1995–2000 period solidified Southern metro areas' dominance as magnets, while at the same time Northern and Western metro areas such as Los Angeles and San Francisco took the lead in net black out-migration. Atlanta began its long reign as the top black migration magnet, outpacing other Southern metro areas such as Dallas; Charlotte, North Carolina; and Orlando, Florida; along with Raleigh, North Carolina; Columbia, South Carolina; and later, Houston, among others. And in the late 1990s, Las Vegas, catching some "spillover" from California, began to show a pattern of black migrant gains that would later proliferate in Western states. During this period, black migration back to the South has largely been driven by younger, college-educated black Americans. They have contributed to the growth in many Southern states, especially in Texas, Georgia, and North Carolina, as well as metropolitan regions such as Atlanta, Dallas, and Houston.

Figure 9.14   CNBC Ranking of States' Business Competitiveness; Comparative
Black Migration

Top 10 Gainers— Black Migration	Business Ranking	Top 10 Losers—Black Migration	Business Ranking
1. Texas	5	1. New York	36
2. Georgia	10	2. Illinois	19
3. North Carolina	1	3. California	29
4. Nevada	39	4. New Jersey	42
5. Florida	11	5. Mississippi	50
6. Maryland	27	6. Louisiana	48
7. Arizona	34	7. District of Columbia	NR
8. Pennsylvania	17	8. Michigan	16
9. Washington	2	9. Massachusetts	24
10. Kentucky	26	10. Wisconsin	23
Average	15	Average	32

Source: Based on Data from "What US States are the Best to do Business In?" by Visual Capitalist and CNBC

When we compare the top black migration gainers and top black migration losers from Figure 9.13 to the state business rankings in Figure 9.14, we find that states with pro-business policies that produce jobs and opportunities generally enjoy greater black and overall immigration. Notice that Nevada and Arizona don't rank well as places to do business. These are the exception and have unique circumstances. So why are blacks moving to Nevada and Arizona? In short—they are not the best places for business, but they are better than California (particularly in the California metro areas) to live. According to Black Excellence Media, most blacks moving to these two states are moving from California.

Blacks from California choose these two states because of their proximity to California—their ability to visit friends and family remaining in California. Next, the opportunity for home ownership and overall cost of living. The average cost of a home in LA and San Francisco is $665K and $1.0 million, respectively; this compares to the average cost of a home in Metropolitan Arizona and Las Vegas of \$269K and \$307K, respectively. Nevada has no state income tax. Arizona's state income tax is 4.2%. California's state income tax is the highest in the country at 13.3%. California is ranked the third worst state in the country to start a new business.[90]

Figure 9.15   California's Black Exodus to Other States

According to Lauren Helper's July 2020 article in *CalMatters*, "The Hidden Toll of California's Black Exodus," 75,000 blacks have left the state since 2018.[91] States receiving the most black relocations are:

1. Nevada (Las Vegas): 10,022
2. Texas (Dallas, Houston and San Antonio): 9,909
3. Georgia (Atlanta): 7,172
4. Arizona: 6,092
5. Michigan (Detroit): 5,108

Again, people vote for opportunity with their feet, even though they may not yet understand that free enterprise economic systems and smart government policies created the opportunity.

Conclusion

The preamble to the Constitution broadly identifies six responsibilities of the U.S. Constitution that civil servants are sworn to uphold. They include:

- Form a more perfect Union.
- Establish Justice.
- Insure domestic Tranquility.
- Provide for the common defense.
- Promote the general Welfare.
- Secure the Blessings of Liberty to ourselves and our Posterity.

Thanks to School House Rock, you want to sing it. The sixth responsibility catches your eye "…secure the Blessings of Liberty to ourselves and our Posterity." Government is responsible for securing (and maintaining) our Liberty. Liberty is a blessing. Liberty recognizes that we as individuals (we the people) know best how to pursue our own well-being. Liberty is choice. Liberty is free enterprise. Socialism is not a choice. It is command and control.

We started this essay with the recognition that poverty is man-made. We conclude with the recognition that reversing poverty is man-made, as well.

1. Discrimination has no place in the free enterprise system. The free enterprise system must be a meritocracy to function optimally. Rewards and success are based on ingenuity, skills, innovation, persistence, sacrifice, and hard work. Skin color, gender, sexual orientation, religion, and age must never be a factor. When they are a factor, we all lose. However, we cannot fight discrimination with discrimination. Beware, seeking equity of outcomes is socialism. We loathe the day when a government bureaucrat gets to choose winners and losers. Nobel Laureate (Economics) Milton Freedman's comments on the topic resonate today.

> A society that puts equality before freedom (or liberty) will get neither. A society that puts freedom (liberty) before equality will get a high degree of both.

Equal opportunity—always. Equal outcome—the shared misery of socialism. Our Founding Fathers got it right when they made the focus of the American experiment Liberty.

2. The viability of the American family is crucial for the survival of the republic, not only sociologically, but financially. We all cumulatively either contribute to, or detract from, the soundness of the familial units comprising our society. We must not

only do our part in our familial microcosms, but electorally, we must elect and support those who favor governmental policy that strengthens the family unit, and who do not buckle to political correctness in redefining our societal building blocks. As a society and stakeholders in the free enterprise system, we must reject any legislation or ideology that seeks to harm the nuclear family.

3. Thus far, free enterprise has proven to be the vastly superior economic system for reversing poverty. Socialism and communism have proven to be vastly superior economic systems for creating poverty. Covetous Socialists and Marxists may argue that entrepreneurs and capitalists are greedy. Again, Milton Freedman's response is valuable:

> Well first of all, tell me: Is there some society you know that doesn't run on greed? You think Russia does not run on greed? You think China does not run on greed? What is greed? Of course, none of us are greedy, it is only the other fellow who's greedy. The world runs on individuals pursuing their separate interests (free enterprise). The great achievements of civilization have not come from government bureaus. Einstein did not construct his theory under order from a bureaucrat. Henry Ford did not revolutionize the automobile industry that way. In the only cases in which the masses have escaped from the kind of grinding poverty you are talking about, the only cases in recorded history, are where they have had capitalism and largely free trade. If you want to know where the masses are worse off, worst off, it is exactly in the kinds of societies that depart from that. So that the record of history is absolutely crystal clear, that there is no alternative way so far discovered of

improving the lot of the ordinary people that can hold a candle to the productive activities that are unleashed by the free-enterprise system.

4. Each stakeholder in the free enterprise ecosystem ought to understand and champion the free enterprise system. These include: the nuclear family, all areas of education (K–universities), the investor/capitalist, financial institutions, the entrepreneur/business owners, and all levels of government. Stakeholders need to know their roles and responsibilities. They must recognize their interdependence and be united in pursuit of their objectives.

5. Poverty is reversed and marginalized zip codes are stabilized when the stakeholders of the free enterprise system fly in formation.

10

MARGINALIZED COMMUNITIES DIDN'T JUST HAPPEN

Curtis Hill

Marginalized communities, particularly black communities, did not just happen. They result from often purposeful, sometimes unintended, and consistently negligent policies of devaluation of the people making up the community.

Are blacks still devalued within the classification of human beings nearly sixty years after the passage of the sweeping Civil Rights Act?

"How else except by becoming a Negro could a white man hope to learn the truth?"

So describes the premise as set forth in the 1961 classic book *Black Like Me* by John Howard Griffin, wherein Griffin determines to experience "the plight of second-class citizens" by presenting as black and thus subjecting himself to the treatment afforded blacks at that time.[1] Initially, Griffin received much general support for his work and for helping people understand the experience. Eventually, threats caused him to move to Mexico for some years for safety. In 1964, while stopped on the side of the road with a flat tire in Mississippi, he was beaten by a group of white men with chains.[2] It took him five months to recover.

How much can the broader society learn from those systematically marginalized over decades to realize a connection in the economic and educational realities that have devastated our urban centers?

What if we could reinforce our American values and free market economy by prioritizing marginalized communities as the center of opportunities for personal, public, and private initiatives? Access to initiatives that create sustainable and profitable growth entities, while achieving informed and intentional unity, would prove essential to demarginalizing black communities.

The Historical Foundation of Marginalization

First, it is necessary to acknowledge that racial marginalization is deeply rooted in American history and its founding. The racism, brutal violence, dehumanization toward blacks, and the various indignities extended to the indigenous American Indians stand out among multiple intolerances that contradict America's founding principles. While it is true that slavery, as a world institution, was not isolated to colonial America in the seventeenth and eighteenth centuries, that other nations practiced human bondage does nothing to lessen the horrors of a nation founded on freedom that was so deeply engaged in the traffic of human beings.

America has a well-documented history that includes clear policy toward the official and sustained inferior treatment of blacks, which has had a pervasive impact on the black and white communities.

Today, we fully recognize, academically, the necessity of compromise required to settle the question of American Independence in 1776 and the adoption of constitutional government in 1789. That "necessity" does not alter the reality that American policy toward blacks and human bondage was not only an acceptable practice but one that was encouraged in the promotion of commerce and required consistent and brutal conditioning of enslaved black people to enforce their position as property rather than persons. The constant conditioning of blacks continued well beyond slavery and to a point where American culture is nearly permanently ingrained with an attitude on race that has proved difficult, if not impossible, to shake.

It is not the point to bring forth this history to generate emotional outbursts or calls of retaliation for past practices, but rather to candidly acknowledge the factual history behind our modern racial attitudes. This collective understanding and acknowledgment must come with rules that demand mutual respect. Our country is simply not moving forward by ignoring where we come from.

To fully understand and fully appreciate current feelings of disenfranchisement or marginalization, twenty-first-century black and white Americans need to have a fundamental understanding of the eighteenth-, nineteenth-, and twentieth-century black experience and its ultimate impact on modern culture.

While it is true that not all slaveholders were as cruel and abusive as others, the cruelty of slavery was not limited to torturous beatings and hard labor. It included intentional degradation and separation of family, the systemic humiliation of the black male, the habitual rape of the black female, and the purposeful indignities designed to inflict mortal wounds on the character of the American blacks.

Generation after generation of conditioning produced a culture of compliance, notwithstanding a spirit of defiance among many American blacks.

For 100 years after slavery, blacks suffered treacherous treatment, and as supposedly free people, blacks were consistently harassed, denigrated, and denied freedoms guaranteed by the Constitution.

It would be the rare black American who doesn't have a recollection of false accusations, an embarrassing story, or a humiliating atrocity from a personal experience or the experience of a family member, simply because of the color of their skin.

If only we could say that racism in America existed only through pockets of individuals too stubborn to let their personal beliefs subside. But no, our government institutions were profoundly engaged in facilitating the condition of race and racism. Segregation of the United States military, the education system, and official housing policies that sanctioned open discrimination put in place a market heavily skewed against black participation, and some of the effects linger today.

Communities like Greenwood, Oklahoma, a suburb of Tulsa, sprung up as a result of forced segregation and proved to be early signs of successful free market capitalism for black Americans despite overt government-sponsored racism. In the face of widespread factors designed to short-circuit black success, blacks have demonstrated a collective tenacity to persevere, but not without considerable cost.

School segregation, neighborhood redlining, and income inequality eventually gave way to integrated schools, fair housing legislation, and affirmative action programs that did little to relieve the centuries of complex race assumptions while increasing black dependency on government. Black men and women are often taught as children to anticipate discriminatory practices to insulate them from routine slights. It is customary for blacks to be constantly aware of their "blackness" in most settings, which is contrary to white Americans, who do not ordinarily think of themselves by racial classification. This alone marks a central understanding point in the relationship between blacks and whites necessary for the encouragement of further engagement.

Until we understand from what depths marginalization has risen, we will not have the empathy and credibility required to form policy initiatives that will continue to reverse the decades of bad outcomes in marginalized neighborhoods across our country.

The original Great Black Migration tracked the steady exodus of Southern blacks living in the segregated South from 1910 to 1970. Black men by the thousands began heading north, in search of the promise of sure economic opportunity brought on by the industrial age and the rise of urban factories.

In the early part of the twentieth century, nine in ten blacks lived in the rural Deep South, toiling as farm labor with little hope or ability to escape to a more economically favorable and less oppressive circumstance. The adoption of the Thirteenth Amendment to the U.S. Constitution abolished slavery, but the overwhelming majority of former slaves were limited to share cropping and menial labor under conditions that rivaled those of their previous servitude, making an exit from the Deep South a welcome priority for many blacks.

The Great Black Migration was made up of two distinct phases:

- The first phase occurred between 1910 and 1930 and was a direct result of the transition from an agricultural economy to an industrial economy. New job availability in Northern factories spurred on by United States participation in World War I and the reduction in European immigrants seemed a far cry from the atrocities suffered by blacks in the South during that time. Cities like Chicago, Detroit, Philadelphia, and New York, among others, became filled with migrating blacks.[3,4]
- The second phase of the Great Migration followed a slowdown during the Great Depression of the 1930s and was attributed to the massive increase in industrial manufacturing during World War II, which produced huge growth in the Western cities of San Francisco and Los Angeles. Following World War II, many black military veterans returning from active duty chose Northern and Western cities as home, instead of returning to the rural South.[5]

Although the black community in America is largely viewed as consistently living in urban centers, including the more marginalized neighborhoods within the urban setting, recent trends have demonstrated that blacks are very willing to move out of the great urban centers and are doing so in large scale.

What has been referred to as the "New Great Migration" is resulting in a black flight away from large cities in the North, Midwest, and West, back to the Deep South.[6] Yet the rate of marginalization has changed little through this process. In fact, the number of Americans living in distressed neighborhoods, primarily blacks, has held constant with no change.[7]

Are Americans becoming economically more divided and polarized? By answering this question, we can set a baseline for deciding what policies, grassroots initiatives, and intentional economic improvements can be initiated and where they can be executed. We can focus on local centers of change that are targeted for investment to demarginalize specific distressed communities. If those communities are ready for the introduction of practices that can foster prosperity, it can reenergize the possibility of attaining opportunity for all.

For "when they enter, we all enter" into the constitutional rights of America.[8]

The Distressed Community Index (DCI) report, created by the Economic Innovation Group (EIG), states:

> At 50.5 million, the number of Americans living in distressed communities held mostly constant since the turn of the century even as the country's population grew significantly. As a result, the share of the total U.S. population residing in economically distressed zip codes fell from 18 percent in 2000 to 16 percent in 2018. By contrast, the middle quintile of well-being added 13.1 million people over the period, triggering a clear shift in the preponderance of the country's population towards higher tiers of well-being. Population now increases as economic well-being

does. At the high end, prosperous communities lead with 82.4 million residents as of 2018, stable at 26 percent of the country's total population.[9]

The DCI sorts U.S. zip codes based on seven complementary economic indicators into five even quintiles of well-being: prosperous, comfortable, mid-tier, at risk, and distressed. It uses seven components to score each community on the index equivalent to its percentile rank across all seven measures combined. In all, the DCI captures 99% of the U.S. population and all 25,400-plus zip codes with at least 500 residents.

- No high-school diploma: percentage of the 25+-year-old population without a high school diploma or equivalent
- Housing vacancy rate: percentage of habitable housing that is unoccupied, excluding properties that are for seasonal, recreational, or occasional use
- Adults not working: percentage of the prime-age (25–54) population not currently employed
- Poverty rate: percentage of the population living under the poverty line
- Median income ratio: median household income as a percentage of metro area median household income (or state, for non-metro areas)
- Change in employment: percent change in the number of jobs from 2014 to 2018
- Change in establishments: percent change in the number of business establishments from 2014 to 2018

Figure 10.1 Total Population in 2000 and 2020 DCI Quintiles

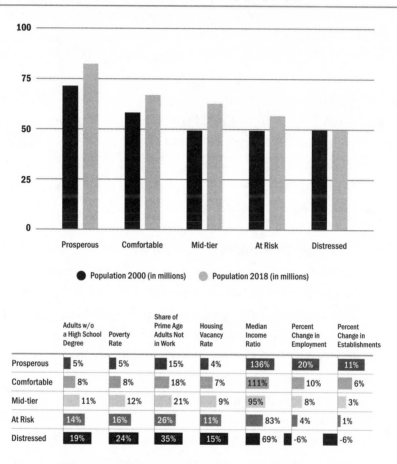

Source: "Distressed Communities: Key Findings." *Economic Innovation Group.* Accessed December 29, 2022. https://eig.org/distressed-communities/key-findings/.

So far in the twenty-first century, national economic growth has failed to lift the country's most vulnerable communities.

"These findings showcase just how many aspects of our lives still break along lines of race and place," said EIG Research Director Kenan Fikri. "While abstract forces such as a pandemic should be colorblind, pre-existing inequalities render this impossible. Prosperous places and the households in them enjoy an intrinsic resiliency that eludes much of the rest of the country."[10]

Here are highlights from the EIG report:

- On measures of income, poverty, joblessness, and vacancy, the typical distressed zip code remained just as far behind the typical prosperous zip code in 2018 as it was in 2000.
- At 50.5 million, the number of Americans living in distressed communities held constant even as the country's population grew significantly.
- A plurality of Americans (82.4 million) calls prosperous zip codes home, but the population increased fastest in the mid-tier category.
- Zip codes that were prosperous in 2000 gained 8.7 million jobs between 2000 and 2018, generating nearly 62% of total U.S. job growth over the period.
- Meanwhile, zip codes that were distressed at the turn of the century lost jobs on the net between 2000 and 2018. The number of jobs and businesses in distressed communities even fell from 2014 to 2018, deep into the national recovery from the Great Recession.
- Community-level advantages and disadvantages tend to perpetuate over time. Two-thirds of zip codes that ranked as prosperous in 2000 were prosperous in 2018. Likewise, two-thirds of zip codes that were distressed at the turn of the century remained so.

The geography of well-being has shifted as cities and the West gain ground.

- The total population of prosperous urban zip codes doubled from 2000 to 2018, and the country's urban geography expanded, especially in the West. These advances were uneven, however, as the number of prosperous zip codes flatlined or declined across 61 of the country's 100 largest cities.

- The share of the country's urban population residing in distressed zip codes fell from 34.3 to 21.7% over the period—still slightly edging out the other quintiles. Meanwhile, the share of rural Americans living in distressed zip codes rose to 23.6%.

- In the West, 53.4% of the population resides in a prosperous or comfortable zip code, a greater share than in any other region. It displaced the Midwest, which led in American economic well-being in 2000 but now trails even the Northeast.

Figure 10.2 Urban-Rural Population Share by 2020 DCI Quintile

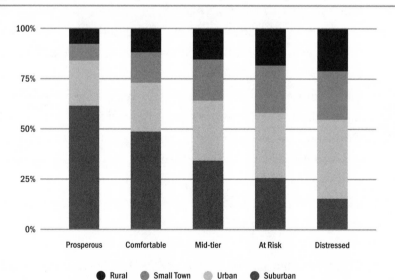

Source: "Distressed Communities: Key Findings." *Economic Innovation Group.* Accessed December 29, 2022. https://eig.org/distressed-communities/key-findings/.

Despite significant progress, Americans' exposure to community prosperity and distress remains profoundly divided along racial lines.

- The minority share of the population in prosperous zip codes jumped from 16.3 to 26.9% between 2000 and 2018 and declined slightly in the distressed quintile to 56.4%, still leaving communities of color significantly overrepresented at the bottom.
- The share of the country's black population living in distressed zip codes declined from 45.6% in 2000 to 35.3% in 2018. But in the Midwest, fully half of the black population still lives in distressed communities.
- Racial inequality is observed at every level of community well-being, but especially in distressed areas, where the median household income (MHI) for the typical black household was only 66% that of the typical white household. Across every quintile, the typical black MHI fell as a share of white MHI between 2000 and 2018.
- An overwhelming 70% of majority-black zip codes are distressed, compared to 20% of zip codes nationally and 16% of majority-white zip codes. Only 19 majority-black zip codes rank as prosperous on the DCI.

Other organizations such as IGI Global[11] find that marginalized communities around the world are those that experience the following characteristics:

- Populations with limited access to digital technology.
- Groups of people that socially and economically experience discrimination and exclusion from activities for different reasons, such as age, physical or mental disabilities, economic status, access to education, or living in isolated places or depressed areas.

Figure 10.3 Race and Ethnicity Composition of the 2020 Quintiles

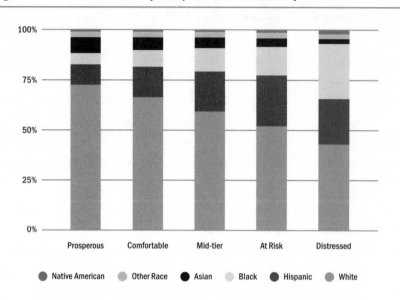

Source: "Distressed Communities: Key Findings." *Economic Innovation Group.* Accessed December 29, 2022. https://eig.org/distressed-communities/key-findings/.

- In general terms, marginalized communities are societies and communities confined to the lower or peripheral edge of society because of unequal power relationships. Such a group is denied involvement in mainstream economic, political, educational, cultural, and social activities due to their living conditions, lifestyles, or exclusion.

Such data demonstrates that even before the pandemic, our divide was still apparent and indicative of our history of marginalization. In that sense, the pandemic should be a wake-up call because the magnitude of our current divides leaves our economy and society more vulnerable in the face of outside shocks.

In her paper, "Demarginalizing the Intersection of Race and Sex," Kimberlé Crenshaw of the University of Chicago Legal Forum (1989) states the follow-

ing conclusion to her article.¹² Such informed and collective unity is perhaps just the answer we need:

> It is somewhat ironic that those concerned with alleviating the ills of racism and sexism should adopt such a top-down approach to discrimination. If their efforts instead began with addressing the needs and problems of those who are most disadvantaged and with restructuring and remaking the world where necessary, then others who are singularly disadvantaged would also benefit. In addition, it seems that placing those who currently are marginalized in the center is the most effective way to resist efforts to compartmentalize experiences and undermine potential collective action.
>
> It is not necessary to believe that a political consensus to focus on the lives of the most disadvantaged will happen tomorrow in order to recenter discrimination discourse at the intersection. It is enough, for now, that such an effort would encourage us to look beneath the prevailing conceptions of discrimination and to challenge the complacency that accompanies belief in the effectiveness of this framework. By so doing, we may develop language which is critical of the dominant view, and which provides some basis for unifying activity. The goal of this activity should be to facilitate the inclusion of marginalized groups for whom it can be said: "When they enter, we all enter."

The Outcomes of Marginalization

To the extent we continue to tolerate the marginalization of distressed and at-risk communities, the economic fabric of our nation will deteriorate. Race is proven to be at the center of marginalization. As we avoid our distressed populations, and don't centralize solutions for implementing growth-focused social and economic policies in black communities, we continue to compromise the realization of the American values of freedom and prosperity for all. We will settle for mediocrity, and it is such settling that will lead to the demise of the American experiment.

Decades of left-driven policies have upended diverse once-vibrant neighborhoods that are now facing significant challenges in urban and rural zip codes. Growth in crime, compromised public safety, low graduation rates, high infant mortality rates, stagnated poverty-level per capita household incomes, increased alcohol, tobacco, and drug-related arrests—as well as overdoses and deaths—are just part of an exhaustive list (shown in Figure 10.4) of possible adverse measures feeding into the cause-and-effect relationship of marginalization in America.[13] These outcomes are simply strangling the sense of hope for opportunity in marginalized distressed, at-risk neighborhoods.

Figure 10.4 Adverse Measures Contributing to Marginalization in America

Infant mortality	Crime rate	Single-parent households	Economic impact of new developments
Preterm births	ER visits for violence, accidents, poisonings	Middle class households	Housing demand rate by type
Voluntary pre-K enrollment	Reported child abuse and neglect cases	Per capita income	Percentage of housing units occupied
Kindergarten readiness	Number of arrest of minors	Rent-burdened households	Percentage of commercial sq ft occupied
Free/reduced lunch	Alchohol, tobacco, drug arrests, overdoses, deaths	Population	Number of new business startups
Cost of child care	Convictions of mothers	Median workforce age	Percent completion of priority initiatives
High school graduation rate	Workforce participation of mothers	Overweight and obesity rate	
College graduates	Labor force participation	Voter turnout	

As our public education system continues to create excuses for a majority of failing schools in more urban school districts, we continue to steer our growing population of minority students away

Figure 10.5 Contributing Factors to Distress in Communities

	Adults without a high school diploma	Poverty rate	Prime-age adults not in work	Housing vacancy rate	Median household income	Change in employment	Change in establishments
Prosperous	5.2%	5.7%	15.4%	4.7%	$90,800	20.8%	11.8%
Comfortable	8.4%	9.0%	18.3%	6.9%	$69,600	10.5%	6.9%
Mid-tier	11.7%	12.7%	21.6%	9.0%	$56,500	8.3%	4.9%
At risk	15.5%	17.3%	26.9%	11.3%	$47,700	4.8%	3.0%
Distressed	20.6%	24.8%	35.3%	15.3%	$37,800	-4.4%	-4.2%

from achieving high school diplomas. This is evidenced by more than 20% of adults in distressed zip codes not having a high school diploma. Over 24% of distressed adults live at or below the poverty level. With over 35% of distressed, prime-age adults not working, we have systematically deactivated a large and growing segment of our population from participating in the active workforce. In 2020 (see Figure 10.5), distressed median incomes were at $37,800, with higher home vacancy rates and lower employment rates than other quintiles.[14] This was occurring even before the full effects of COVID took hold.

Distressed communities have not been prime beneficiaries of workforce training, development, and job growth initiatives. Yet strengthening them could dramatically boost the economic prosperity of local economies and the country at large.

Much of the challenge to activating distressed community members in the workforce can be attributed to workforce development services and educational organizations not going to those communities. Traditional bureaucracies expect residents to find them rather than assembling and collaborating within the neighborhoods to offer and demonstrate real solutions designed to integrate each community's needs with local employment opportunities.

While people within prosperous and comfortable quintiles (see Figure 10.6) know where to seek and find jobs and have the trans-

Figure 10.6 Real Median Household Income by Race and Hispanic Origin: 1967 to 2020 (Households as of March of the following year)

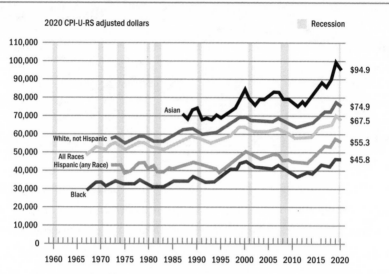

Notes: The data for 2017 and beyond reflect the implementation of an updated processing system. The data for 2013 and beyond reflect the implementation of the redesigned income questions. The data points are placed at the midpoints of the respective years. Median household income data are not available prior to 1967. Information on confidentiality protection, sampling error, nonsampling error, and definitions is available at <https://www2.census.gov/programs-surveys/cps/techdocs/cpsmar21.pdf>.

Source: U.S. Census Bureau, Current Population Survey, 1968 to 2021 Annual Social and Economic Supplements (CPS ASEC).

portation to get to them, distressed communities often do not have the infrastructure and leadership to know about, prepare for, and encourage the same opportunities.

Free Markets and Conservative Principles Can Save America

How do we reintroduce American values and the belief that opportunity is available to majority black communities that have experienced decades of empty promises?

Several factors have gone into the making of marginalized communities and vary widely from community to community: systemic institutionalized racism, the legacy of Jim Crow segregation, income inequality, and educational deficiencies, among others. While the causes may be many, the solutions begin with acknowledging the truth about what got us here and relying upon free market principles to move these communities forward.

The free market is defined by adherence to Jefferson's immortal words "Life, liberty, and the pursuit of happiness" as the basis of American truth and justice.[15]

As we acknowledge the history of marginalization and the injustices therein, we must also assert that truth means objective truth and recognizing reality.

The meaning of justice must be defined in the biblical sense of you reap what you sow. This is a different view from "social justice," which Nobel prize laureate Friedrich Hayek described as "treating different people unequally to make them equal."[16]

Our American values and the conservative principles that have built this country still stand strong, and they work for everyone. So, too, should the expectation of achieving success by earning it and demonstrating the commitment and self-discipline required to live the American dream.

What we should be teaching and reinforcing in marginalized communities is the restoration of fundamental American principles that, for a blip in time, were the exact practices that raised black communities such as Tulsa to prosperity.

First, marriage, followed by family, reinforces responsibility and vocation. The most significant contributor to marginalized communities is single-parent family structures that result in disproportionate incarceration rates, sporadic and long-term unemployment, failing education standards, and economic instability.[17,18]

Black Americans make up 13% of the United States population.[19] Yet the incarceration rate for blacks is a disproportionate 38%.[20] The percentage of white babies born with no fathers in the home is approximately 30%, while the percentage of no fathers in the home of black births is a disproportionate 72%.[21] Nationally, only 11% of black prison inmates are married, compared to 25% for blacks not incarcerated.[22] Approximately 62% of black prisoners do not have a high school diploma.

The data suggests that one of the best ways to improve stability within marginalized neighborhoods is to encourage blacks to graduate from high school, pursue a vocation, marry, and live with their children.

The detrimental lack of quality education in marginalized communities should not be much of a shock and is partly a result of missing family structure. Inner-city urban schools face the challenge of a higher percentage of single parents who have less time to engage with teachers, administrators, and yes, even their children. These realities contribute to creating a problematic learning environment, even for children who come from more stabilized backgrounds.

It only makes sense that someone who graduated from high school has achieved a fundamental educational goal, suggesting a stick-to-it-ness that is crucial to furthering one's academic pursuits or career opportunities. Suffice it to say that a married man has less incentive to take the time to commit crimes or engage in other poor life choices because that individual has a wife and family to consider.

Religion and faith play another vital role in providing moral guidance, often lacking in marginalized zip codes. Although most urban centers, especially black neighborhoods, have no shortage of church facilities and services, too many churches have failed to provide the moral leadership required to inspire economic stability. Black churches that apply faith as the vehicle for hope and preservation of self-worth, family values, and the pursuit of education and vocation will have a direct economic and moral impact in their immediate neighborhoods. The church's expansion as a resource for prosperity can change the fabric of core black culture and activate its inherent resilience to thrive and earn equality in such times when America most seeks redemption.

Economic independence is challenging to achieve if the essential ingredients of intact family structure, educational opportunity, and faith or moral guidance are significantly inferior to that of the more stable zip code areas.

A Seven-Point Plan for Demarginalizing Distressed Communities and Achieving Informed, Collective Unity

Decades of black oppression and migration leading to no improvement in distressed living conditions have led to evident and problematic social and economic measured outcomes signifying the deep sense of defeat branded into the core of American black culture. This pain and anger can evolve to be perhaps the most powerful source of human strength that we have yet to see in modern times. However, this strength will be realized only if we centralize resources to help it evolve.

The practical, elegant, non-autocratic effort of aligning swift investment and action toward redeeming projects is the only way to prove meaning and intent to marginalized communities. In many ways, existing federal, state, and local policies and funding sources can be directed toward evolving marginalized neighborhoods. The roadblocks often lie in the lack of local leadership and skills required to operationalize such policies and funding into distinct capital projects with aligned programming that is relevant and meaningful to each marginalized neighborhood.

Reducing marginalization requires successfully assembling a broad set of federal, state, and local public-private resources to implement neighborhood projects. These must be deeply intentional initiatives that encourage collaborative personal, public, and private partnerships. Such arrangements can transcend political bureaucracies that too often undercut projects and kick the can down the road.

The following plan outlines the critical elements to achieving sustainable and economically responsible initiatives in marginalized communities.[23] As a result, the economic impact can grow by providing relevant opportunities to individual communities within distressed and at-risk neighborhoods—one neighborhood at a time.

1. **Courageous Personal Commitment**

   Anyone, regardless of race, who cares about their community and wants to help overcome the challenges of marginalization compromising local economic growth and development, must be willing to openly express commitment to change. Today, this can be difficult. Stepping forward and seeking to unify diverse groups to work together can cause one to be ridiculed, targeted, judged, and even called a racist.

   Like-minded, thick-skinned partners can leverage their strengths to identify and implement meaningful reforms. Empty promises and lack of follow-through are the roots of demise. Strong leadership skills must include the ability to navigate the complexities of transformative projects.

2. **Engaged Community Leadership**

Neighborhood transformation initiatives will get minimal traction without solid community engagement and the establishment of a respected leadership group. Local black leadership is necessary and should be identified and engaged from the very start. Black pastors, business and community leaders, and residents who are trusted and able to set personal agendas aside are critical to building knowledge and trust within the community.

Expert partners must also be aligned to inform and guide the planning process. Regular communication and a transparent work plan instill the trust leaders need to maintain community trust and continuity of project objectives.

3. **A Target Location for a Neighborhood Opportunity Hub**

There often is a disconnect for our more impoverished neighborhoods between the unmet needs of their residents and the available opportunities to address them. Access to essential services and opportunities is difficult due to limited transportation and childcare options, lack of financial resources, and a general lack of confidence and sometimes trust in engaging with foreign institutions or organizations. Too often, there are very real and personal roadblocks that prevent struggling households from taking advantage of the available opportunities.

Neighborhood Opportunity Hubs are intended to establish a convenient, visible, and inviting front door to a wide range of opportunities (see Figure 10.7). It, first and foremost, should be a comfortable gathering place for residents of all ages. It may serve as a place for neighbors to socialize and recreate and engage in accessing needed services and opportunities. An Opportunity Hub may be integrated into an existing community center, education facility, or easily accessible public space.

A critical element, in keeping with the 15-minute Complete Neighborhood concept, is that an Opportunity Hub must be designed to be a neighborhood-based resource, hub, and new "town center" that is easily accessed. Depending on a specific neighborhood's needs, capital and programming resources can include any of the following common elements designed to serve the community's journey towards prosperity:

- Vibrant town centers with retail and commerce
- Entrepreneurship/business startups
- Education
- Health and wellness
- Parks and recreation
- Childcare
- Transportation
- Training
- Counseling
- Job placement
- Food access
- Mental health services
- Banking and financial services
- Organized sports
- Community theater
- Youth programs
- Adult programs
- Speakers, forums, and lectures
- Transitional housing
- Homeownership
- Social and human rights organizations

- Emergency shelter
- Homeless services
- English as a second language training
- Technology training

4. **A Focused Work Plan for a Needed Initiative**
   Great neighborhood design comes down to distilling the character and personality of a neighborhood and translating it authentically through its continued construction of architecture, street design, housing configurations, recreation, commerce, and community programming.

   The neighborhood needs ongoing community leadership to guide the integration of revenue-generating business startups, services, events, programs, and activities that connect community members to invest in themselves and feel pride and the desire to live, work, and play where they share a bond as neighbors.

5. **Informed Private-Public Collaboration and Accountability**
   It's important to stress that most successful projects in marginalized neighborhoods are led by private-sector leadership members working together to orchestrate a responsible investment stack and a revenue stream that assures long-term success. It is critical that the entity generates revenue from its collaborative businesses, services, and programs for long-term sustainability that isn't reliant on ongoing fundraising and government handouts.

6. **Diversified Funding Stack**
   Funding a neighborhood transformation can be enhanced by tapping into various sources of local, state, federal, public, private, and institutional funding. The collaboration of these

254 ☙ THE STATE OF BLACK PROGRESS

funding sources can create strength and assurance of project success. Achieving a more complex funding stack isn't easy, and must strategically align agendas, requirements, and fund-matching opportunities. Due to COVID, millions of dollars are still available for projects at local, state, federal, and private levels for urban, distressed, and low-income neighborhoods. Working carefully and intentionally to match these funds with the corporations needing a qualified workforce and small businesses needing dedicated employees can foster an economic pull that sustains for years.

7. **Measure Neighborhood Success**
   Each community project will have different measurements for success and may include those listed earlier in this essay. While city leadership may measure economic impact with a citywide dashboard, neighborhoods should post a scorecard to track the impact measures outlined in their work plan objectives. Without reporting measured outcomes, it is impossible to prove success, build trust, gain more investments, or adapt to modify actions and achieve a more significant impact.

Redefining Economic Impact

Marginalized communities often have a broad list of needs that run deep with various cause-and-effect relationships. As demonstrated, black crime often results from deteriorated family structure caused by less marriage and low relevant engagement by churches in their communities.

As the priority needs and desired impacts for each community shape the vision for change, leaders must go beyond the traditional ways to measure economic impacts, such as household income, employment, housing, and demographic changes.

Figure 10.7 Neighborhood Opportunity Hub Services

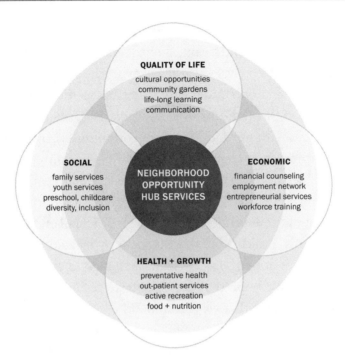

Leadership teams must evolve and expand to include specific lifestyle, psychographic, and quality of place measures. Primary areas for impact typically include quality of life, economic, health, growth, and social effects. These clarify what demarginalization should look like when people are living their lives differently and achieving prosperity. A community can only identify what it measures. With a scorecard showing a more expanded view of outcomes for the future, leadership can facilitate a movement toward and have a greater impact on community retention and prosperity.

Conclusion

As much as our history of oppressing blacks has kept too many from achieving the American Dream, that adversity has forged stronger human bonds and a revival towards achieving the prosperity intended by our forefathers. Our American values of freedom and equality can be realized through instilling conservative principles into our daily practices with our families, faith communities, and the work that we commit to in transforming our local communities.

We can see this work being tried in distressed neighborhoods such as the transformation to a Neighborhood Opportunity Hub from the long-abandoned John Marshall High School on the east side of Indianapolis. Projects in Gary, Kenosha, Milwaukee, Cleveland, and other cities are striving to achieve change in their distressed communities. We hope they can integrate some of the essential elements for success that we recommend.

Knowing and understanding the truth of our history can bring justice by achieving collective unity and putting marginalized neighborhoods at the forefront of economic growth initiatives. While the work is not easy and requires much courage from principled community leaders, such work can responsibly bridge grassroots needs to federal, state, and local public-private resources.

Suppose such work can unify the full potential, cultural strength, and desire for community in marginalized zip codes. In that case, we will find a new workforce, establish stronger families, reduce crime, achieve quality education, and increase household incomes to achieve greater prosperity for all.

"When they enter, we all enter."[24]

11

SOCIAL SECURITY ROBS BLACK AMERICANS OF THEIR LIFETIME SAVINGS—THERE'S A BETTER WAY

Every Black Worker Could Retire with $1 Million or More of Retirement Income

Stephen Moore

Few federal programs have had a more a deleterious effect on the economic advancement and wealth accumulation opportunities of minorities in America than Social Security.

The 12% tax on the first dollar earned in worker paychecks to pay for Social Security has robbed all young Americans—especially black Americans—of the chance to build up real wealth over their working years. A study published in 2020 found that if black workers who retired in 2020 (with 40 hours worked per week at an average wage) had been allowed to take 10% of their paychecks and invest them in an index fund of stocks over the prior 40 years, they would have accumulated nearly $1 million of wealth and up to $2 million with higher earnings.[1] They could have then paid themselves twice as large a monthly benefit as Social Security and left an inheritance of up to one-quarter million dollars or more from this fund to their children.

There is no turning back the clock to make up for the terrible mistake that we didn't allow this option for today's retirees. But there is not a moment to lose in allowing Americans under the age of 40 to shift to a new voluntary retirement program.

Every year we wait to give workers the option of choosing an individual 401(k) type of account, the potential for building up ownership and wealth is further diminished.

One major cause of income inequality in America is the lack of real wealth held by the bottom 50% of Americans.[2] This group of Americans already has tight family budgets, and so the money to put in real savings is constrained. To alleviate this problem and to solve the long-term unfunded liabilities of Social Security, Congress should amend the Federal Insurance Contributions Act (FICA) tax to give every worker the option to shift up to 10% of his or her paycheck away from Social Security and deposit that money into a new, personal "Own America Account."

You own it. You keep it. The government can't take it away from you. This may sound too good to be true. But it isn't.

Here is how the program would work. Each worker's individually owned account would be invested in an index fund of roughly two-thirds stocks and one-third bonds, and would mature at the federal retirement age of 67. But if you wanted to keep working to 68, or 70, or even 75, you would continue to accumulate real wealth through the almost magical power of compounding the returns on your investment dollars.

Under this program, every working American—from the minimum-wage waiter to the truck driver to the store manager—would become a genuine owner, building real wealth for himself and his family with each paycheck. Investment in the private market would deliver far better retirement savings than the current government-mandated structure. We estimate that over the past 40 years, Social Security's real annual return for a typical middle-class worker has been about 1% a year.[3]

Given the program's growing deficits, returns may be even lower or even negative for today's young workers. In contrast, stocks returned more than 6% annually in the same 40-year period—as they have over the last 100 years. Over a career of saving, the difference amounts to a literal lifetime's worth of additional income.

This study (relying on an analysis from the nonpartisan Tax Foundation) finds that the average American who retired in 2016 after 40 to 45 years of work could have saved more than $1 million in balanced index accounts.[4]

To be sure, the stock market is risky and highly volatile in the short term, as tens of millions of Americans discovered painfully during the Great Recession and during the COVID-19 pandemic. But over periods of 40 or 50 years the market offers remarkably stable and robust real returns of 6% or more—and that's been true since the New York Stock Exchange first opened its doors.

With Own America Accounts, even stock and bond returns half as large as the historical average would still leave workers with bigger retirement incomes. This means the government could guarantee that payments wouldn't fall below the minimum Social Security benefit.

Own America Accounts would make black Americans wealthier— not through a government giveaway, but by simply allowing them to invest money taken from their own paychecks and collect the high returns brought by true ownership. These personal accounts are also the best possible means to address inequality, as working people all across America would together be accumulating trillions in their personal accounts. These personal accounts would consequently provide working people a substantial, direct, personal ownership stake in America's business and industry. Freeing working people to choose personal savings, investment, and insurance accounts for their Social Security benefits would eliminate all future deficits in Social Security, without cutting benefits or raising taxes, as documented by the Chief Actuary of Social Security.

How Social Security Rips Off Minorities

Social Security is a bad deal for all Americans, but it is especially a rip-off for most minorities.[5]

One reason Social Security is unfair to black Americans is variations in life expectancy based on race. For example: the life expectancy of black Americans was 70.8 in 2021. The life expectancy of white Americans was 76.4 years.[6] Some of this life expectancy difference is due to more blacks dying at younger ages than whites.

Let us say the average worker retires at age 65. But even at the age of 65, blacks live several fewer years than whites at that age. This means that blacks get substantially less lifetime benefits from Social Security than whites (or Asians) do.

Let's say that a black woman, who is a mother of three children, dies at the age of 45. That woman has worked perhaps 20 to 25 years and paid Social Security taxes on nearly every dollar earned. But her family/children get almost no benefits (except for small survivor benefits) when she dies even though she paid tens of thousands of dollars in taxes into the system. With an Own America Account her children would immediately get the money she paid in plus the stock market return that could have easily doubled her money.

Another reason Social Security is unfair to black Americans is that blacks tend to start working full-time at an earlier age than whites. For example, blacks are more likely to join the workforce straight out of high school at age 19, whereas whites and Asians are more likely to go to college and even graduate school. Yes, whites and Asians will generally have higher lifetime earnings, but those four to five years of earnings early in life and invested in the market at such a young age mean that there is a bigger compounding effect over the 40-to-45-year period of working. At retirement age, the value of the account for the worker who started working at a younger age will be substantial because of the power of compound interest year after year after year.

Social Security is not *intentionally* discriminatory. But its effect is to deprive black and Hispanic workers of a fair return on their Social Security taxes, which—by the way—is the number one tax that minorities pay.

A Million-Dollar Legacy for One's Children

Most black Americans would be able to leave a substantial inheritance to their children when they die under the Own America Accounts. This is because the individual *owns* the account and the nest egg of savings can be left to one's children. Not so with Social Security. Those who die at an earlier age do not get to transfer unused benefits to their children. This could mean benefits to many future generations of black, Hispanic, and low-income whites who would not otherwise be able to leave money to their children under conventional Social Security.

How the Own America Accounts Would Work

Personal account freedom of choice would empower all workers and their families to earn much higher benefits, often double or more what Social Security even promises, let alone what it can pay, through a lifetime of personal account savings and investment.[7] Over a generation, this shift from public financing of Social Security benefits to private financing of higher retirement benefits through free-market savings and investment would involve the greatest reduction of government spending in world history!

Once the personal accounts are phased in over a generation to assume responsibility for paying future benefits, the payroll tax, which is the highest tax most working people pay, can and should be eliminated altogether. That would amount to the greatest tax cut in world history! The personal accounts are actually a means of fundamentally transforming Social Security from a tax-and-redistribution, pay-as-you-go system to a fully funded, savings and investment system.

It is vitally important for readers to understand that the Social Security "Trust Fund" does not have the money to pay the benefits that have been promised.[8] There will be trillions of dollars of deficits in the system because Congress has already spent those dollars on other programs.[9] This means that if we stay with conventional Social Security in the future, the benefits will have to be cut or the taxes will have to be raised. Or both. This makes a bad deal even worse for young people.

The current Social Security program does not save the funds workers and their employers are paying in today to finance their future benefits. Social Security uses the tax payments coming in today to immediately finance the benefits for today's retirees. Social Security expects the future tax payments of future workers to finance the future benefits for today's workers. Almost 90% of the money coming in is paid out within the year to beneficiaries. Unfortunately, those annual surpluses are not saved and invested, because that's not what government does. The federal government borrows the money for other government programs, from foreign aid to bridges to nowhere. In return, the Social Security trust funds receive federal IOUs. These IOUs are all that is held by the so-called Social Security trust funds, now totaling more than $4 trillion.

As a result, Social Security is not a savings and investment system. It is a tax and redistribution system, where money is taken from one group of people through taxes and immediately redistributed to other people in benefits and other government spending. Blacks, as discussed above, pay a lot in and don't get a fair deal on the way out.

How Bad a Deal Is Social Security?

Let us say that a black couple makes an above-average-income and will continue to do so for the next 30 years. These workers would actually receive a negative real return from Social Security even assuming all promised benefits are somehow paid out in the future. A negative real return is like depositing your money in the bank, and instead of the bank paying you interest, you pay the bank interest on your deposit. This is Social Security for a lot of people today. There are workers who along with their employers today are paying more than $10,000 a year, each and every year, into Social Security.

The nonpartisan Tax Foundation conducted the calculations[10] comparing the benefits that could be paid through personal savings, investment, and insurance accounts with the benefits promised by Social Security. The results were calculated for different hypothetical family combinations, with varying family compositions (single or married, with or without children, one-earner- or two-earner-couples), work histories (low wage starting work after high school, middle class starting work after college, higher wage starting work after graduate or professional school), earnings histories (25%, 45%, 100%, 160%, 300% of median income, with differing combinations among two-earner couples), investment strategies (e.g., 60% stocks and 40% bonds, 100% stock index).

What the Tax Foundation found was that virtually every demographic and income group does considerably better from a financial point of view with the personal account.[11]

The study also found that the government could guarantee that every worker would get the minimum amount Social Security offers even if their accounts didn't have enough money—which would be highly unlikely. In other words, families could only benefit from this program. They couldn't lose money.

Is the Stock Market Too Risky? No, And Here's Why

Senator Cory Booker (D-NJ), who is black, was exactly right when he said: "Paychecks help you get by. But wealth equity, having resources—creates generational wealth."[12] Nothing creates wealth like ownership, and the best way to expand ownership is to broaden participation in the stock and bond markets.

Congress should facilitate such ownership by amending FICA to give every worker the option to shift up to 10% of his paycheck away from Social Security and into a new, personal "Own America Account."

A recent study commissioned by the Committee to Unleash Prosperity found that the average American who retired in 2016 after 40 to 45 years of work could have saved more than $1 million in balanced index accounts, and many middle-class families could have accumulated closer to $2 million.[14]

Some say, the stock market is too risky. It is true that the stock market is risky and highly volatile in the short term, as tens of millions of Americans discovered painfully during the Great Recession. But, as previously noted, over periods of 40 or 50 years the market offers remarkably stable and robust real returns of 6% or more. With Own America Accounts, even stock and bond returns half as large as the historical average would leave workers with bigger retirement incomes. This means the government could guarantee that payments wouldn't fall below the minimum Social Security benefit.

For those who are completely risk averse, the government could guarantee that no worker would do worse than the promised Social Security benefit. The government would still collect a 2% payroll tax to protect anyone who falls through the cracks.

Anyone who cares about the national debt should also love this plan. Over several decades it would reduce the national debt significantly. Every dollar paid to a retiree from his Own America

Account would be matched by a dollar of reduced Social Security liabilities in the future. Over decades, tens of trillions of dollars of liabilities could be eliminated. So it's a win-win for workers and government.[15]

Own America Accounts would make Americans wealthier— not through a government giveaway, but by simply allowing them to invest money taken from their own paychecks and collect the high returns brought by true ownership. The accounts would build significant wealth over a lifetime for American workers, regardless of their income. Minorities would do best, because under the current system, they get the worst deal of all. And for the first time in American history, every black American would be an owner/investor in American companies.

12

SOCIAL SECURITY REFORM AND MARKET ALTERNATIVES

Raheem Williams

Introduction

In 1935, President Franklin Roosevelt signed the Social Security Act to create a national public retirement program, which primarily exists to provide a basic level of retirement funding for workers. The program achieves this via a pay-as-you-go structure, transferring funds from the earnings of current workers to fund current retirees. The original bill included unemployment insurance, old-age assistance, aid to dependent children, and grants to the states to provide various forms of medical care. Over the decades the programs have been expanded. In 1956, the Disability Insurance program was established for aged and disabled Social Security recipients, and in 1965, Medicare was added.[1] All the aforementioned expansions were primarily financed by increasing payroll taxes. Social Security taxes are also referenced collectively as the Old Age, Survivors, and Disability Insurance (OASDI) tax, although these are technically two distinct taxes for two distinct funds.

Since its inception, Social Security has been hailed by many proponents as a phenomenal anti-poverty weapon. Proponents of the program point out that minority communities have come to depend on Social Security as a vital source of retirement income.[2] Although these arguments have merit, they must be placed in the proper context when debating potential reforms. When the system was first devised, the retirement planning industry was in its infancy and most Americans did not have the knowledge or tools to plan out their golden years. In this context, Social Security was a powerful anti-poverty tool by simply being better than nothing for millions of poor Americans. However, a lot has changed since 1935.

Understanding the Problem

Today the Social Security program has become problematic for a host of reasons. Social Security operates two distinct funds: the Old-Age and Survivors Insurance (OASI) Trust Fund pays retirement and survivors benefits, and the Disability Insurance (DI) Trust Fund pays disability benefits. The two funds will be referred to collectively as the OASDI program. Over the lifetime of the program, Social Security has collected $25.2 trillion and paid out $22.3 trillion, leaving the combined trust funds asset reserves of $2.9 trillion. In 2021, the OASI trust fund took in over $942 billion but dispersed over $1 trillion in payments.[3] The DI fund has similar struggles as its asset reserves peaked in 2008 near $215 billion but subsequently have since plummeted to $99 billion in 2021.[4]

The OASDI program's cash-flow deficit was $126 billion in 2021 and is projected to be $452 billion in 2034 (in current dollars). This will leave Social Security unable to pay full scheduled benefits by 2035. This could result in more than a 20% reduction in benefits for recipients, a potentially devastating blow to the retirement security of millions.[5]

The shortfall facing Social Security arises from the structuring method used to finance the program. The pay-as-you-go method inherently assumes there will be more people working at a given time than retirees. However, the original drafters didn't foresee

America's demographic changes as birth rates declined after the baby boomer generation, causing slower growth in the pool of eligible workers.

For example, in 1940, there were 159.4 workers for every retiree receiving benefits; by 2020, this number had dropped to 2.6.[6] This long slide has exposed a critical flaw in the design of the system. Social Security is not designed to save money on behalf of retirees. Structurally, the program takes on the form of a government-mandated Ponzi scheme as it is dependent on new workers paying for current retirees instead of wealth accumulation from investing.

Similarly, longer life expectancies are great for spending more time with the people we love but challenging for the deficient financing scheme employed by the Social Security program.[7] Social Security benefits are paid out until the death of the beneficiary and eligible survivors. This feature of the program will force Congress to make difficult decisions to keep the program functioning as the number of retirees grows.[8]

Another issue with Social Security is the opportunity cost. In economics, opportunity cost forces us to consider the next best use of resources. Any honest evaluation of Social Security retirement benefits would have to consider the potential benefits of alternatives. For example. If investment "A" yields a 3% return and investment "B" yields a 6% return, going with option "A" will cost you 3% in gains you otherwise would have realized. This is admittedly an oversimplification of investing to illustrate the concept of opportunity cost. When making decisions on resource allocation, one must also consider risk.

Social Security offers what many consider to be a safe and guaranteed payout but at substantially lower returns. Yet, in the past the United States Supreme Court has refused to guarantee benefit payouts.[9] Furthermore, it's no secret that private retirement accounts often create more wealth in retirement.[10] This calls into question the wisdom of forcing American workers to pay into a low-yielding retirement program when they could potentially build more wealth faster for themselves and their families by utilizing alternatives. The payroll taxes used to fund Social Security have been consistently rising to offset the increasing cost of the declining worker-to-retiree ratio. In 1937, payroll taxes were just 1% of pre-tax income. Today, this has ballooned to 12.4% (not including the Medicare tax); this represents a 1,140% increase, which will likely go higher if nothing is done to fix the inherent structural issues within the program.[11] Social Security siphons funds that could be going towards higher-yielding private investment accounts.

Currently, Social Security benefits are paid out using the average indexed monthly earnings (AIME). To calculate benefits, we take the average annual income over the last 35 years of a worker's life, adjust it to inflation, and divide it by 420 (the number of months in 35 years) to get the AIME. Intuitively, higher-income earners will have higher AIME. This makes sense because those earners pay more into the system. However, Social Security employs inflation-adjusted Benefit Formula Bend Points, to make the payouts more progressive. For example, using 2023 bend points, this is accomplished by allowing workers to keep 90% of the first $1,115 of the AIME, 32% of his or her average indexed monthly earnings over $1,115, and 15% of his or her average indexed monthly earnings over $6,721. Although bend points help low-earning retirees keep more of their AIME, the system pays more to those who make more.[12]

This system is particularly problematic for black Americans, who tend to have lower incomes, lower life expectancy, higher rates of incarceration, and higher rates of unemployment when compared to white Americans. A study on Social Security utilization for black Americans confirmed that black Americans are less likely than whites to be OASDI beneficiaries, and when they are

OASDI beneficiaries, they generally have lower benefit payouts as a function of the aforementioned factors.[13] Admittedly, some of these problems are outside the scope of the Social Security program, but as we dive deeper into the design of the program, it becomes increasingly clear that the program creates structural limitations to building wealth.

Social Security has arguably done nothing to reduce racial wealth inequities by forcing the limited funds that people of color have into a subpar retirement program. The evidence of this can be seen in the persistent and hard-to-close black–white wealth gap.

According to the Federal Reserve, the average black and Latino household earns about 50% less than the average white household. Black and Latino households have about 15 to 20% of the average wealth found in white households. If black and Latino households had similar wealth distribution to that of white families, black households would hold over five times the amount of wealth they currently do, and Hispanic households would hold nearly four times as much.[14]

Black people are far less likely to have retirement savings and pension benefits than their white peers, making them particularly dependent on Social Security for retirement income. According to the National Academy of Social Insurance, 47% of white people over the age of 65 received income outside of Social Security compared to 30% of black people in the same age group.[15]

Researchers at the National Bureau of Economic Research found that the black–white wealth gap saw rapid declines after slavery, slowing dramatically in the 1950s and reversing in the 1990s. The same researchers found that black households hold 67% of their wealth in non-financial assets compared to just 41% for white households.[16]

It's fair to say black Americans, who are disproportionately poor, pay high opportunity costs by being required to pay into Social Security with funds that could fetch higher returns on the market.

Proposed Solutions

Now that we've established the scope of the problem, we can begin to explore solutions. The most intuitive solution for those who favor the program's current structure is to advocate for tax hikes. This could be as simple as raising the OASDI payroll tax paid by both employees and employers. Understandably, this would immediately increase the funds flowing into the program. Similarly, removing the cap on top incomes or increasing the retirement age could increase revenues and potentially add decades of solvency.

However, higher payroll taxes are problematic. Increasing these taxes would be highly regressive and disproportionately harm low-income workers. Although payroll taxes are presented as being paid in equal shares by the employee and employer, the real world of tax incidence is far more complicated than basic accounting.

Research shows that employees incur the cost of the employers' portion through lower wages. This could be particularly detrimental for low-income workers who struggle to make ends meet. Dorian Carloni of the Congressional Budget Office found that 62% of the tax burden from an increase in the OASDI tax rate would be shifted to employees.[17] The prospect of asking workers, particularly poor workers who are disproportionately people of color, to sacrifice more of their income to prop up current retirees at the expense of their current and future consumption needs such as housing, food, and child-rearing is ethically troublesome and raises significant equity concerns.

Another often-discussed intervention is removing the income cap on payroll taxes. In 2022, payroll taxes were only paid on the first $147,000 of income.[18] Removing this limitation would spread the cost to high-income earners and it could extend the current shortfall projections.

However, removing the income cap would only delay cuts, not prevent them. Furthermore, such an action would be a massive tax hike that would have ripple effects throughout the economy by distorting labor markets and reducing consumption.[19] Likewise, this could prove less than optimal if demographic and economic growth assumptions fall short of expectations. Additionally, there is a fairness question to taking this approach.

Contrary to popular belief, high-income earners already pay a disproportionate share of federal taxes, and removing the payroll tax contribution cap without raising the benefits cap would effectively ensure that high-income earners don't get what they paid into the system. This would effectively turn Social Security into more of a welfare program without fixing any structural issues or opportunity costs associated with forgoing more attractive investment vehicles.

Another idea is to force all workers to pay into Social Security. Throughout America, many state and local government employees do not pay Social Security payroll taxes. Instead, these workers contribute to public sector pensions and defined contribution plans. Forcing these workers into our Social Security system is fraught with issues. Many of these workers prefer the retirement plans they have in place, and forcing them to change could spark a massive backlash from public unions.

Similarly, there is more than $1.3 trillion in public pension debt in the United States that would have to be accounted for in such a plan.[20] Transferring those liabilities to the federal government would force Americans everywhere to pay for poor planning made by officials in states and cities in which they never lived or worked.

Another proposed solution would be to raise the retirement age for full benefits. Although this could also help delay the projected shortfall, it presents an entirely new set of issues. Poor people, who are disproportionately black, have lower life expectancies.[21] Raising the retirement age would rob the working poor of financial resources during a crucial time in their golden years. This would hurt the very people the program was devised to help—poor retirees.

Another means to partially address the Social Security shortfall is to invest the Social Security Trust Funds more aggressively. When Social Security was first devised and implemented, it was during the backdrop of the Great Depression with events like the 1929 stock market crash being very well remembered during the initial phases of designing the system. This led to a very conservative investment strategy for the fund.

Today, the fund is invested 100% in U.S. Treasury bonds. In finance, these investments are considered to be risk-free because the U.S. government underwrites the bonds being issued in U.S. dollars, a currency the federal government also controls. This means the only way to default on the bonds would be a lack of political will to pay them.

However, this, too, comes at an immense opportunity cost and slight risk. The risk-free strategy almost guarantees sub-optimal returns. The annual effective interest rate (the average rate of return on all investments over one year) for the OASI and DI Trust Funds, combined, was 2.45% in 2021. Conversely, the S&P 500 returned 26.89% in 2021 and has averaged over 10.22% annual returns since its inception in 1928.[22] OASDI Trust Fund returns peaked at 11.6% in 1984 and have been slowly declining ever since.[23] Investing the payroll taxes in higher-yield securities could open the door to higher returns and bolster the Social Security trust funds, delaying future shortfalls and tax hikes.

Implementing a private retirement account system that functions similarly to the current Social Security system should be an attractive option for all reformers. A private account system could provide a stable income for retirees via financial instruments while lowering the risk of creating new public debt and massive benefit shortfalls.

A private account system would reduce long-term tax risk for beneficiaries. According to an analysis by the Tax Foundation, only single-income households make less than 25% of the average wage of the benefit from the current structure when compared to a 60-stock 40-bond profile. However, this advantage disappears when aggressively investing in stocks.[24]

One of the most common misconceptions about switching from pay-as-you-go Social Security to a market-invested retirement account is the erroneous idea that such an account would be highly vulnerable to market downturns and other investment risks. Proponents of the current structure of Social Security often point to market declines as a reason to be skeptical of market-based individual retirement accounts. The argument many make is that once adjusting for risk, there's not much to gain from private market-based accounts. Although this concern has some merit, it isn't an issue without a solution.

First, it's important to note that no rule would require anyone to withdraw their investments during a downturn. In general, personal finance practitioners advise against selling during a downturn because investors who do so generally miss out on the wealth accumulation of the market rebound. Any alternative design for Social Security would have to account for these risks.

Similar to waiting to receive full Social Security benefits, a market alternative could be designed with safeguards that would prevent people from panic selling in a decline, investing in unregulated securities, or taking on too much risk.

Over the past few decades, the retirement industry has learned and adapted from the shortcomings of poorly designed private retirement plans. The adoption of the modern defined contribution plan was an accidental outcome of the Revenue Act of 1978, which created a section of the Internal Revenue Code—401(k)—that allowed employees to avoid being taxed on deferred compensation.

Benefits consultant Ted Benna saw an opportunity to create a new retirement benefits plan and birthed the first 401(k)–style plans—also known as defined contribution plans—in 1980.[25] This ushered in a new era of retirement planning. At first, these were simply taxed-deferred savings accounts often too inadequate to serve as primary retirement savings vehicles. These plans have since evolved into formidable investment vehicles.

The most prominent of these changes is target-date funds that address the issue of market risk. These funds are designed to optimize the investor's returns by a specific date aligned with the worker's retirement goal or target age.[26] A targeted date fund builds on gains made in the early years of a worker's life by focusing on riskier growth stocks, then slowly pivoting to low-risk investments to retain those gains as the investor ages. This ensures that those near or at retirement are not exposed to stock market volatility during a downturn.

Similarly, private investment accounts could be annuitized to ensure that gains are locked in to provide structured lifetime payments to the beneficiary. In most cases, this will beat the current investment method employed by the Social Security trust of 100% risk-free, low-yield Treasury securities.

Although pivoting from Social Security's current pay-as-you-go model of individual retirement accounts would look very similar to private retirement accounts, the governance and rules of such may differ.

In short, Social Security is a subpar program that doesn't outperform its market alternatives. There's a real opportunity cost to taking money from poor people and investing it poorly. Tax hikes and benefit reductions can extend the financial solvency of the program. However, these reforms do not attempt to address the structural issue inherent in the design of the Social Security program, the pay-as-you-go funding method, and the lackluster expected returns.

Pay-as-you-go ensures that the program will always be subject to the very same issues it has today, meaning that the history of the program consuming more and more of our income is likely to continue. Similarly, as elites amass massive amounts of wealth by employing private sector market-based retirement planning, the working poor fall further and further behind, and our wealth inequality statistics grow.

Social Security is a primary culprit. We take money from the poor and invest it in low-yield assets while the upper class and rich enjoy a plethora of investment options. The opportunity cost of Social Security relative to motivating investment accounts is immense.

Critics of the pay-as-you-go model for funding Social Security have proposed bold structural reform to the program, such as shifting to an entirely new retirement model. This would have far-reaching ramifications for our national retirement system. To better understand how such a pivot could be managed, we can look abroad at places that have either made the switch or utilized a completely different funding method.

Case Studies

The Government Pension Fund of Norway (GPFN), which should not be confused with the country's larger oil fund, is an example of a hybrid-funded national pension system.[27] Back in 1966, Norway created a pay-as-you-go model called the National Insurance Scheme (NIS). This system operates similarly to Social Security by taxing the earnings of current workers to pay for retirees.

Norway did not simply buy low-yielding securities like U.S. Treasury bonds. In 1967, they established GPFN and used the surpluses from the NIS payroll taxes to actively invest in equity markets. The nation launched the Government Pension Fund Global (GPFG) in 1990 to turn oil wealth into lasting financial wealth. Like

GPFN, the Global Fund invests in equities, but unlike GPFN, these investments are made exclusively outside of Norway. Today, both these funds are worth a combined $1.2 trillion or about $244,000 per citizen. In contrast, U.S. Social Security trust funds are worth less than $9,000 per citizen.[28]

Trying to replicate Norway's approach in the U.S. would be difficult. The size of our Social Security trust fund could make whoever manages it an economic kingmaker. This could exacerbate the problem of private firms lobbying the government for preferential treatment and dramatically expand government power over private markets.

All these factors can become problematic distortions in our market system. Furthermore, the United States is unlikely to nationalize its oil companies, given the current emphasis on green energy and the longstanding traditions of economic management.

Another oft-cited example of a well-managed national retirement plan can be found in Singapore.

Singapore is a multi-ethnic city-state that can offer American reformers insight when examining market-based alternatives to our Social Security system. In 1955, while under colonial rule, the city-state established the Central Provident Fund (CPF).[29] Singapore mandates the use of individual retirement accounts. Similar to our Social Security system, these accounts are funded by worker and employer contributions and there are restrictions on withdrawals.

Unlike our system in the United States, which is primarily a transfer between current workers and retirees, contributions to the CPF are set aside in individual investment accounts. The CPF Investment Scheme (CPFIS) allows Singaporeans to invest their retirement account savings into a multitude of instruments such as insurance products, unit trusts, fixed deposits, bonds, housing, and equities. All these instruments have strict rules in place to discourage and prevent fraud. Fund managers are vetted, and members are given a list of vetted products that meet strict criteria laid out by regulators. Likewise, the members themselves must meet a certain threshold saved before they can engage in more speculative investments.[30] The CPF design is a stark contrast to the U.S. Social Security system, which makes it nearly impossible to make individual investment decisions.

Advocates for market-based retirement systems frequently point to the success of countries like Singapore in implementing quasi-public funding models. However, the path to individual accounts in the U.S. would require a challenging transition from pay-as-you-go. For guidance on how to accomplish such a transition, the country of Chile offers us some insights.

Chile successfully navigated the transition from unfunded pension liabilities to a quasi-public system. They instituted a two-pillar approach in the 1980s. This two-pillar approach guarantees a minimum standard of benefits to current retirees by continuing some version of the pay-as-you-go system while a fraction of payroll taxes from current workers are channeled to mandated individual retirement accounts.[31]

Chile accomplished their transition by allowing workers already in the system to choose between privately invested funds and the old pay-as-you-go system. Most workers chose to participate in the privately managed system. New hires were automatically enrolled in the newly created private plans.[32]

However, Chile's transition wasn't perfect. Research shows the shift from a centralized public system to decentralized private accounts led to a loss of efficiency in Chile due to increased administrative costs. However, this loss was negated by higher returns.[33] While Chile's system is imperfect, it provides an outline for nations seeking to pivot away from pay-as-you-go. Since 1990, Argentina (1994), Bolivia (1997), Colombia (1993), Costa Rica (1995), Dominican

Republic (2003), El Salvador (1998), Mexico (1997), Panama (2008), Peru (1993), and Uruguay (1996) have adopted similar "Chilean Model" reforms.

In the United States, it is unclear how Chile's approach would affect current payroll taxes and beneficiaries. Public policy is not perfectly transitive. As with all major reform efforts, the devil is in the details. The inconvenient truth is the Social Security trust funds are no longer running large surpluses. With each passing day, it becomes more difficult to shift away from pay-as-you-go without reducing the benefits of current and future retirees or increasing taxes on current workers to cover the cost.

Individual retirement accounts won't automatically fix all our social equity issues. However, unlike Social Security, these accounts would be instantly vested, meaning that workers would not have to meet certain thresholds to become eligible for retirement or survivor benefits. Although withdrawal restrictions would likely exist, workers would own these accounts and would be able to leave the assets to family members upon death, whether at a young or older age.

All the aforementioned reform options have their pros and cons. Furthermore, a combination of multiple reform options can be used to either buy time or fundamentally transform the U.S. Social Security system.[34] Ultimately, what happens will be a product of the political process.

The Politics of Social Security Reform

According to polling from Data for Progress, a left-leaning think tank, 84% of Americans are worried about the ability of Social Security to cover its projected shortfall. The same polling found strong support for increasing benefits. Although it's impossible to parse through the minds of each respondent, it's clear that Americans are worried about Social Security and want more from the system.[35] Similarly, the problems aren't news to most in the policy world.

We've been debating this issue for decades now, and the problem has only gotten worse. So we need to be clear as to why that is.

The politics of entitlement reform is tricky. Rival factions have often mischaracterized the other side's arguments. This makes it very hard for voters to understand what is being proposed and support or oppose the legislation. Social Security reform plans are often attacked in an attempt to scare elderly Americans and win their votes. Elderly voters tend to vote at higher rates and are the primary recipients of retirement benefits, making them a key constituency for any reform efforts. These political attacks make for effective campaign commercials but often obscure the truth and exacerbate the problem. For example, when Senator Rick Scott (R-FL) unveiled a plan to review and reauthorize Social Security that didn't propose any benefit cuts to current recipients, his political opposition mounted a nationwide campaign to claim that his political party wanted to eliminate Social Security.[36] These claims were proven false.[37]

If the political atmosphere continues to favor shallow sound bites over honest discussions on the merits of reform, our national retirement system will continue to suffer. Current and future beneficiaries will be the primary victims of ongoing political obfuscation.

Unfortunately, the short-term benefits of solving an issue that will take more than ten years to manifest create little incentive for politicians to act. If the proposed reforms are unpopular or controversial, they could negatively impact the careers of those proposing and voting for the changes. However, if successful, the positive impacts of such reforms would not be apparent in the short term and not necessarily understood in the long term. In short, it is challenging to generate the political will to solve these problems.

Those who truly believe in helping low-income Americans— including millions of black Americans—overcome poverty and build long-term wealth need to step up and lead on this critical issue. These problems can't be ignored indefinitely, and with each passing day, the consequences of doing nothing become increasingly untenable.

The American people hunger for visionary and bold leaders. It is our job to identify such leaders and help them achieve the critical goals of retirement security and the ability to transfer intergenerational wealth to those who have too often been disadvantaged by our current Social Security system.

Conclusion

Each plausible reform option has different equity considerations for black workers and different cost considerations for our nation. Raising the payroll tax and/or age of retirement would harm poor workers, who are disproportionately black and generally have lower life expectancies.

Transitioning to a different system based on private accounts would likely help poor workers amass wealth more quickly but would cause the Social Security system to incur substantial transition costs, as current retirees will still be dependent on the pay-as-you-go system. However, private accounts would reduce the long-term financial obligations of the Social Security system by more closely mirroring a private sector-defined contribution plan.

The noted racial wealth disparities discussed in previous sections can be addressed by reforming Social Security and providing an option for real ownership and wealth accumulation through personal retirement accounts. This would empower low-income Americans, who are disproportionately people of color, and provide them an alternative to the current subpar pay-as-you-go government transfer system.

Given the cumbersome challenges of reforming the entire Social Security system, we should consider allowing Americans up to age 30, earning up to $30,000 annually, to opt out of paying payroll taxes and instead require that they invest up to 10% of their taxable income in a personally owned retirement account.

This would enable low-income individuals to accumulate wealth throughout their working careers faster. Owned wealth changes personal reality and behavior.[38] Similarly, ownership of one's retirement account means that this wealth can be more easily transferred to heirs. This would undoubtedly help narrow the current racial gap in intergenerational wealth due to the fact that blacks tend to inherit less wealth from their parents.[39]

Countries that have the most economic freedom create the most wealth and grow the fastest. Individual ownership gives every American a chance to share in the gains of a free and growing country.

A reasonable transition could be piloted by allowing young workers with low income a choice between the current Social Security system and a private account. The cost of doing such would be contingent on how many low-income workers exercise such an option.

There are no easy answers, but it's clear the current status quo has not allowed low-income black workers to accumulate the savings necessary for a secure retirement or to provide their children with an equal opportunity for a more prosperous future.

CONTRIBUTORS

W. B. ALLEN, General Editor of *The State of Black of America* (2022), is a resident scholar and former chief operating officer of the Center for Urban Renewal and Education. He is emeritus professor of political philosophy and dean of James Madison College at Michigan State University, and he served as chairman of the US Commission on Civil Rights. Recognized for excellence in liberal education on the 1997 Templeton Honor Roll (individually and institutionally), Allen has published extensively, including *George Washington: A Collection* (Liberty Fund, Inc.), *Rethinking Uncle Tom: The Political Philosophy of H. B. Stowe* (Lexington Books), and *George Washington: America's First Progressive* (Peter Lang, Inc.).

JANICE ROGERS BROWN served on the United States Court of Appeals for the DC Circuit from 2005 through 2017. She previously served as a deputy in the Office of Legislative Counsel for the State of California, as a California deputy attorney general, and as deputy secretary and general counsel for California's Business, Transportation and Housing Agency; and as legal affairs secretary to California Governor Pete Wilson. Judge Brown earlier served as an associate justice of the California Court of Appeals and as an associate justice of the California Supreme Court.

GRACE-MARIE TURNER runs the Galen Institute, a public policy research organization that promotes free-market ideas for health reform, including the transfer of health care decision making to doctors and patients through a more competitive, patient-centered health sector.

Turner has been named one of "Washington's 500 Most Influential People" by *Washingtonian* magazine and has been published in many newspapers, including the *Wall Street Journal*, the *New York Times*, and *USA Today*, and appears frequently on radio and television programs. She testifies before Congress and speaks widely, including at Harvard University, Princeton, the London School of Economics, Oxford University, and the Gregorian University at the Vatican. Grace-Marie facilitates the Health Policy Consensus Group, a forum for market-oriented health policy experts to analyze and develop policy recommendations.

SALLY C. PIPES is president, CEO, and Thomas W. Smith Fellow in Health Care Policy at the Pacific Research Institute. Encounter Books published Pipes's book, *False Premise, False Promise: The Disastrous Reality of Medicare for All*, a number one Amazon.com bestseller for Health Law books. Pipes is frequently called upon for media interviews, speeches, debates, and meetings with policymakers to share her ideas for better quality and access to health care while lowering costs. She writes for Forbes.com, Newsmax, and the *Washington Examiner*'s "Beltway Confidential" blog. Pipes received an honorary PhD from Pepperdine University's School of Public Policy for her work on health care reform.

IAN V. ROWE is the founder of Vertex Partnership Academies and a senior fellow at the American Enterprise Institute. He served as CEO of Public Prep and held leadership positions at Teach for America, the Bill & Melinda Gates Foundation, the White House, and MTV, where he earned two Public Service Emmys. In his book *Agency* (Templeton Press), Rowe seeks to inspire young people of all races to build strong families and become masters of their own destiny. He earned an MBA from Harvard Business School, a BS from Cornell University's College of Engineering, and he graduated from Brooklyn Tech as part of a K–12 New York City public education.

LESLIE HINER is EdChoice vice president of legal affairs, where she strives to empower parents with funded choice of how and where their children are educated. In Indiana, Hiner was chief of staff to the Speaker of the House, counsel to the Senate President Pro Tempore, and general counsel and elections deputy to the Secretary of State. She was a founding member and board chair of the Irvington Community Charter School. Hiner was a commissioner on the Indiana Advisory Committee to the US Commission on Civil Rights, and she served on the Indianapolis City-County Ethics Commission. Hiner also served as president of the Federalist Society's Indianapolis Lawyers Chapter.

HOWARD HUSOCK is a senior fellow in Domestic Policy Studies at the American Enterprise Institute, where he focuses on municipal government, urban housing policy, civil society, and philanthropy. Husock was vice president for research and publications at the Manhattan Institute. He has been a director of case studies in public policy and management at the Harvard Kennedy School, a board member of the Corporation for Public Broadcasting, a journalist, and an Emmy-winning documentary filmmaker. Husock has been widely published in policy journals and the popular press. His books include *The Poor Side of Town: And Why We Need It* (Encounter Books); *Who Killed Civil Society? The Rise of Big Government and Decline of Bourgeois Norms* (Encounter Books), "Philanthropy Under Fire" (Encounter Broadsides), and *America's Trillion-Dollar Housing Mistake: The Failure of American Housing Policy* (Ivan R. Dee).

EDWARD J. PINTO is a senior fellow and director of the American Enterprise Institute's Housing Center, which uses a unique set of housing market indicators to monitor US markets. Pinto is researching ways to improve wealth building opportunities and outcomes for low-income and minority homebuyers and approaches to increase the supply of market-rate economical apartments for hourly wage earners. Active in housing finance for nearly 50 years, he was an executive vice president and chief credit officer for Fannie Mae. Pinto is frequently interviewed on radio and television and often testifies before Congress. His writings have been published in trade publications and the popular press.

CRAIG SCHEEF co-founded Texas Security Bank (TSB) in 2008 and serves as chairman and CEO. TSB's mission is Elevating the Champions of Free Enterprise. The bank has about $1 billion in assets and is annually ranked one of the healthiest banks in America. Scheef previously served as president of business banking at the Bank of Texas. He and TSB have been honored by multiple organizations. TSB's service during the COVID-19 PPP loan application process earned them a 2021 Silver Stevie Award for Sales and Customer Service, and 2021 All-Star recognition from the National Customer Service Association. TSB has also been recognized as a four-year certified best workplace by the Best Workplace Institute.

CURTIS HILL served as Indiana Attorney General from 2017 through 2021. He focused on protecting life, defending freedom, and encouraging Hoosiers' pursuit of happiness. In 2002, Hill won the first of four elections as Elkhart County prosecuting attorney with 78 percent of the vote. He took on corruption, organized crime, and drug traffickers, establishing and supervising the Interdiction and Covert Enforcement unit. Hill testified before Congress on "Methamphetamine in the Heartland" and represented Northern Indiana at an Office of National Drug Control Policy methamphetamine summit. Hill is an advisor to the Douglass Leadership Institute and the Unity Project, and served as a senior fellow at the Center for Urban Renewal and Education.

STEPHEN MOORE is a conservative economist and author. He is currently a senior economist at FreedomWorks, a distinguished fellow at the Heritage Foundation, and a Fox News analyst. From 2005 to 2014, Moore served as a senior economics writer for the *Wall Street Journal* and as a member of the *Journal*'s editorial board. He still contributes regularly to the *Journal*'s editorial page. He is a frequent lecturer to business investment and university audiences around the world on US economic conditions and the political outlook in Washington, DC

RAHEEM WILLIAMS is a former senior policy analyst at the Center for Urban Renewal and Education. He has worked for several liberty-based academic research centers and think tanks. Raheem taught Intro to Microeconomics at North Dakota State University before joining the Reason Foundation's Pension Integrity Project. As a writer, Raheem covers tax and social policy issues. His work has appeared in conservative media and the popular press. Williams serves on the Louisiana Advisory Board for the US Commission on Civil Rights and is a member of the New Orleans Federalist Society. He has served as a Koch Fellow, a Republican Leadership Initiative Fellow, an America's Future Writing Fellow, and an American Conservatism & Governing Fellow at the Manhattan Institute.

NOTES

CHAPTER 1

1 Ireland, Robert. "The Reconstruction Amendments' Debates. Edited by Alfred Avins." *Washington and Lee Law Review* 25, no. 2 (1968): 342–60. https://scholarlycommons.law.wlu.edu/cgi/viewcontent.cgi?article=3686&context=wlulr.

2 Allen, W.B., with Mikael Rose Good. "Yesterday and Tomorrow." In *The State of Black America: Progress, Pitfalls, and the Promise of America*, ed. W.B. Allen (New York: Encounter Books, 2022), 11–68.

3 *Brown v. Board of Education*, 347 U. S. 490 (1954).

4 Funk, Isaac, and Charles Funk. *Funk & Wagnall's New Standard Dictionary of the English Language* (London: Wavery Book Company, 1946).

5 Wilson, James. *Collected Works of James Wilson*, vol. 2, ed. James DeWitt Andrews (Chicago: Callaghan and Company, 2007), p. 426.

6 *Regents of Univ. of California v. Bakke*, 438 U.S. 265 (1978).

7 "Deep Divisions in Americans' Views of Nation's Racial History—and How to Address It." *Pew Research Center.* August 12, 2021. https://www.pewresearch.org/politics/2021/08/12/deep-divisions-in-americans-views-of-nations-racial-history-and-how-to-address-it/.

8 This theory maintains that the Court is required to show special solicitude for the rights of minorities inasmuch as one could not expect majoritarian political institutions to forward their interests. The Court promised, accordingly, that while it would show decreasing alertness to public abuses of economic liberties, it would exhibit increasing vigilance to sniff out "prejudice against discrete and insular minorities." See *United States v. Carolene Products Co*, 304 U.S. 144 (1938).

9 Allen, William. "Multiculturalism and Diversity: Same Origins, Different Ends." Racism on Campus Forum, Emory University, 1991.

10 This and immediately following discussion appeared previously in my essay, William Allen, "Black and White Together: A Reconsideration." In *Reassessing Civil Rights*, eds. Ellen Frankel Paul, Fred D. Miller, Jr., and Jeffrey Paul (Cambridge, MA: Blackwell Publishers for the Social Philosophy and Policy Center, Bowling Green State University, 1991), 172–95.

11 *City of Richmond v. J.A. Croson Co*, 488 U.S. 469 (1989).

12 *Plessy v. Ferguson*, 163 U.S. 537 (1896).

13 Compare my discussion in the essay, William Allen, "A New Birth of Freedom: Fulfillment or Derailment." In *Slavery and Its Consequences: The Constitution, Equality, and Race*, eds. Robert A. Goldwin and Art Kaufman (American Enterprise Institute, 1988), especially pages 79–80 and 85–86.

14 A full discussion of a path the Court might have followed is laid out in my essay, William Allen, "Let's Re-Do Runyon: Questions to Guide Justice White." *Rutgers Law Review* 41, no. 3 (1989): 893. The argument that a robust contract scheme would license discrimination gives too little credence to the notion that certain contracts are ruled beyond the pale from the beginning. Yet this is not a novel theory. We do not enforce contracts for murder; we punish such contracts even in the case that nothing more than the contract has been executed. The willingness to distinguish rightful from impermissible contracts gives even greater scope to the regulation of conduct by rightful contracts. Persons will naturally divide their activities into those they are unwilling to undertake without an enforceable contract (and therefore on a non-discriminatory basis) and those regarding which they do not find a contract reassuring. Surely, it will pose no burden for society to establish that same line of division respecting discrimination, regarding as impermissible only that discrimination that cannot attain its end without relying on the common force of society for the purpose.

15 The United States Commission on Civil Rights has correctly described the fallacy of that argument in its "Report of the United States Commission on Civil Rights on The Civil Rights Act of 1990." The authors show that "Settlement amounts represent a cost to defendants and a benefit to plaintiffs. On net, they represent neither a cost nor a [financial] benefit to society," p. 71n. See: "Report of the United States Commission on Civil Rights on the Civil Rights Act of 1990." *U.S. Commission on Civil Rights.* July 1990. https://www2. law.umaryland.edu/marshall/usccr/documents/cr12c4910.pdf. Moreover, one may find even a very recent example of this in the case reported in the *New York Times*, in which a woman won a $1 million judgment against the firm whose station attendant denied gas service with the declaration that "I don't wait on blacks" (Oregon requires stations attendants to fill tanks, disallowing self-service). See Oxenden, McKenna. "Jury Awards $1 Million to Woman Who Was Told, 'I Don't Serve Black People.'" *New York Times.* January 28, 2023. https://www.nytimes.com/2023/01/28/us/oregon-woman-gas-station-discrimination.html. And in prior years I have personally counseled such plaintiffs in even more dramatic cases.

16 One of the mysteries in the debate over racial preference is the clear decision by political conservatives in general to argue against preferences, not by reason of a defense of their own rights but rather on the spurious and paternalistic grounds of the harm racial preferences cause for the "disadvantaged." There seems to be an unspoken and awkward embarrassment that inhibits white males above all from simply declaring, "I got my rights." Indeed, I made this observation quite tellingly in a bastion of political conservatism in Washington, D.C., in 1989. Recommending that one pose the rights of white males rather than the specter of quotas as the real issue in dispute, the response I drew consisted largely of personal abuse directed at me (*in absentia*) by a Republican Congressman who had drafted legislation inconsistent with the goal I had espoused, followed by the general publication and distribution of that abuse by the conservative think-tank involved, although it had

not published my statement to which the response was directed. The message seemed clear to me: The strategy of avoiding the issue in the debate about civil rights had the highest blessings. I cannot help but believe, however, that that strategy is doomed to the failure that had greeted the American Revolution if the Founders, instead of saying "The tax hurts!" had insisted instead on "India's need for trade!"

17 *City of Richmond v. Croson*, 57 U.S.L.W. 4132 (1989).

18 This argument was set forth most persuasively by a gathering of legal and constitutional scholars, summoned to Cambridge, Massachusetts, by Drew S. Days, III, and other defenders of affirmative action. On March 30, 1989, this conference produced a "Constitutional Scholars' Statement on Affirmative Action After City of Richmond v. Croson," in which the participants announced, upon reflection, that although "some have recently argued that race-conscious remedies by local and state governments should be regarded as conflicting with the Constitution, [a]s long-time students of constitutional law, we regard this assessment as wrong." What followed was a resounding defense of racial set-asides but also of federal government supervision of local and state recourse to that remedy (as provided in the article by Days). The signatories to this remarkable document were: Judith C. Areen, Philip C. Bobbitt, Paul Brest, Denise Carty-Bennia, Jesse Choper, Peggy C. Davis, Drew S. Days III, Walter E. Dellinger III, Norman Dorsen, Christopher F. Edley, Jr., Yale Kamisar, Patricia A. King, Frank J. Michelman, Susan W. Prager, John E. Sexton, Laurence H. Tribe, James Vorenberg, Lee C. Bollinger, Barbara A. Black, Guido Calabresi, John Hart Ely, Herma Hill Kay, Gerald P. Lopez, Eleanor Holmes Norton, Robert M. O'Neil, Dean Rusk, Geoffrey R. Stone, Cass R. Sunstein.

19 Bast, Diane et. al. "Disadvantaged Business Set-Aside Programs: An Evaluation." *Heartland Policy Institute*. June 26, 1989. https://heartland.org/publications/disadvantaged-business-set-aside-programs-an-evaluation/.

20 In order to understand the implications of this constitutional prescription for public bodies or agencies, one should first (1) construct a policy geography that describes the unreformed situation. When that is accomplished, one may assess (2) how far it is necessary to change policy or practice, distinguishing those that are inconsistent with the constitutional prescription from those that are consistent with it. Finally (3), in the spirit of the constitutional prescription, one should enumerate the kinds of active initiatives that would be required to give the fullest meaning to the positive command of inclusiveness, the resources that would be pertinent to enacting those initiatives, and the persons and/or agencies that should undertake those initiatives.

21 The transition from what Diane Ravitch labeled "pluralistic multiculturalists" to "particularism" is well nigh complete. Whereas "[p]luralistic multiculturalists seek to enrich our common culture, to make it more inclusive and less parochial by incorporating elements of other cultures," adherents of particularism "reject the notion of a common culture altogether.... From the particularist perspective, education must recognize that students are culture-bound and teach them, not an oppressive or illusory common culture, but

their own culture—or as academicians reconstruct it." See Bonevac, Daniel. "Leviathan U." In *The Imperiled Academy*, ed. Howard Dickman (New Brunswick: Transaction Publishers, 1993), 2–3.

CHAPTER 2

1 Circuit Judge, District of Columbia Circuit, retired.

2 Kolakowski, Leszek. "The Idolatry of Politics." May 7, 1986. 15th Annual Jefferson Lecture, Washington, DC. https://neh.dspacedirect.org/bitstream/ handle/11215/3767/LIB37_002-public.pdf?sequence=1&isAllowed=y.

3 Ibid.

4 Jefferson, Thomas. "Letter to Henry Lee." *Teaching American History*. May 8, 1825. https://teachingamericanhistory.org/document/letter-to-henry-lee/.

5 Ibid.

6 Ibid.

7 Watson, Bradley. "Progressivism and the New Science of Jurisprudence." The Heritage Foundation. February 24, 2009. https://www.heritage.org/political-process/report/progressivism-and-the-new-science-jurisprudence.

8 Brutus. "Brutus XI." *Teaching American History*. January 31, 1788. https:// teachingamericanhistory.org/document/brutus-xi/.

9 Brutus. "Brutus XV." March 20, 1788. https://teachingamericanhistory.org/ document/brutus-xv-2/.

10 Washington, George. "Circular to the States: George Washington to the States, June 8, 1783." *George Washington's Mount Vernon*. Accessed March 4, 2023. https://www.mountvernon.org/education/primary-source- collections/ primary-source-collections/article/circular-to-the-states-george-washington-to-the-states-june-8-1783/.

11 Fornieri, Joseph, editor. *The Language of Liberty: The Political Speeches and Writings of Abraham Lincoln, Revised Bicentennial Edition* (Getaway Heritage, 2009).

12 Douglass, Frederick. "What to the Slave Is the Fourth of July?" *Teaching American History*. July 5, 1852. https://teachingamericanhistory.org/document/ what-to-the-slave-is-the-fourth-of-july/.

13 Fehrenbacher, Don E. *The Dred Scott Case: Its Significance in American Law and Politics* (Oxford University Press, 1978), pp. 41–42.

14 "Dred Scott v. Sandford (1857)." *National Archives*. Accessed March 4, 2023. https://www.archives.gov/milestone-documents/dred-scott-v-sandford.

15 Alexander M. Bickel, *The Least Dangerous Branch* (New Haven: Yale University Press, 1962), p. 259.

16 Lincoln, Abraham. "Peoria Speech, October 16, 1854." *National Park Service*. Accessed March 4, 2023. https://www.nps.gov/liho/learn/historyculture/peoriaspeech.htm.

17 Lincoln, Abraham. "Speech at Chicago." *Teaching American History*. July 10, 1858. https://teachingamericanhistory.org/document/speech-at-chicago-illinois/.

18 Kesler, Charles. *Crisis of the Two Constitutions* (New York: Encounter Books, 2021), p. 116.

19 Lincoln, Abraham. "Address in Independence Hall." *National Park Service.* Accessed March 4, 2023. https://www.nps.gov/liho/learn/historyculture/independence-hall.htm.

20 Lincoln, Abraham. "Peoria Speech, October 16, 1854."

21 Brodie, Fawn. *Thaddeus Stevens: Scourge of the South* (New York: W. W. Norton & Company, 1966), p. 132.

22 Lincoln, Abraham. "Protest in Illinois Legislature on Slavery, 3 March 1837," in *Collected Works of Abraham Lincoln. Volume 1* (Ann Arbor: University of Michigan Digital Library Production Services, 2001), pp. 125–26.

23 Brodie, Fawn. *Thaddeus Stevens: Scourge of the South*, p. 20.

24 Ibid., p. 193.

25 Ibid.

26 Ibid., pp. 193–94.

27 Ibid., p. 202

28 Litwick, Leon. *Been in the Storm So Long: The Aftermath of Slavery* (New York: Vintage Books, 1980), pp. 271–72, 404.

29 McCammon, Sarah. "The Story Behind '40 Acres and a Mule.'" *National Public Radio.* January 12, 2015. https://www.npr.org/sections/codeswitch/2015/01/12/376781165/the-story-behind-40-acres-and-a-mule.

30 Brodie, Fawn. *Thaddeus Stevens: Scourge of the South*, p. 212.

31 Harris, Robert. *The Quest for Equality*, p. 53–54.

32 Fehrenbacher, Don E. *The Dred Scott Case*, p. 579; and Raoul Berger, *Government by Judiciary: The Transformation of the Fourteenth Amendment*, (Indianapolis: Liberty Fund, 1997), p. 246.

33 "Slaughter-House Cases." *Oyez.* Accessed March 4, 2023. https://www.oyez.org/cases/1850-1900/83us36.

34 Harris, Robert. *The Quest for Equality: The Constitution, Congress, and the Supreme Court* (Baton Rouge: Louisiana State University Press, 1960), p. 108.

35 Berger, Raoul. *Government by Judiciary: The Transformation of the Fourteenth Amendment* (Indianapolis: Liberty Fund, 1997), p. 65.

36 Ibid., pp. 65–66.

37 Miller, Loren. *The Petitioners: The Story of the Supreme Court of the United States and the Negro* (New York: Pantheon Books, 1966).

38 Quarles, Benjamin. *Frederick Douglass* (New York: Da Capo Press, 1997), p. 272.

39 Berger, Raoul. *Government by Judiciary*, pp. 33–34.

40 Ibid., p. 35.

41 "United States v. Cruikshank, 92 U.S. 542 (1875)." *Justia Law.* Accessed March 4, 2023. https://supreme.justia.com/cases/federal/us/92/542.

42 "The Enforcement Acts of 1870 and 1871." *United States Senate.* Accessed March 4, 2023. https://www.senate.gov/artandhistory/history/common/generic/EnforcementActs.htm#:~:text=In%20its%20first%20effort%20to,intention%20of%20violating%20citizens'%20constitutional.

43 Ibid.

44 "United States v. Harris, 106 U.S. 629 (1883)." *Justia Law*. Accessed March 4, 2023. https://supreme.justia.com/cases/federal/us/106/629.

45 Fehrenbacher, Don E. *The Dred Scott Case*, p. 582.

46 Ibid., quoting Miller, Loren. *The Petitioners*, p. 116.

47 Canellos, Peter. *The Great Dissenter: The Story of John Marshall Harlan, America's Judicial Hero* (New York: Simon & Schuster, 2021), p. 134.

48 Du Bois, W. E. B. *The Souls of Black Folk* (New York: Barnes and Noble, 2003), p. 13.

49 "Civil Rights Cases, 109 U.S. 3 (1883)." *Justia Law*. Accessed March 4, 2023. https://supreme.justia.com/cases/federal/us/109/3.

50 Fehrenbacher, Don E. *The Dred Scott Case*.

51 "Handout #3: The Civil Rights Cases (1883). *Thirteen WNET New York*. Accessed March 4, 2023. https://www.thirteen.org/wnet/supremecourt/educators/print/lp2-org4.html.

52 Abbott, Everett. *Justice and the Modern Law* (New York: Houghton Mifflin, 1913), pp. 75–76.

53 Alexander, Jordon. "Trailblazer: The Legacy of Bishop Henry M. Turner During the Civil War, Reconstruction, and Jim Crowism. *Liberty University*. May 2016. https://digitalcommons.liberty.edu/cgi/viewcontent.cgi?article=1416&context=masters.

54 Litwick, Leon. *Been in the Storm So Long*, p. 73.

55 Ibid., p. 72.

56 Canellos, Peter. *The Great Dissenter*, p. 268.

57 "Proceedings of the Civil Rights Mass-Meeting held at Lincoln Hall, October 22, 1883." *Speeches of Hon. Frederick Douglass and Robert G. Ingersoll* (Washington, DC: C. P. Farrell, 1883).

58 "Hall v. DeCuir, 95 US 485 (1877)." *Justia Law*. Accessed March 4, 2023. https://supreme.justia.com/cases/federal/us/95/485.

59 "Civil Rights Cases, 109 U.S. 3 (1883)."

60 "Separate Car Act." *Britannica*. Accessed March 4, 2023. https://www.britannica.com/topic/Separate-Car-Act.

61 Canellos, Peter. *The Great Dissenter*, pp. 332–33.

62 Ibid., p. 324.

63 Ibid., p. 342.

64 "Separate But Equal." *Cornell Law School Legal Information Institute*. Revised January 2022. https://www.law.cornell.edu/wex/separate_but_equal.

65 Canellos, Peter. *The Great Dissenter*, p. 343.

66 Ibid., pp. 477–78.

67 Little, Becky. "How Woodrow Wilson Tried to Reverse Black American Progress." History. July 14, 2020. https://www.history.com/news/woodrow-wilson-racial-segregation-jim-crow-ku-klux-klan.

68 Leonard, Thomas. *Illiberal Reformers: Race, Eugenics & American Economies in the Progressive Era*. (Princeton, NJ: Princeton University Press, 2016), p. 49.

69 Leonard, Thomas. *Illiberal Reformers*, p. 50.

70 "Brown v. Board of Education of Topeka, 347 U.S. 483 (1954)." *Justia Law.* Accessed March 4, 2023. https://supreme.justia.com/cases/federal/us/347/483.

71 "Justice Harlan Concurring." *New York Times.* May 23, 1954. https://www.nytimes.com/1954/05/23/archives/justice-harlan-concurring.html.

72 Caldwell, Christopher. *The Age of Entitlement: America Since the Sixties* (New York: Simon and Schuster, 2020), p. 15

73 Morgan, Richard. "Coming Clean About Brown." *City Journal.* Summer 1996. https://www.city- journal.org/html/coming-clean-about-brown-12007.html.

74 Ibid., p. 10.

75 Wechsler, Herbert. "Toward Neutral Principles of Constitutional Law." *The Harvard Law Review Association* 73, no.1 (1959): 1–35. https://www.jstor.org/stable/1337945.

76 Bell Jr., Derrick. "Brown v. Board of Education and the Interest-Convergence Dilemma." *The Harvard Law Review Association* 93, no. 3, (1980): 518–33. https://www.jstor.org/stable/1340546.

77 Bickel, Alexander. *The Least Dangerous Branch: The Supreme Court at the Bar of Politics* (New Haven: Yale University Press, 1962), p. 255.

78 Ibid.

79 Ibid., p. 267.

80 Ibid.

81 Klarman, Michael. *From Jim Crow to Civil Rights: The Supreme Court and the Struggle for Racial Equality* (Oxford University Press, 2006); and Harris, Robert. *The Quest for Equality*, p. 1235.

82 Morgan, "Coming Clean About Brown," p. 8.

83 Ibid., pp. 1–2.

84 Coolidge, Calvin. "Speech 150th Anniversary of the Declaration of Independence." *Teaching American History.* July 5, 1926. https://teachingamericanhistory.org/document/speech-on-the-occasion-of-the-one-hundred-and- fiftieth-anniversary-of-the-declaration-of-independence/.

85 Ibid.

86 Ibid.

87 Canellos, Peter. *The Great Dissenter.* p. 343.

88 "Martin Luther King, Jr., Letter from Birmingham Jail, 1963." Bill of Rights Institute. Accessed March 4, 2023. https://billofrightsinstitute.org/activities/martin-luther-king-jr-letter-from-birmingham-jail-1963-pdj.

CHAPTER 3

1 Grace-Marie Turner is president of the Galen Institute, which works to promote ideas putting doctors and patients at the center of our health sector.

2 "New HHS Report Shows National Uninsured Rate Reached All-Time Low in 2022." *Department of Health and Human Services.* August 2, 2022. https://www.hhs.gov/about/news/2022/08/02/new-hhs-report-shows-national-uninsured-rate-reached-all-time-low-in-2022.html. Data from the first quarter of 2022, based on new data from the National Health Interview Survey.

3   "Health Insurance Coverage and Access to Care Among Black Americans: Recent Trends and Key Challenges." *Assistant Secretary for Planning and Evaluation Office of Health Policy.* February 22, 2022. https://aspe.hhs.gov/sites/default/files/documents/08307d793263d5069fdd6504385e22f8/black-americans-coverages-access-ib.pdf.

4   Ibid.

5   CDC Vital Signs. "African American health: Creating equal opportunities for health." *Centers for Disease Control and Prevention.* May 2017. https://www.cdc.gov/vitalsigns/pdf/2017-05-vitalsigns.pdf.

6   Vespa, Jonathan, Lauren Medina, and David Armstrong. "Demographic Turning Points for the United States: Population Projections for 2020 to 2060." *US Census Bureau.* Modified February 2020. https://www.census.gov/content/dam/Census/library/publications/2020/demo/p25-1144.pdf.

7   Artiga, Samantha, et al. "Health Coverage by Race and Ethnicity, 2010–2019." *Kaiser Family Foundation.* July 16, 2021. https://www.kff.org/racial-equity-and-health-policy/issue-brief/health-coverage-by-race-and-ethnicity/.

8   "Racial and Ethnic Disparities in Medicaid: An Annotated Bibliography." *Medicaid and CHIP Payment and Access Commission.* April 2021. https://www.macpac.gov/wp-content/uploads/2021/04/Racial-and-Ethnic-Disparities-in-Medicaid-An-Annotated-Bibliography.pdf.

9   "Infant Mortality and African Americans." *US Department of Health and Human Services Office of Minority Health.* July 8, 2021. https://minorityhealth.hhs.gov/omh/browse.aspx?lvl=4&lvlid=23.

10 Ibid.

11 "Mental and Behavioral Health—African Americans." *US Department of Health and Human Services Office of Minority Health.* May 18, 2021. https://www.minorityhealth.hhs.gov/omh/browse.aspx?lvl=4&lvlid=24.

12 Ibid.

13 Baicker, Katherine, et al. "The Oregon Experiment—Effects of Medicaid on Clinical Outcomes." *New England Journal of Medicine* 368, no. 18 (2013): 1713–22. https://www.nejm.org/doi/full/10.1056/nejmsa1212321.

14 Kirzinger, Ashley, Cailey Munana, and Mollyann Brodie. "The Public on Next Steps for the ACA and Proposals to Expand Coverage." *Kaiser Family Foundation.* January 23, 2019. https://www.kff.org/health- reform/poll-finding/kff-health-tracking-poll-january-2019/.

15 "CAHC Presents to House Education and Labor Committee to Advocate for a New Small Business Health Care Platform." *Council for Affordable Health Coverage.* April 29, 2022. https://www.cahc.net/newsroom/2022/4/29/cahc-presents-to-house-education-and-labor-committee-to-advocate-for- a-new-small-business-health-care-platform.

16 Sowell, Thomas. *Ever Wonder Why? And Other Controversial Essays.* Hoover Institute Press, 2006.

17 Pauly, Mark. "Will Health Care's Immediate Future Look a Lot like the Recent Past?" *American Enterprise Institute.* June 7, 2019. https://www.aei.org/wp-content/uploads/2019/06/Will-Health-Cares-Immediate-Future- Look-a-Lot-Like-the-Recent-Past.pdf.

18   "CURE 2021 Annual Report." *Center for Urban Renewal and Education.* Accessed November 7, 2022. https://curepolicy.org/2021-in-review/#pdf-2021-annual-report/1.

19   And what problem are they trying to solve? More than 90% of Americans have health coverage now, and most of the remaining 30 million uninsured are eligible for public or private health coverage but aren't signed up—that or they are not legally in the U.S., which is an immigration, not a health reform problem.

20   "Key Design Components and Considerations for Establishing a Single-Payer Health Care System." *Congressional Budget Office.* May 2019. https://www.cbo.gov/system/files/2019-05/55150-singlepayer.pdf.

21   Turner, Grace-Marie. "Marching Toward Socialism." *Galen Institute.* August 11, 2022. https://galen.org/2022/marching-toward-socialism%ef%bf%bc/.

22   Blase, Brian. "Expanded ACA Subsidies: Exacerbating Health Inflation and Income Inequality." *Galen Institute.* June 11, 2021. https://galen.org/assets/Expanded-ACA-Subsidies-Exacerbating-Health-Inflation-and-Income-Inequality.pdf.

23   Blase, Brian. "Testimony of Brian C. Blase, PhD—'Exploring Pathways to Affordable, Universal Health Coverage.'" *House Committee on Education and Labor Subcommittee on Health, Employment, Labor, and Pensions.* February 17, 2022. https://edlabor.house.gov/imo/media/doc/BlaseBrianTestimony%20 0217221.pdf.

24   Badger, Doug. "Obamacare Subsidies: Six Reasons Congress Should Not Make Temporary Increases Permanent." *Heritage Foundation.* May 26, 2021. https://www.heritage.org/health-care-reform/report/obamacare-subsidies-six-reasons-congress-should-not-make-temporary.

25   Perry, Andre, et al. "Black-Owned Businesses in U.S. Cities: The Challenges, Solutions, and Opportunities for Prosperity." *Brookings Institute.* February 14, 2022. https://www.brookings.edu/research/black-owned-businesses- in-u-s-cities-the-challenges-solutions-and-opportunities-for-prosperity/.

26   Riley, Jason. "Black Politics—An Excerpt from 'Please Stop Helping Us' by Jason L. Riley." *Forbes.* October 15, 2014. https://www.forbes.com/sites/realspin/2014/10/15/black-politics-an-excerpt-from-please-stop-helping-us-by-jason-l-riley/?sh=6a084f1a511d.

27   "CURE 2021 Annual Report."

28   Parker, Tan. *Making American Health Care Great: A Conservative Agenda for States to Create Innovative Health Care Markets.* Regnery Publishing, 2020.

29   "CURE: Healthcare." *Center for Urban Renewal and Education.* Accessed October 25, 2022. https://curepolicy.org/policy/healthcare/.

30   Rasmussen, Scott. "Scott Rasmussen's Number of the Day for May 10, 2022." *Ballotpedia.* May 10, 2022. https://ballotpedia.org/Scott_Rasmussen%27s_Number_of_the_Day_for_May_10,_2022.

31   "Health Care Choices 20/20: A Vision for the Future." *Health Policy Consensus Group.* Published October 2020. https://www.healthcarechoices2020.org/.

32   Ibid.

33 Schaefer, Nina Owcharenko. "Health Care: Time to Go on Offense." *Heritage Foundation*. May 31, 2022. https://www.heritage.org/health-care-reform/report/health-care-time-go-offense.

34 Ibid.

35 Schaefer, Nina Owcharenko. "Medicaid at 55: Understanding the Design, Trends and Reforms Needed to Improve the Health Care Safety Net." *Heritage Foundation*. April 14, 2021, https://www.heritage.org/sites/default/files/2021- 04/BG3604_0.pdf.

36 Ibid.

37 Cueto, Isabella. "Medicare Is Using One of Its Biggest Hammers to Try to Fix the Dialysis System: How Providers Are Paid." STAT. September 19, 2022. https://www.statnews.com/2022/09/19/medicare-is-using-one-of-its-biggest-hammers-to-try-to-fix-the-dialysis-system-how-providers-are-paid/.

38 "Top Challenges 2021: #1 Administrative burdens and paperwork." Medical Economics 98, no. 1 (2021). https://www.medicaleconomics.com/view/top-challenges-2021-1-administrative-burdens-and-paperwork.

39 Schaefer, Nina Owcharenko. "U.S. Health Care Policy: 2022 Will Be a Really Confusing Year." *Heritage Foundation*. February 17, 2022. https://www.heritage.org/health-care-reform/commentary/us-health-care-policy- 2022-will-be-really-confusing-year.

40 Primis, Rebecca. "Care For (Not Just Covered)." *State Policy Network*. October 5, 2015. https://spn.org/blog/cared-for-not-just-covered/.

41 Kirshbaum, Eli. "Legislative Update on Texas House Health Care Package." *State of Reform*. April 30, 2021. https://stateofreform.com/featured/2021/04/legislative-update-on-texas-house-health-care- package/#:~:text="Healthy%20Families%2C%20Healthy%20Texas%20is,improve%20healthcare%20for%20every%20Texan.".

42 "Surgery Center of Oklahoma." *Surgery Center of Oklahoma*. Accessed October 25, 2022. https://surgerycenterok.com/.

43 "Oklahoma City Hospital Posts Surgery Prices Online; Creates Bidding War." *Oklahoma News 4*. July 9, 2013. https://kfor.com/news/okc-hospital-posting-surgery-prices-online/.

44 "Reforming America's Healthcare System Through Choice and Competition." *US Department of Health and Human Services, US Department of the Treasury, US Department of Labor*. December 3, 2018. https://www.hhs.gov/sites/default/files/Reforming-AmericasHealthcare-System-Through-Choice-and-Competition.pdf. Pg.74.

45 Miller, Brian, et al. "Reversing Hospital Consolidation: The Promise of Physician-Owned Hospitals." *Health Affairs*, April 12, 2021. https://www.healthaffairs.org/do/10.1377/forefront.20210408.980640/.

46 Miller, Brian. "Testimony of Brian Miller—'Antitrust Applied: Hospital Consolidation Concerns and Solutions'." *House Committee on Judiciary Subcommittee on Competition Policy, Antitrust, and Consumer Rights*. May 19, 2021. https://www.judiciary.senate.gov/imo/media/doc/Brian%20J%20Miller%20Senate%20Judiciary%20testimony%20of or%2005%2019%202021.pdf.

47 Badger, Doug and Grace-Marie Turner. "Rescuing Seniors and Part D from Congress." *The Hill.* May 11, 2018. https://thehill.com/blogs/congress-blog/healthcare/387332-rescuing-seniors-and-part-d-from-congress/.

48 The average premium in 2022 is $30. See: O'Brien, Sarah. "Here's What to Know About Your 2022 Medicare Costs." *CNBC.* December 31, 2021. https://www.cnbc.com/2021/12/31/heres-what-to-know-about-your-2022- medicare-costs.html#:~:text=would%20be%20%2411%2C300.-,Part%20D,in%20 2022%20up%20from%20%24445.

49 Georgia is working to create a private exchange through a pending waiver.

50 CMS fined two Georgia hospitals for failing to disclose their prices, the first time it's enforced a price transparency rule launched last year. See: Matthews, Anna, Melanie Evans, and Tom McGinty. "Hospitals Face Penalties for First Time for Failing to Make Prices Public." *Wall Street Journal.* June 8, 2022. https://www.wsj.com/articles/hospitals-face-penalties-for-first-time-for-failing-to-make-prices-public-11654731977.

51 Pauly, Mark. "Will Health Care's Immediate Future Look a Lot Like the Recent Past?"

CHAPTER 4

1   Elizabeth Arias et al., "Provisional Life Expectancy Estimates for 2021," *National Vital Statistics System*, August 2022, https://www.cdc.gov/nchs/data/vsrr/vsrr023.pdf.

2   Ibid.

3   Ibid.

4   Ibid.

5   Ibid.

6   Elizabeth Arias et al., "Provisional Life Expectancy Estimates for 2020," *National Vital Statistics System*, July 2021, https://www.cdc.gov/nchs/data/vsrr/vsrr015-508.pdf.

7   "Top Ten Leading Causes of Death in the US for Ages 1-44 from 1981-2020," *Centers for Disease Control and Prevention*, updated February 28, 2022, https://www.cdc.gov/injury/wisqars/animated-leading-causes.html.

8   Elizabeth Arias et al., "Provisional Life Expectancy Estimates for 2021."

9   "Overdose Death Rates Increased Significantly for Black, American Indian/Alaska Native People in 2020," *Centers for Disease Control and Prevention*, updated July 18, 2022, https://www.cdc.gov/media/releases/2022/s0719- over-dose-rates-vs.html.

10 Ibid.

11 Ibid.

12 "An Analysis of Traffic Fatalities by Race and Ethnicity," *Governors Highway Safety Association*, June 2021, https://www.ghsa.org/resources/Analysis-of-Traffic-Fatalities-by-Race-and-Ethnicity21.

13 "Early Estimates of Motor Vehicle Traffic Fatalities and Fatality Rate by Sub-Categories in 2020," *National Center for Statistics and Analysis*, updated June 2021, https://crashstats.nhtsa.dot.gov/Api/Public/ViewPublication/813118, table 2;

Amanda Malie and Mina Kaji, "Traffic Deaths Increased Among Black People More than Any Other Race During Pandemic: Study," *ABC News*, June 22, 2021, https://abcnews.go.com/Politics/traffic-deaths-increased-black-people-race-pandemic-study/story?id=78423808.

14 Latoya Hill, Nambi Ndugga, and Samantha Artiga, "Key Data on Health and Health Care by Race and Ethnicity," *Kaiser Family Foundation*, March 15, 2023, https://www.kff.org/report-section/key-facts-on-health-and-health-care- by-race-and-ethnicity-health-status-outcomes-and-behaviors/.

15 "African American Health," *Centers for Disease Control and Prevention*, updated July 3, 2017. https://www.cdc.gov/vitalsigns/aahealth/index.html.

16 Ibid.

17 Latoya Hill, Nambi Ndugga, and Samantha Artiga, "Key Data on Health and Health Care by Race and Ethnicity."

18 Ibid.

19 "Table 26, Normal Weight, Overweight, and Obesity Among Adults Aged 20 and Over, by Selected Characteristics: United States, Selected Years 1988–1994 Through 2015–2018," *Centers for Disease Control and Prevention*, accessed August 15, 2023, https://www.cdc.gov/nchs/data/hus/2019/026-508.pdf.

20 Sofia Carratala and Connor Maxwell, "Health Disparities by Race and Ethnicity," *American Progress*, May 7, 2020, https://www.americanprogress.org/article/health-disparities-race-ethnicity/.

21 Karilyn T. Larkin et al., "High Early Death Rates, Treatment Resistance and Short Survival of Black Adolescents and Young Adults with AML," *American Society of Hematology* 6, no. 19 (2022): 5570–581, https://ashpublications.org/bloodadvances/article/6/19/5570/485729/High-early-death-rates-treatment-resistance-and.

22 "Cancer and African Americans," *Office of Minority Health*, updated November 30, 2022, https://minorityhealth.hhs.gov/omh/browse.aspx?lvl=4&lvlid=16.

23 "HIV/AIDS and African Americans," *Office of Minority Health*, updated February 17, 2023, https://minorityhealth.hhs.gov/omh/browse.aspx?lvl=4&lvlid=21.

24 Ibid.

25 John Creamer et al., "Poverty in the United States: 2021," *U.S. Census Bureau*, September 2022, https://www.census.gov/content/dam/Census/library/publications/2022/demo/p60-277.pdf.

26 "Profile: Black/African Americans," *Office of Minority Health*, updated February 24, 2023, https://minorityhealth.hhs.gov/omh/browse.aspx?lvl=3&lvlid=61.

27 Steven H. Woolf et al., "How Are Income and Wealth Linked to Health and Longevity?," *Urban Institute*, April 2015, https://www.urban.org/sites/default/files/publication/49116/2000178-How-are-Income-and-Wealth-Linked-to-Health-and-Longevity.pdf, p. 1.

28 Ibid.

29 Paula A. Braveman et al., "Socioeconomic Disparities in Health in the United States: What the Patterns Tell Us," *American Journal of Public Health* 100,

no. 1 (2010): S186–S196, https://doi.org/10.2105/AJPH.2009.166082. https://pubmed.ncbi.nlm.nih.gov/20147693/.

30 Kanetha B. Wilson, Roland J. Thorpe, and Thomas A. LaVeist, "Dollar for Dollar: Racial and Ethnic Inequalities in Health and Health-Related Outcomes Among Persons with Very High Income," *Preventative Medicine* 96 (2017): 149–53, https://pubmed.ncbi.nlm.nih.gov/28237367/.

31 "Addressing Social Determinants of Health Through Community Research," *Centers for Disease Control and Prevention*, last reviewed April 24, 2023, https://www.cdc.gov/prc/research-in-action/issue-briefs/addressing-social-determinants-of-health.html.

32 "Social Determinants of Health," *Office of Disease Prevention and Health Promotion*, accessed August 5, 2023, https://health.gov/healthypeople/priority-areas/social-determinants-health.

33 Ruqaijah Yearby, Brietta Clark, and Jose F. Figueroa, "Structural Racism in Historical and Modern US Health Care Policy," *Health Affairs* 41, no. 2 (2022), https://www.healthaffairs.org/doi/10.1377/hlthaff.2021.01466.

34 Tara O'Neill Hayes and Rosie Delk, "Understanding the Social Determinants of Health," *American Action Forum*, September 4, 2018, https://www.americanactionforum.org/research/understanding-the-social-determinants-of-health/#ixzz7YC4LPLvP.

35 Xavier Pi-Sunyer, "The Medical Risks of Obesity," *Postgraduate Medical Journal* 121, no. 6 (2009): 21–33, https://www.ncbi.nlm.nih.gov/pmc/articles/PMC2879283/.

36 "Burden of Cigarette Use in the US," *Centers for Disease Control and Prevention*, updated May 4, 2023, https://www.cdc.gov/tobacco/campaign/tips/resources/data/cigarette-smoking-in-united-states.html.

37 "Adult Obesity Facts," *Centers for Disease Control and Prevention*, updated May 17, 2022, https://www.cdc.gov/obesity/data/adult.html.

38 James H. Price et al., "Racial/Ethnic Disparities in Chronic Diseases of Youths and Access to Health Care in the United States," *BioMed Research International* (2013), https://www.ncbi.nlm.nih.gov/pmc/articles/PMC3794652/.

39 Samantha Artiga, Latoya Hill, and Anthony Damico, "Health Coverage by Race and Ethnicity, 2010–2021," *Kaiser Family Foundation*, December 20, 2022, https://www.kff.org/racial-equity-and-health-policy/issue-brief/health-coverage-by-race-and-ethnicity/.

40 Ibid.

41 "Racial and Ethnic Disparities in Medicaid: An Annotated Bibliography," *Medicaid and CHIP Payment and Access Commission*, April 2021, https://www.macpac.gov/wp-content/uploads/2021/04/Racial-and-Ethnic-Disparities-in-Medicaid-An-Annotated-Bibliography.pdf.

42 Tamar Oostrom, Liran Einav, and Amy Finkelstein, "Outpatient Office Wait Times and Quality of Care for Medicaid Patients," *Health Affairs* 36, no. 5 (2017), https://doi.org/10.1377/hlthaff.2016.1478.

43 Matt Kuhrt, "Medicaid Patients Wait Longer at Office Visits than Those with Private Insurance," *Fierce Healthcare*, May 2, 2017, https://www.fiercehealthcare.com/practices/study-finds-medicaid-patients-wait-longer-than-those-private-insurance.

44 "Outpatient Office Wait Times and Quality of Care for Medicaid Patients."

45 "Summary of Research: Medicaid Physician Payment and Access to Care," *American Medical Association*, 2020, https://www.ama-assn.org/system/files/2020-10/research-summary-medicaid-physician-payment.pdf.

46 Kayla Holgash and Martha Heberlein, "Physician Acceptance of New Medicaid Patients," *Medicaid and CHIP Payment and Access Commission*, January 24, 2019, https://www.macpac.gov/wp- content/uploads/2019/01/Physician-Acceptance-of-New-Medicaid-Patients.pdf.

47 Ibid.

48 Dylan Scott, "Medicaid Is a Hassle for Doctors. That's Hurting Patients," *Vox*, June 7, 2021, https://www.vox.com/2021/6/7/22522479/medicaid-health-insurance-doctors-billing-research.

49 Les Masterson, "Doctors Less Likely to Accept Medicaid than Other Insurance," *Healthcare Dive*, January 29, 2019, https://www.healthcaredive.com/news/doctors-less-likely-to-accept-medicaid-than-other-insurance/546941/.

50 "Colorado's Unmet Demand for Specialty Care," *Colorado Health Institute*, June 2019, https://www.coloradohealthinstitute.org/sites/default/files/file_attachments/Telligen%20Specialty%20Care%20Acce ss%20Report.pdf.

51 Ibid.

52 Michael R. Daly and Jennifer M. Mellor, "Racial and Ethnic Differences in Medicaid Acceptance by Primary Care Physicians: A Geospatial Analysis," *Medical Care Research and Review* 77, no. 1 (2020): 85–95, https://journals.sagepub.com/doi/pdf/10.1177/1077558718772165.

53 Masterson, "Doctors Less Likely to Accept Medicaid than Other Insurance."

54 Katherine Baicker et al., "The Oregon Experiment—Effects of Medicaid on Clinical Outcomes," *New England Journal of Medicine* 368 (2013): 1713–22, https://www.nejm.org/doi/full/10.1056/NEJMsa1212321.

55 Joseph Kwok et al., "The Impact of Health Insurance Status on the Survival of Patients with Head and Neck Cancer," *Cancer* 116, no. 2 (2010): 476–85, https://www.ncbi.nlm.nih.gov/pmc/articles/PMC3085979/.

56 "Marginal Tax Rate," *Tax Foundation*, accessed August 5, 2023, https://taxfoundation.org/tax-basics/marginal- tax-rate/.

57 Alan Cole, "High Implicit Marginal Tax Rates Make Life Difficult for the Poor," *Tax Foundation*, November 15, 2013, https://taxfoundation.org/high-implicit-marginal-tax-rates-make-life-difficult-poor/.

58 Gizem Kosar and Robert A. Moffitt, "Trends in Cumulative Marginal Tax Rates Facing Low-Income Families," *National Bureau of Economic Research*, October 2016, https://www.nber.org/papers/w22782.

59 Lucy Chen et al., "HealthCare.gov Enrollment by Race and Ethnicity, 2015–2022," *Office of Health Policy*, October 25, 2022, https://aspe.hhs.gov/sites/default/files/documents/c070089ad329eeed43dcab36ca80d18f/aspe- oep-2022-race-ethnicity-marketplace.pdf.

60 Shelby Livingston, "Most ACA Exchange Plans Feature a Narrow Network," *Modern Healthcare*, December 3, 2018, https://www.modernhealthcare.com/article/20181204/NEWS/181209976/most-aca-exchange-plans-feature-a- narrow-network.

61   "Cost-Sharing for Plans Offered in the Federal Marketplace, 2014–2023," *Kaiser Family Foundation*, February 13, 2023, https://www.kff.org/slideshow/cost-sharing-for-plans-offered-in-the-federal-marketplace/.

62   "Affordable Care Act Deductibles," *Healthcare Insider*, updated June 11, 2021, https://healthcareinsider.com/affordable-care-act-deductibles-367400.

63   "Annual Family Premiums for Employer Coverage Average $22,463 This Year, with Workers Contributing an Average of $6,106, Benchmark KFF Employer Health Benefit Survey Finds," *Kaiser Family Foundation*, October 27, 2022, https://www.kff.org/press-release/annual-family-premiums-for-employer-coverage-average-22463-this-year/.

64   "The Unsubsidized Uninsured: The Impact of Premium Affordability on Insurance Coverage," *Centers for Medicare and Medicaid Services*, January 2021, https://www.cms.gov/CCIIO/Resources/Forms-Reports-and-Other-Resources/Downloads/Uninsured-Affordability-in-Marketplace.pdf.

65   Philip L. Swagel, "Letter to Senator Mike Crapo—Re: Health Insurance Policies," Congressional Budget Office, July 21, 2022, https://www.cbo.gov/system/files/2022-07/58313-Crapo_letter.pdf.

66   "HHS Poverty Guidelines for 2023," *Office of the Assistant Secretary for Planning and Evaluation*, accessed August 5, 2023, https://aspe.hhs.gov/topics/poverty-economic-mobility/poverty-guidelines.

67   Brian Blase, "Expanded ACA Subsidies: Exacerbating Health Inflation and Income Inequality," *Galen Institute*, updated June 11, 2021, https://galen.org/assets/Expanded-ACA-Subsidies-Exacerbating-Health-Inflation-and-Income-Inequality.pdf.

68   "Report: Half of Latinx, Black Medicare Beneficiaries Choose Medicare Advantage," *Better Medicare Alliance*, June 16, 2021, https://bettermedicarealliance.org/news/report-half-of-latinx-black-medicare-beneficiaries-choose-medicare-advantage/.

69   "Your Coverage Options," *Medicare*, accessed August 14, 2023, https://www.medicare.gov/health-drug-plans/health-plans/your-coverage-options

70   Ibid.

71   "Study: Medicare Advantage Saves Beneficiaries $1,640 Year, Delivering 40% Lower Cost Burden than Traditional Medicare," *Better Medicare Alliance*, March 30, 2021, https://bettermedicarealliance.org/news/study- medicare-advantage-saves-beneficiaries-1640-year-delivering-40-lower-cost-burden-than-traditional-medicare/.

72   "Report: Positive Outcomes for High-Need, High-Cost Beneficiaries in Medicare Advantage Compared to Traditional Fee-for-Service Medicare," *Better Medicare Alliance*, December 2020, https://bettermedicarealliance.org/wp- content/uploads/2020/12/BMA-High-Need-Report.pdf.

73   Mary Ann Sevick et al., "Patients with Complex Chronic Diseases: Perspectives on Supporting Self-Management," *Journal of General Internal Medicine* 22, no. 3 (2007): 438–44, https://www.ncbi.nlm.nih.gov/pmc/articles/PMC2150604/.

74   Meredith Freed et al., "Dental, Hearing, and Vision Costs and Coverage Among Medicare Beneficiaries in Traditional Medicare and Medicare Advantage," *Kaiser Family Foundation*, September 21, 2021, https://www.kff.

org/health-costs/issue-brief/dental-hearing-and-vision-costs-and-coverage-among-medicare- beneficiaries-in-traditional-medicare-and-medicare-advantage/.

75 Nancy Ochieng et al., "Medicare Advantage in 2023: Premiums, Out-of-Pocket Limits, Cost Sharing, Supplemental Benefits, Prior Authorization, and Star Ratings," *Kaiser Family Foundation*, August 9, 2023, https://www.kff.org/medicare/issue-brief/medicare-advantage-in-2023-premiums-out-of-pocket-limits-cost-sharing- supplemental-benefits-prior-authorization-and-star-ratings/.

76 Kenton J. Johnston et al., "Association of Race and Ethnicity and Medicare Program Type with Ambulatory Care Access and Quality Measures," *Journal of the American Medical Association* 326, no. 7 (2021): 628–36, https://jamanetwork.com/journals/jama/article-abstract/2783067.

77 Thomas Sowell, "The Mindset of the Left: Part II," *Creators*, June 30, 2013, https://www.creators.com/read/thomas-sowell/06/13/the-mindset-of-the-left-part-ii.

78 Jason Riley, *Please Stop Helping Us: How Liberals Make It Harder for Blacks to Succeed* (New York: Encounter Books, 2016).

79 Jason L. Riley, "Black Politics—An Excerpt from 'Please Stop Helping Us' by Jason L. Riley," *Forbes*, October 15, 2014, https://www.forbes.com/sites/realspin/2014/10/15/black-politics-an-excerpt-from-please-stop-helping-us- by-jason-l-riley/.

80 Thomas Sowell, "Blame the Welfare State, Not Racism for Poor Blacks' Problems: Thomas Sowell," *Penn Live*, May 7, 2015, https://www.pennlive.com/opinion/2015/05/poor_blacks_looking_for_someon.html.

81 David Altig et al., "The Marginal Net Taxation of Americans' Labor Supply," *National Bureau of Economic Research*, updated June 2023, https://www.nber.org/papers/w27164.

82 Christopher Jacobs, "New Study Confirms That the Welfare State Discourages Work," *The Federalist*, June 16, 2020, https://thefederalist.com/2020/06/16/new-study-confirms-that-the-welfare-state-discourages-work/.

83 "The HSA Option: Allowing Low-Income Americans to Use a Portion of Their ACA Subsidy as a Health Savings Account Contribution," *Paragon Institute*, November 2022, https://paragoninstitute.org/wp- content/uploads/2022/07/The-HSA-Option_web.pdf.

84 "Making HSA-Qualified Health Plans Work for Low-Income Employees," *Health Equity Remark Blog*, November 8, 2018, https://blog.healthequity.com/making-hsas-work-for-low-income-employees.

85 "HSA Contribution Limits and Eligibility Rules," *Fidelity*, July 10, 2023, https://www.fidelity.com/learning- center/smart-money/hsa-contribution-limits.

86 Michael F. Cannon, "Large Health Savings Accounts: A Step Toward Tax Neutrality for Health Care," *Forum for Health Economics and Policy* 11, no. 2 (2008), https://www.cato.org/sites/cato.org/files/articles/cannon-large- health-savings-accounts.pdf.

87 Jackie Stewart, "Roth IRA Contribution Limits for 2022," *Kiplinger*, updated November 21, 2022, https://www.kiplinger.com/retirement/retirement-plans/roth-iras/603954/roth-ira-contribution-limits-for-2022.

88 "Facts About the US Black Population," *Pew Research Center*, March 2, 2023, https://www.pewresearch.org/social-trends/fact-sheet/facts-about-the-us-black-population/#age-structure. See downloadable spreadsheet. 46.8 million total. 5.25 million over the age of 65.

89 "Matching Rates," *Medicaid and CHIP Payment and Access Commission*, accessed August 5, 2023, https://www.macpac.gov/subtopic/matching-rates/.

90 Brian Blase, "Individual Health Insurance Markets Improving in States that Fully Permit Short-Term Plans," *Galen Institute*, February 2021, https://galen.org/assets/Individual-Health-Insurance-Markets-Improving-in-States-that-Fully-Permit-Short-Term-Plans.pdf.

91 Internal Revenue Service, Employee Benefits Security Administration, and Department of Health and Human Services, "Final Rule: Short-Term, Limited-Duration Insurance," *Federal Register*, August 3, 2018, https://www.federalregister.gov/documents/2018/08/03/2018-16568/short-term-limited-duration-insurance.

92 Louise Norris, "Short-Term Health Insurance Availability by State," *Health Insurance*, March 3, 2023, https://www.healthinsurance.org/short-term-health-insurance/.

93 "Black Population by State," *Black Demographics*, accessed August 5, 2023, https://blackdemographics.com/population/black-state-population/.

94 "Fact Sheet: President Biden Announces New Actions to Lower Health Care Costs and Protect Consumers from Scam Insurance Plans and Junk Fees as Part of Bidenomics' Push," *White House*, July 7, 2023, https://www.whitehouse.gov/briefing-room/statements-releases/2023/07/07/fact-sheetpresident-biden-announces-new-actions-to-lower-health-care-costs-and-protect-consumers-from-scam-insurance-plans-and-junk-fees-as-part-of-bidenomics-push/.

95 Chris Pope, "Renewable Term Health Insurance: Better coverage than Obamacare," *Manhattan Institute*, May 2019, https://media4.manhattan-institute.org/sites/default/files/R-0519-CP.pdf?mod=article_inline.

96 Brian Blase, "Individual Health Insurance Markets Improving in States that Fully Permit Short-Term Plans," 16.

97 Darrell J. Gaskin et al., "Residential Segregation and the Availability of Primary Care Physicians," *Health Services Research* 47, no. 6 (2012), 2353–76, https://www.ncbi.nlm.nih.gov/pmc/articles/PMC3416972/.

98 Tony Abraham, "'Trauma Deserts' More Likely in Black Communities: JAMA," Healthcare Dive, March 11, 2019, https://www.healthcaredive.com/news/trauma-deserts-more-likely-in-black-urban-communities-jama/550098/.

99 "'Pharmacy Deserts' Disproportionately Affect Black and Latino Residents in Largest US Cities," *USC Schaeffer Center*, May 3, 2021, https://healthpolicy.usc.edu/article/pharmacy-deserts-disproportionately-affect-black-and-latino-residents-in-largest-u-s-cities/.

100 Matthew D Mitchell, Anne Philpot, and Jessice McBirney, "CON Laws in 2020: About the Update," *Mercatus Center*, February 19, 2021, https://www.mercatus.org/publications/healthcare/con-laws-2020-about-update.

101 "Certificate of Need State Laws," *National Conference of State Legislature*, January 1, 2023, https://www.ncsl.org/research/health/con-certificate-of-need-state-laws.aspx.

102 "Black Population by State."

CHAPTER 5

1 "Brown v. Board of Education of Topeka, 347 U.S. 483 (1954)." *Justia Law*. Accessed March 4, 2023. https://supreme.justia.com/cases/federal/us/347/483/.

2 "*Plessy v. Ferguson* (1896)." *National Archives*. Accessed March 4, 2023. https://www.archives.gov/milestone- documents/plessy-v-ferguson.

3 "*Brown v. Board of Education of Topeka*, 347 U.S. 483 (1954)."

4 Sowell, Thomas. "Where Rhetoric Beats Reasoning." *The Wall Street Journal*. May 13, 2004. https://www.wsj.com/articles/SB108440405457410141.

5 "Kansas: *Brown v. Board of Education* National Historic Site." National Parks Service. Accessed March 4, 2023. https://www.nps.gov/places/brown-v-board-of-education-national-historic-site.htm.

6 Van Delinder, Jean. "*Brown v. Board of Education*: A Landmark Case Unresolved Fifty Years Later." *Prologue Magazine* 36, no. 1, 2004. https://www.archives.gov/publications/prologue/2004/spring/brown-v-board-1.html.

7 Romo, Vanessa. "Linda Brown, Who Was at Center of *Brown v. Board of Education*, Dies." *National Public Radio*. March 26, 2018. https://www.npr.org/sections/thetwo-way/2018/03/26/597154953/linda-brown-who-was-at- center-of-brown-v-board-of-education-dies.

8 Brown, DeNeen L. "The Determined Father Who Took Linda Brown by the Hand and Made History." *The Washington Post*. March 27, 2018. https://www.washingtonpost.com/news/retropolis/wp/2018/03/27/the- determined-black-dad-who-took-linda-brown-by-the-hand-and-stepped-into-history/.

9 Davey, Monica. "The Reluctant Icons." *The New York Times*. January 18, 2004. https://www.nytimes.com/2004/01/18/education/the-cases-the-reluctant-icons.html.

10 Brown, DeNeen L. "The Determined Father Who Took Linda Brown by the Hand and Made History."

11 "Linda Brown on Her Involvement in *Brown v. Board of Education* Supreme Court Case." C-SPAN. April 3, 2004. https://www.c-span.org/video/?c4720634%2Flinda-brown-involvement-brown-v-board-education-supreme-court- case.

12 "Monroe Elementary School: Cultural Landscapes Inventory." *National Park Service*. July 2014. http://www.npshistory.com/publications/brvb/cli-monroe-elementary.pdf.

13 "Kansas: *Brown v Board of Education* National Historic Site."

14 Chesney, Charles. "The *Brown v. Board of Education* Case Didn't Start How You Think It Did." PBS. May 19, 2019. https://www.pbs.org/newshour/education/the-brown-v-board-of-education-case-didnt-start-how-you-think-it- did.

15 "*Brown v. Board of Education.*" National Archives. Accessed March 4, 2023. https://www.archives.gov/education/lessons/brown-v-board.

16 "*Brown v. Board of Education of Topeka*, 347 U.S. 483 (1954)."

17 "*Brown v. Board*: The Significance of the 'Doll Test.'" Legal Defense Fund. Accessed March 4, 2023. https://www.naacpldf.org/brown-vs-board/significance-doll-test/.

18 "*Brown v. Board of Education.*"

19 "Transcript of Record: Supreme Court of the United States October Term, 1952." *Black Freedom.* Accessed March 4, 2023. http://blackfreedom.proquest.com/wp-content/uploads/2020/09/briggs12.pdf, p. 207

20 Neale, Rick. "Shuttered Rosenwald Schools Still Have Lessons to Teach." *USA Today.* February 6, 2017. https://www.usatoday.com/story/news/nation-now/2017/02/03/rosenwald-school-education-segregation- era/97423432/.

21 Solender, Michael J. "Inside the Rosenwald Schools." *Smithsonian Institution.* March 30, 2021. https://www.smithsonianmag.com/history/how-rosenwald-schools-shaped-legacy-generation-black-leaders- 180977340/.

22 Granat, Diane. "Saving the Rosenwald Schools: Preserving African American History." *Alicia Patterson Foundation.* May 5, 2011. https://aliciapatterson.org/stories/saving-rosenwald-schools-preserving-african- american-history.

23 Aaronson, Daniel and Bhash Mazumder. "The Impact of Rosenwald Schools on Black Achievement." (Revised September 2011). *Federal Reserve Bank of Chicago.* Accessed March 4, 2023. https://www.chicagofed.org/publications/working-papers/2009/wp-26.

24 Sowell, Thomas. "Sowell: Did Court-Ordered 'Diversity' Really Improve Schools?" *The Columbian.* October 4, 2016. https://www.columbian.com/news/2016/oct/04/sowell-did-court-ordered-diversity-really-improve-schools/.

25 Sowell, Thomas. "Dunbar High School After 100 Years." *Creators.* October 4, 2016. https://www.creators.com/read/thomas-sowell/10/16/dunbar-high-school-after-100-years.

26 Solender, Michael J. "Inside the Rosenwald Schools."

27 "Rosenwald Schools." National Trust for Historic Preservation. Accessed March 4, 2023. https://savingplaces.org/places/rosenwald-schools.

28 "State Achievement-Level Results." The Nation's Report Card. Accessed March 4, 2023. https://www.nationsreportcard.gov/reading/states/achievement/?grade=4.

29 "Explore Assessment Data." *The Nation's Report Card.* Accessed March 4, 2023. https://nces.ed.gov/nationsreportcard/data/.

30 "Reading and Mathematics Scores Decline During COVID-19 Pandemic." *The Nation's Report Card.* Accessed March 4, 2023. https://www.nationsreportcard.gov/highlights/ltt/2022/.

31 "Illinois's Shocking Report Card." *The Wall Street Journal.* October 4, 2022. https://www.wsj.com/articles/illinois- shocking-report-card-reading-math-grade-level-decatur-teachers-school-board-11664722519.

32 "Report Shows School Segregation in New York Remains Worst in Nation." The Civil Rights Project. June 10, 2021. https://www.civilrightsproject.ucla.

edu/news/press-releases/2021-press-releases/report-shows-school- segregation-in-new-york-remains-worst-in-nation.

33   "Home Page." *Vertex Partnership Academies.* Accessed March 4, 2023. https://www.vertexacademies.org/.

CHAPTER 6

1   Douglass, Frederick. "The Blessings of Liberty and Education." (Keynote address, Manassas Industrial School for Colored Youth, Manassas, Virginia. September 3, 1894).

2   Jacobson, Linda. "The 74 Interview: After Two Years of Pandemic Schooling, Nashville Parent Advocate Sonya Thomas Asks, 'What Has Changed?'" *The 74.* March 2, 2022. https://www.the74million.org/article/the-74- interview-after-two-years-of-pandemic-schooling-nashville-parent-advocate-sonya-thomas-asks-what-has-changed/.

3   Veney, Debbie. "Never Going Back: An Analysis of Parent Sentiment in Education." *National Alliance for Public Charter Schools.* August 2022. https://www.publiccharters.org/our-work/publications/never-going-back-analysis-parent-sentiment-education.

4   "First COVID-Era NAEP Assessment Shows Steep Declines In Mathematics and Reading for 9-Year-Olds." *National Assessment Governing Board.* September 1, 2022. https://www.nagb.gov/content/dam/nagb/en/documents/newsroom/press-releases/2022/2022-ltt-press-release- final.pdf.

5   "NAEP Report Card: 2022 NAEP Mathematics Assessment." *The Nation's Report Card.* Accessed December 14, 2022. https://www.nationsreportcard.gov/highlights/mathematics/2022/.

6   Binkley, Colin. "Test Scores Show Historic COVID Setbacks for Kids Across US." *Associated Press News.* October 24, 2022. https://apnews.com/article/science-health-government-and-politics-covid-education- 39e01a570b-560c685b5340078c8dcdee.

7   Lewis, Karyn, et al. "The Widening Achievement Divide During COVID-19." *NWEA.* November 2022. https://www.nwea.org/research/publication/the-widening-achievement-divide-during-covid-19.

8   McCluskey, Neal. "Public Schooling Battle Map." *CATO Institute.* Accessed December 14, 2022. https://www.cato.org/public-schooling-battle-map.

9   Tarnowski, Ed, and Marc LeBlond. "Families Prevail in West Virginia School-Choice Fight." *National Review.* October 12, 2022. https://www.nationalreview.com/2022/10/families-prevail-in-west-virginia-school-choice-fight/.

10   Garland, Merrick. "Partnership Among Federal, State, Local, Tribal, and Territorial Law Enforcement to Address Threats Against School Administrators, Board Members, Teachers, and Staff." *Office of the Attorney General.* October 4, 2021. https://www.justice.gov/media/1170056/dl?inline=.

11   "Historical Timeline of Public Education in the US." *Race Forward: The Center for Racial Justice Innovation.* Accessed December 14, 2022. https://www.race-forward.org/research/reports/historical-timeline-public-education- us.

12 Swift, Fletcher Harper. *A History of Public Permanent Common School Funds in the United States, 1795–1905* (University of Michigan Library, 1911).

13 Usher, Alexandra. "Public Schools and the Original Federal Land Grant Program." *Center on Education Policy.* April 2011. https://files.eric.ed.gov/fulltext/ED518388.pdf.

14 Thomson, Charles. "An Ordinance for the Government of the Territory of the United States, North-west of the River Ohio." *Library of Congress.* July 13, 1787. https://www.loc.gov/item/90898154/.

15 Washington, George. "Washington's Inaugural Address of 1789." *National Archives and Records Administration.* April 30, 1789. https://www.archives.gov/exhibits/american_originals/inaugtxt.html.

16 Washington, George. "Washington's Farewell Address, 1796." *George Washington's Mount Vernon.* September 19, 1796. https://www.mountvernon.org/education/primary-source-collections/primary-source- collections/article/washington-s-farewell-address-1796/.

17 Warder, Graham. "Horace Mann and the Creation of the Common School." *Disability History Museum.* Accessed December 14, 2022. http://www.disabilitymuseum.org/dhm/edu/essay.html?id=42.

18 "Woodstock Letters: Volume 18." *Jesuit Archives Digital Collections and Resources.* Accessed December 14, 2022. https://jesuitarchives.omeka.net/items/show/917.

19 Donahoe v. Richards, 38 Me. 379 (1854).

20 "Dastardly Outrage in Ellsworth, ME." *The Liberator* (Boston, MA). October 27, 1854. https://www.newspapers.com/clip/72240465/1854-the-liberator-boston-oct-27/.

21 Douglass, Margaret. *Personal Narrative of Mrs. Margaret Douglass, A Southern Woman, Who Was Imprisoned for One Month in the Common Jail of Norfolk, Under the Laws of Virginia, For the Crime of Teaching Free Colored Children to Read* (Boston: John P. Jewitt; Jewitt, Proctor, and Worthington, 1854).

22 Douglass, Frederick. *Narrative of the Life of Frederick Douglass, An American Slave* (Boston: Anti-Slavery Office, 1845).

23 Dred Scott, Plaintiff in Error v. John Sandford, 60 U.S. 393 (1856).

24 Clark v. Board of Directors, 24 Iowa 266 at 277 (1868).

25 Plessy v. Ferguson, 16 S.Ct. 1138 (1896).

26 "African American Cultural Heritage Action Fund: Rosenwald Schools." *National Trust for Historic Preservation.* Accessed December 14, 2022. https://savingplaces.org/places/rosenwald-schools#.Y5EgHnZKiUk.

27 Pietrusza, David. "The Ku Klux Klan in the 1920's." *Bill of Rights Institute.* Accessed December 14, 2022. https://billofrightsinstitute.org/essays/the-ku-klux-klan-in-the-1920s.

28 Pierce v. Society of Sisters, 45 S.Ct. 571 (1925).

29 Brown v. Board of Education, 74 S.Ct. 686 (1954).

30 Richer, Matthew Richer. "Bussing's Boston Massacre." *Hoover Institution.* November 1, 1998. https://www.hoover.org/research/busings-boston-massacre.

31 Ibid.

32 Reardon, Sean, et al. "Is Separate Still Unequal? New Evidence on School Segregation and Racial Academic Achievement Gaps." *Stanford Center for Education Policy Analysis.* Last modified August 2022. http://cepa.stanford.edu/wp19-06.

33 Ibid.

34 "National Tracking Poll #2211081: November 10-14, 2022." *EdChoice.* Accessed December 14, 2022. https://edchoice.morningconsultintelligence.com/assets/201430.pdf.

35 "School Choice in America." *EdChoice.* Last modified April 17, 2023. https://www.edchoice.org/school-choice-in-america-dashboard-scia/.

CHAPTER 7

1 *Public Housing,* directed by Frederick Wiseman (Zipporah, 1997), film.

2 Feifei Sun. "Brownsville: Inside One of Brooklyn's Most Dangerous Neighborhoods." *Time.* January 31, 2012. https://time.com/3785609/brownsville-brooklyn/.

3 "Resident Data Book 2021: All Programs." *City of New York.* Accessed March 6, 2023. https://www.nyc.gov/assets/nycha/downloads/pdf/Resident-Data-Book-Summary-2021.pdf.

4 "Picture of Subsidized Households." *US Department of Housing and Urban Development.* Accessed October 2, 2022. https://www.huduser.gov/portal/datasets/assthsg.html.

5 Bart M. Schwartz. "Monitor's First Quarterly Report for the New York City Housing Authority: Pursuant to the Agreement Dates January 31, 2019." *New York City Housing Authority Federal Monitor.* July 30, 2019. https://nychamonitor.com/wp-content/uploads/2019/07/NYCHA-First-Report-7.22.19.pdf.

6 "Detroit History Primer—What was Hastings Street? Paradise Valley? Black Bottom?" *University of Michigan.* Accessed March 4, 2023. https://static1.squarespace.com/static/58042680e3df288140a8a145/t/58518c4129687f7b59 49e183/1481739329747/ Detroit+history+primer+for+Mosaic+2001+Hastings +Street--summer+2000.pdf.

7 Marian Morton. "Deferring Dreams: Racial and Religious Covenants in Shaker Heights, Cleveland Heights and East Cleveland, 1925 to 1970." *Teaching Cleveland.* February 27, 2010. https://teachingcleveland.org/deferring- dreams-racial-and-religious-covenants-in-shaker-heights-and-cleveland-heights-1925-to-1970-by-marian-morton/.

8 Howard Husock. "How New York's Public Housing Fails the City's New Poor." *Manhattan Institute.* October 2017. https://media4.manhattan-institute.org/sites/default/files/IB-HH-1017-v2.pdf.

9 "U.S. Homeownership Rate Experiences Largest Annual Increase on Record, Though Black Homeownership Remains Lower Than a Decade Ago, NAR Analysis Finds." *National Association of Realtors.* February 23, 2022. https://www.nar.realtor/newsroom/u-s-homeownership-rate-experiences-largest-annual-increase-on-record-though- black-homeownership-remains-lower-than-decade-ago.

10   Barbara Penner. "The (Still) Dreary Deadlock of Public Housing." *Places Journal*. October 2018. https://placesjournal.org/article/catherine-bauer-and-the-need-for-public-housing/.

11   Michael Karp. "The St. Louis Rent Strike of 1969: Transforming Black Activism and American Low-Income Housing." *Journal of Urban History* 40, no. 4 (2014): 648–70. doi: 10.1177/0096144213516082.

12   Housing and Urban Development Act of 1969. PL 91-152, 91st Cong. (1969).

13   "Picture of Subsidized Households."

14   Ibid.

15   Jung Hyun Choi. "Breaking Down the Black-White Homeownership Gap. *Urban Institute*. February 21, 2020. https://www.urban.org/urban-wire/breaking-down-black-white-homeownership-gap.

16   "Moving to Work Program (MTW)." *Delaware State Housing Authority*. Accessed October 2, 2022. https://laborfiles.delaware.gov/main/det/one-stop/MTW%20Program.pdf.

17   "Moving to Work." *Housing Authority of the County of San Bernardino*. Accessed October 2, 2022. https://hacsb.com/moving-to-work/.

18   Howard Husock. "Atlanta's Public-Housing Revolution." *City Journal*. Autumn 2010. https://www.city-journal.org/html/atlanta%E2%80%99s-public-housing-revolution-13328.html.

19   "FY 2021 Moving to Work Annual Report." *Housing Authority of the City of Atlanta, Georgia*. September 30, 2021. https://www.atlantahousing.org/wp-content/uploads/2021/10/HA-GA006-FY2021-Ann.-MTW-Report.pdf.

20   Nathalie Baptiste. "Staggering Loss of Black Wealth Due to Subprime Scandal Continues Unabated." *The American Prospect*. October 13, 2014. https://prospect.org/justice/staggering-loss-black-wealth-due-subprime- scandal-continues-unabated/.

21   Edward Pinto. "Triggers of the Financial Crisis." *Financial Crisis Inquiry Commission*. Revised March 15, 2010. https://fcic-static.law.stanford.edu/cdn_media/fcic-docs/2010-03- 15%20Triggers%20of%20the%20Financial%20Crisis%20(Pinto%20memo%20revised).pdf.

22   Christina Hughes Babb. "10 Most-Threatened Metros Based on FHA Delinquency Rates." *DS News*. March 25, 2021. https://dsnews.com/daily-dose/03-25-2021/10-most-threatened-metros-based-on-fha-delinquency-rates.

23   Herbert J. Gans. "The Balanced Community: Homogeneity or Heterogeneity in Residential Areas." *Journal of the American Institute of Planners* 27, no. 3 (1961): 176–84. doi.org/10.1080/01944366108978452.

24   Texas Department of Housing and Community Affairs v. Inclusive Communities Project, Inc. 576 U.S. 519 (2015).

CHAPTER 8

1   "Reagan Quotes and Speeches: News Conference August 12, 1986." *Ronald Regan Presidential Foundation and Institute*. Accessed October 2, 2022. https://www.reaganfoundation.org/ronald-reagan/reagan-quotes- speeches/news-conference-1/.

2 Pinto, Edward, Tobias Peter, and Emily Hamilton. "Light Touch Density: A Series of Policy Briefs on Zoning, Land Use, and a Solution to Help Alleviate the Nation's Housing Shortage." *American Enterprise Institute.* January 2022. https://www.aei.org/wp-content/uploads/2022/01/Light-Touch-Density-Compiled-FINAL-1.12.2022.pdf?x91208.

3 Badger, Emily and Quoctrung Bui. "Cities Start to Question an American Ideal: A House with a Yard on Every Lot." *The New York Times.* June 18, 2019. https://www.nytimes.com/interactive/2019/06/18/upshot/cities-across- america-question-single-family-zoning.html.

4 Advisory Committee on Zoning. "A Zoning Primer." *Department of Commerce.* 1922. https://www.govinfo.gov/content/pkg/GOVPUB-C13-cf208d8edodda43ed677acd6cad8be81/pdf/GOVPUB-C13- cf208d8edod-da43ed677acd6cad8be81.pdf. Note: Committee members included the president of the National Association of Real Estate Boards (now National Association of Realtors), two representatives from the U.S. Chamber of Commerce, president of the American Civic Association, president of the American Society of Landscape Architects (and past president of the American City Planning Institute), secretary and director of the National Housing Association, counsel of the Zoning Committee of New York, and a representative of the National Conference on City Planning and National Municipal League (and past president of the American City Planning Institute). The president of the American Society of Landscape Architects was Frederick Law Olmsted Jr., son of famed landscape architect Frederick Law Olmsted Sr. Three members of the committee were involved in promoting and crafting New York City's first zoning ordinance.

5 Ibid.

6 Advisory Committee on Zoning. "A Standard State Zoning Enabling Act: Under Which Municipalities Can Adopt Zoning Regulations." *Department of Commerce.* 1922, revised 1926. https://www.govinfo.gov/content/pkg/GOVPUB-C13-18b3b6e632119b6d94779f558b9d3873/pdf/GOVPUB-C13- 18b3b6e6321 19b6d94779f558b9d3873.pdf.

7 Advisory Committee on Zoning. "A Zoning Primer."

8 Ibid.

9 Advisory Committee on Zoning. "A Standard State Zoning Enabling Act."

10 Ibid.

11 Ibid.

12 Frank Backus Williams, *The Law of City Planning and Zoning* (New York: Macmillan, 1922), 200. Note: This compendium runs over 700 pages and was the most authoritative book on planning and zoning at the time.

13 Advisory Committee on Zoning. "The Preparation of Zoning Ordinances: A Guide for Municipal Officials and Others in the Arrangement of Provisions of Zoning Regulations." *Department of Commerce.* July 1, 1931. https://www.govinfo.gov/content/pkg/GOVPUB-C13-9c587bf052f6b4aa22cb29d0299d029a/pdf/GOVPUB-C13- 9c587bf052f6b4aa22cb29d0299d029a.pdf.

14 Seymour I. Toll, *Zoned American* (Grossman Publishers, 1969), 193.

15 Stanley L. McMichael and Robert Fry Bingham, *City Growth and Values* (Cleveland: Stanley McMichael Publishing Organization, 1923), 326.

16 Ibid., 200.

17 Ibid., 340–49.

18 Ibid., 200.

19 Ibid., 370.

20 Village of Euclid v. Ambler Realty Co., 272 U.S. 365, 1926.

21 Ernest McKinley Fisher, *Principles of Real Estate Practice* (New York: Macmillan, 1923), 216–19.

22 Toll, Zoned American, 216.

23 Zahn v. Board of Public Works, 274 U.S. 325 (1927).

24 U.S. Department of Commerce, Standard State Zoning Enabling Act, 1922.

25 "Underwriting Manual: Underwriting and Valuation Procedure Under Title II of the National Housing Act." Federal Housing Administration. April 1, 1936. Part II, Section 2: Rating of Location, Section 233. Note: The forward to City Growth Essentials was written by Ernest McKinley Fisher, former assistant executive secretary to the National Association of Real Estate Boards (whose president was appointed to the Advisory Committee on Zoning in 1921) and later the first chief economist at the Federal Housing Administration in 1934, where he was a key author of the FHA Underwriting Manual.

26 Ibid., Section 227.

27 Ibid., Section 210.

28 Ibid., Section 266.

29 Ibid., Section 284.

30 Rothstein, *The Color of Law: A Forgotten History of How Our Government Segregated America*, (New York: Liveright, 2017), 77.

31 Whittemore, Andrew H. "How the Federal Government Zoned America: The Federal Housing Administration and Zoning," *Journal of Urban History* 39, no. 4 (2012). https://doi.org/10.1177/009614421247024.

32 Ibid., Note: This is about 13,000 square feet per one-unit detached structure. This amount of land could comfortably accommodate 4 to 20 LTD units.

33 Pinto, Edward J. "Bibliography of Historically Significant Valuation, Land Use, and Mortgage Risk Documents, and Multifamily and Community Development Federal Housing Enactments." *American Enterprise Institute*. March 13, 2023. https://www.aei.org/research-products/report/bibliography-of-historically-significant-valuation-land-use- and-mortgage-risk-documents-and-multifamily-and-community-development-federal-housing-enactments/.

34 "Richard Lee's Urban Renewal in New Haven." *Connecticut History*. Accessed October 2, 2022. https://connecticuthistory.org/richard-lees-urban-renewal-in-new-haven/.

35 Brian D. Boyer, *Cities Destroyed for Cash: The FHA Scandal at HUD* (Westchester: Follett, 1973)

36 Oatman-Stanford, Hunter. "Demolishing the California Dream: How San Francisco Planned Its Own Housing Crisis." *Collectors Weekly*. September 21, 2018. https://www.collectorsweekly.com/articles/demolishing-the- california-dream/.

37 "Tract Housing in California, 1945–1973: A Context for National Register Evaluation." *California Department of Transportation*. 2011. https://dot.ca.gov/-/

media/dot-media/programs/environmental-analysis/documents/ser/tract-housing-in-ca-1945-1973-a11y.pdf.

38 Stray-Gundersen, Karen M. "Regulatory Responses to the Condominium Conversion Crisis," *Washington University Law Review* 59, no. 2 (1981): 513–34. Note: California's state laws that limit and delay housing construction include the California Land Conservation Act of 1965, the California Environmental Quality Act of 1970, and the California Coastal Control Act and Commission (1972 and 1976).

39 Beitel, Karl. "Did Overzealous Activists Destroy Housing Affordability in San Francisco?: A Time-Series Test of the Effects of Rezoning on Construction and Home Prices, 1967–1998." *Urban Affairs Review* 42, no. 5 (2007): 741–56. doi: 10.1177/1078087406296795.

40 William Fischel, "An Economic History of Zoning and a Cure for its Exclusionary Effects," *Urban Studies* 41, no. 2, February 2004.

41 Moore, Natalie. "Chicago Tax Credit Program Mostly Produces Affordable Housing in Poor, Black Areas." *WBEX Chicago.* March 15, 2021. https://www.wbez.org/stories/chicago-tax-credit-program-mostly-produces-affordable-housing-in-poor-black-areas/a5012638-c6b3-41c3-9632-9522bb5cbb98.

42 Cortright, Joe. "The End of the Housing Supply Debate (Maybe). *City Commentary.* August 11, 2017. https://cityobservatory.org/the-end-of-the-housing-supply-debate-maybe/. Note: The battle cry of the low-income housing advocates is "you can't build your way to affordability." Sightline Institute has tackled that notion directly. Not only can you build your way to affordable housing, in fact, building more supply may be the only effective way to reduce the pressure that is driving up rents and producing displacement. There's ample evidence for this position, but there's still the strong sense that addressing our housing problem by building more high-end housing is a cynical and ineffective kind of "trickle down" economics. . . . When there isn't enough supply, demand from higher-income households floods down to older housing stock, driving up rents and reducing housing options for those with lesser means. Which, is why, as we've observed, in some markets, modest 1950s-era ranch homes are a mainstay of affordability, while in others, they cost more than a million bucks. Also see Alan Durning. "Yes, You Can Build Your Way to Affordable Housing." *Sightline Institute.* September 21, 2017. https://www.sightline.org/2017/09/21/yes-you-can-build-your-way-to-affordable-housing/.

43 "Mortgage Default Rate." *American Enterprise Institute.* Accessed October 2, 2022. https://www.aei.org/housing/mortgage-risk-index/.

44 LIFT loans should be structured as an interest rate buydown on a 20-year loan made to first-generation homebuyers, rather than down payment assistance. The rate buydown, combined with a slightly lower rate due to the shorter term, along with a lower mortgage insurance cost, allows LIFT Home to have the same buying power as a 30-year loan. For the rate buydown, assistance should be provided as compensation to HUD/Rural Housing/Treasury for buying a below-market-yield Ginnie MBS.

45 Applies the same concepts as LIFT Home, but for conventional loans and without federal subsidy.

CHAPTER 9

1 Burton, David. "Comparing Free Enterprise and Socialism." *The Heritage Foundation*. April 30, 2019. https://www.heritage.org/economic-and-property-rights/report/comparing-free-enterprise-and-socialism.

2 Berman, Sheri. "Unheralded Battle: Capitalism, the Left, Social Democracy, and Democratic Socialism." *Dissent*. Winter 2009. https://www.dissentmagazine.org/article/unheralded-battle-capitalism-the-left-social-democracy-and-democratic-socialism; "[W]e are not a separate party. Like our friends and allies in the feminist, labor, civil rights, religious, and community organizing movements, many of us have been active in the Democratic Party. We work with those movements to strengthen the party's left wing, represented by the Congressional Progressive Caucus." "What Is Democratic Socialism." *Democratic Socialists of America*, accessed February 26, 2019. https://www.dsausa.org/about-us/what-is-democratic-socialism/; "The Party of European Socialists (PES) brings together the Socialist, Social Democratic, Labour and Democratic Parties from all over the European Union and Norway." "About Us." *Party of European Socialists*. Accessed February 26, 2019. https://www.pes.eu/en/about-us/; Roemer, John E. *Egalitarian Perspectives: Essays in Philosophical Economics*. Cambridge, UK: Cambridge University Press, 1996.

3 Bruenig, Elizabeth. "It's Time to Give Socialism a Try." *Washington Post*. March 6, 2018. https://www.washingtonpost.com/opinions/its-time-to-give-socialism-a-try/2018/03/06/c603a1b6-2164-11e8-86f6- 54bfff693d2b__story.html?noredirect=on&utm_term=.ce216f60b5b6

4 Burton, David. "Comparing Free Enterprise and Socialism."

5 For a recent survey of socialism's record, see "The Opportunity Costs of Socialism." *The Council of Economic Advisers*. October 2018. https://trumpwhitehouse.archives.gov/wp-content/uploads/2018/10/The-Opportunity-Costs-of-Socialism.pdf; Niemietz, Kristian. *Socialism: The Failed Idea That Never Dies*. London, U.K: Institute for Economic Affairs, 2019.

6 Muravchik, Joshua. "Appendices I & II." In *Heaven on Earth: The Rise and Fall of Socialism*. New York, NY: Encounter Books, 2002; Bauer, Peter Tamas. *Equality, the Third World, and Economic Delusion*. Cambridge, MA: Harvard University Press, 1981.

7 The People's Republic of China (approximately 35 million to 65 million deaths), The Union of Soviet Socialist Republics (20 million to 62 million deaths) and the other Council for Mutual Economic Assistance (COMECON) countries (including the People's Republic of Bulgaria [0.1 million deaths]; the Republic of Cuba; the Czechoslovak Socialist Republic [0.2 million deaths]; the German Democratic Republic [East Germany] [0.1 million deaths]; the Hungarian People's Republic; the Mongolian People's Republic [0.1 million deaths]; the Polish People's Republic [0.6 million deaths]; the Socialist Republic of Romania [0.1 million to 0.3 million deaths]; the Socialist Republic of Vietnam [1 million to 1.7 million deaths]; the People's Socialist Republic of Albania; Khmer Rouge Cambodia [2 million deaths]; the Democratic People's Republic of Korea [North Korea] [1.7 million to 2 million deaths]; and Yugoslavia [1 million deaths]) have the most horrendous records. In addition, National Socialist Germany murdered approximately 21

million people (excluding war dead). See: Rummel, Rudolph. *Death by Government*. Piscataway, NJ: Transaction Publishers, 1994; Courtois, Stéphane et al. *The Black Book of Communism: Crimes, Terror, Repression*. Cambridge, MA: Harvard University Press, 1999; Valentino, Benjamin. *Final Solutions: Mass Killing and Genocide in the 20th Century*. Ithaca, NY: Cornell University Press, 2004; Dikötter, Frank. *Mao's Great Famine*. London, U.K.: Walker, 2010; Conquest, Robert. *The Harvest of Sorrow: Soviet Collectivization and the Terror-Famine*. Oxford, UK: Oxford University Press, 1986; Goodkind, Daniel, Loraine West, and Peter Johnson. "A Reassessment of Mortality in North Korea, 1993–2008." *US Census Bureau*. March 28, 2011. https://paa2011.populationassociation.org/papers/111030.

8 Depending on the egalitarian theory, income (annual or lifetime), wealth, consumption (annual or lifetime), resources, welfare, happiness or utility, capability, opportunity, power or influence, and dignity are all candidates. There is no consensus among proponents of socialist or progressive policies. Measurement of these attributes poses intractable problems with these various theories in the real world.

9 "A government can't control the economy without controlling people. And they know when a government sets out to do that, it must use force and coercion to achieve its purpose. They also knew, those Founding Fathers, that outside of its legitimate functions, government does nothing as well or as economically as the private sector of the economy." See: Reagan, Ronald. *A Time for Choosing*. October 27, 1964. Speech. Los Angeles, C.A.

10 Friedman, Milton, and Rose Friedman. *Free to Choose: A Personal Statement*. San Diego, CA: Harcourt Brace Jovanovich, 1979; Brennan, Jason. *Why Not Capitalism?* Abingdon-on-Thames, UK: Routledge, 2014.

11 Burton knows that some would argue that this is, in principle, a consequentialist rather than an ethical or moral argument. But given the utterly overwhelming evidence of the adverse consequences of adopting socialist policies, it is, in reality, a moral argument: to knowingly take actions that will substantially harm large numbers of people is immoral.

12 When something is owned by "everybody," it is really owned by nobody. Accordingly, no one has an incentive to steward or protect the resource. See: Hardin, Garrett. "Tragedy of the Commons." *The Library of Economics and Liberty*. Accessed February 27, 2019. https://www.econlib.org/library/Enc/TragedyoftheCommons.html; Booth, Phillip. "Property Rights and Conservation: The Missing Theme of Laudato si.'" *The Independent Review* 21, no. 3 (2017): 399–418. http://www.independent.org/pdf/tir/tir_21_03_05_booth.pdf; Block, Walter. *Economics and the Environment: A Reconciliation*. Vancouver, BC: Fraser Institute, 1990.

13 Shaw, Jane, and Richard Stroup. "The Free Market and the Environment." *The Public Interest* (1989): 30–43. https://www.nationalaffairs.com/storage/app/uploads/public/58e/1a4/989/58e1a4989e591657155549.pdf; Peterson, DJ. *Troubled Lands: The Legacy of Soviet Environmental Destruction*. Boulder, CO: Westview Press, 1993; Anderson, Terry, and Laura E. Huggins. *Property Rights: A Practical Guide to Freedom and Prosperity*. Stanford, CA: Hoover Institution Press,

2008; Leal, Donald, and Roger E. Meiners, et al. *Government vs. Environment.* Lanham, MD: Rowman & Littlefield, 2002; Anderson, Terry, and Donald Leal, et al. *Free Market Environmentalism for the Next Generation.* Basingstoke, U.K.: Palgrave Macmillan, 2015; DiLorenzo, Thomas. "Why Socialism Causes Pollution." *Foundation for Economic Education.* March 1, 1992. https://fee.org/articles/why-socialism-causes-pollution/; Satre Ahlander, Anni-Mari. *Environmental Problems in the Shortage Economy: The Legacy of Soviet Environmental Policy.* Cheltenham, U.K.: Edward Elgar, 1994; Sahakyan, Armine. "The Grim Pollution Picture in the Former Soviet Union." *Huffington Post.* December 6, 2017. https://www.huffingtonpost.com/armine-sahakyan/the-grim-pollution-pictur_b_9266764.html.

14   Saint Thomas Aquinas. "Part II, Questions 23–27." In *Summa Theologica: Translated by the Fathers of the English Dominican Province; Volume II.* Pinnacle Press, 2017; Smith, Adam. *The Theory of Moral Sentiments.* Gutenberg Publishers, 2011.

15   Nisbet, Robert. *The Quest for Community: A Study in the Ethics of Order and Freedom.* Wilmington, DE: Intercollegiate Studies Institute, 2010; Putnam, Robert. *Bowling Alone: The Collapse and Revival of American Community.* New York, NY: Touchstone Books, 2001; Otteson, James. *The End of Socialism.* Cambridge, UK: Cambridge University Press, 2014.

16   "The two consequences of this [highly progressive income taxation] which seem to me the most serious are, on the one hand, that it makes for social immobility by making it practically impossible for the successful man to rise by accumulating a fortune and that, on the other, it has come near eliminating that most important element in any free society—the man of independent means, a figure whose essential role in maintaining a free opinion and generally the atmosphere of independence from government control we only begin to realize as he is disappearing from the stage." Hayek, Friedrich. "Chapter VI, Section 6." In *Individualism and Economic Order.* Chicago, IL: University of Chicago Press, 1948.

17   "[E]nvy, which, accordingly, is nothing else but hatred, in so far as it is regarded as disposing a man to rejoice in another's hurt, and to grieve at another's advantage." See: de Spinoza, Benedict. "Part III, Prop. XXIV." In *The Ethics*, translated from the Latin by R. H. M. Elwes, 1887. Project Gutenberg: 2017. Some authors refer to jealousy or covetousness. The latter word is particularly associated with those discussing the biblical injunctions against covetousness found in the Ten Commandments. (See Exodus 20: 17; Deuteronomy 5:21) or the Christian New Testament (See, for example, Luke 12:15; Romans 13:9.). See also Gregorios, Hieromonk. *The Vice of Envy.* Columbia, MO: Newrome Press, 2016; and Dick, Thomas. *An Essay on the Sin and Evils of Covetousness.* New York, NY: Robinson, Pratt & Co, 1836.

18   Schoeck, Helmut. *Envy: A Theory of Social Behavior.* Carmel, IN: Liberty Fund, 1969; Feldman, Allan and Alan Kirman. "Fairness and Envy," *The American Economic Review* 64, no. 6 (1974): 995–1005; Smith, Richard. *Envy: Theory and Research.* Oxford, UK: Oxford University Press, 2008; Clanton, Gordon. "Jealousy and Envy." in Sets, Jan, and Jonathan Turner, eds.

Handbook of the Sociology of Emotions. Springer, 2007; de la Mora, Gonzalo Fernandez. *Egalitarian Envy: The Political Foundations of Social Justice.* Saint Paul, MN: Paragon House, 1987; Hunt, Lester. "The Politics of Envy." Original Papers No. 2, Social Philosophy and Policy Center, 1983; de Jasay, Anthony. "Chapter 3.6." In *The State.* Carmel, IN: Liberty Fund, 1998; Smith, Richard, *The Joy of Pain: Schadenfreude and the Dark Side of Human Nature.* Oxford, UK: Oxford University Press, 2013; "You would rather have the poor poorer provided that the richer were less rich. That is the liberal policy." See: Thatcher, Margaret. "Thatcher's Last Stand Against Socialism." MyNameIsWhatever. November 22, 1990. Video, 1:18–1:23. https://www.youtube.com/watch?time_continue=9&v=rv5t6rC6yvg. Some authors describe a productive, "Keeping Up with the Joneses" envy, which is perhaps better characterized as ambition or emulation since the objective is, and satisfaction is drawn from, improving the agent's well-being rather than deriving displeasure from another's success or good fortune. The ancient Greeks, for example, distinguished between Phthonos [jealousy and envy] and Zelos or Zelus (Ζῆλος) [emulation, zeal, and dedication]. See Sanders, Ed. *Envy and Jealousy in Classical Athens: A Socio-Psychological Approach.* Oxford, UK: Oxford University Press, 2014.

19 Locke, John. *Second Treatise of Government.* Gutenberg Publishers, 2021; Alchian, Armen. "Property Rights." *The Library of Economics and Liberty.* Accessed February 26, 2019. https://www.econlib.org/library/Enc/PropertyRights.html?highlight=%5B%22property%22%5D.

20 Epstein, Richard. "Contracts Small and Contract Large: Contract Law Through the Lens of Laissez-Faire." *Coase-Sandor Institute for Law & Economics.* 1997. https://chicagounbound.uchicago.edu/cgi/viewcontent.cgi?article=1121&context=law_and_economics.

21 A negative externality is a cost imposed by economic activity on a third party that did not agree to incur that cost. See Caplan, Bryan. "Externalities." *The Library of Economics and Liberty.* Accessed February 26, 2019. https://www.econlib.org/library/Enc/Externalities.html; Pigou, Arthur Cecil. "Part II, Chapter II." In *The Economics of Welfare.* New York, NY: MacMillan, 1920. Coase, Ronald. "The Problem of Social Cost." *Journal of Law and Economics* 3, (1960): 1–44. http://home.cerge-ei.cz/ortmann/UpcesCourse/Coase%20-%20The%20problem%20of%20Social%20Cost.pdf. This is analogous to the common law tort of nuisance. See Sir William Blackstone. "Book III, Chapter XIII." In *Commentaries on the Laws of England.* 1765.

22 Public goods exhibit nonexcludability and nonrivalrous consumption. See Cowen, Tyler. "Public Goods." *The Library of Economics and Liberty.* Accessed February 26, 2019. https://www.econlib.org/library/Enc/PublicGoods.html.

23 Nansen McCloskey, Deirdre. "The Great Enrichment: A Humanistic and Social Scientific Account." *Social Science History* 40, no. 4 (2016): 583–98, http://deirdremccloskey.org/docs/pdf/McCloskey_ASSA2016.pdf; Phelps, Edmund. *Mass Flourishing: How Grassroots Innovation Created Jobs, Challenge and Change.* Princeton, NJ: Princeton University Press, 2013.

24 Hall, Joshua, and Robert Lawson. "Economic Freedom of the World: An Accounting of the Literature." *Contemporary Economic Policy* 32, no. 1 (2014):

1–19; Miller, Terry, Anthony B. Kim, and James M. Roberts. "Societies Thrive as Economic Freedom Grows." *The Heritage Foundation*. February 2, 2018. https://www.heritage.org/index/pdf/2018/book/chapter2.pdf; Miller, Terry, and Anthony B. Kim. "The Growth and Impact of Economic Freedom." *The Heritage Foundation*. February 16, 2017. https://www.heritage.org/index/pdf/2017/book/chapter1.pdf; Williamson, Claudia, and Rachel Mathers. "Economic Freedom, Culture, and Growth." *Mercatus Center*. October 2009. https://www.mercatus.org/system/files/Economic_Freedom_Culture_and_Growth.pdf. "Doing Business 2019: Training for Reform." World Bank Group. 2019. http://www.doingbusiness.org/content/dam/doingBusiness/media/Annual- Reports/English/DB2019-report_web-version.pdf; Gwartney, James, Robert Lawson, Joshua Hall, and Ryan Murphy. "Economic Freedom of the World: 2018 Annual Report." *Fraser Institute*. 2018. https://www.fraserinstitute.org/sites/default/files/economic- freedom-of-the-world-2018.pdf.

25 James A. Dorn. "China's March Toward the Market." In *Making Poor Nations Rich: Entrepreneurship and the Process of Economic Development*. Stanford University, 2008; Shah, Parth J., and Renuka Sane. "India: The Elephant in the Age of Liberation." In *Making Poor Nations Rich: Entrepreneurship and the Process of Economic Development*. Stanford University, 2008; Bhagwati, Jagdish and Arvind Panagariya. *Why Growth Matters: How Economic Growth in India Reduced Poverty and the Lessons for Other Developing Countries*. Washington, DC: Public Affairs, 2014; Coase, Ronald, and Ning Wang, *How China Became Capitalist*. Basingstoke, U.K.: Palgrave Macmillan, 2012.

26 Powell, *Making Poor Nations Rich*; Buscaglia, Edgardo, and William Ratliff. *Law and Economics in Developing Countries*. Stanford, CA: Hoover Institution Press, 2000. East Asian poverty rates dropped as these countries adopted pro-market reforms. For data, see "Table 1" in Pinkovskiy, Maxim, and Xavier Sala-i-Martin. "Parametric Estimations of the World Distribution of Income." *National Bureau of Economic Research*. October 2009. https://www.nber.org/papers/w15433.

27 For good introductions to these ideas, see Murphy, Robert, Jason Clemens, Milagros Palacios, and Niels Veldhuis. "Economic Principles for Prosperity." *Fraser Institute*. 2014. https://www.fraserinstitute.org/sites/default/files/economic-principles-for- prosperity.pdf; Butler, Eamonn. *The Best Book on the Market*. Mankato, MN: Capstone, 2008; Sowell, Thomas. *Basic Economics*, 5th ed. New York, NY: Basic Books, 2014; Hazlitt, Henry. *Economics in One Lesson, 50th anniversary edition*. New York, NY: Laissez Faire Books, 1996.

28 McCloskey, Deirdre. *The Bourgeois Virtues: Ethics for an Age of Commerce*. Chicago, IL: University of Chicago Press, 2006.

29 "The recognition of the insuperable limits to his knowledge ought indeed to teach the student of society a lesson of humility which should guard him against becoming an accomplice in men's fatal striving to control society—a striving which makes him not only a tyrant over his fellows, but which may well make him the destroyer of a civilization which no brain has designed but which has grown from the free efforts of millions of individuals." See Hayek, Friedrich. *A Free-Market Monetary System and the Pretense of Knowledge*. Ludwig von Mises Institute, 2008.

30 Kroese, Janique, Wim Bernasco, Aart Liefbroer, and Jan Rouwendal. "Growing Up in Single-Parent Families and the Criminal Involvement of Adolescents: A Systematic Review." *Psychology, Crime & Law* 27, no. 1 (2020): 61–75. https://www.tandfonline.com/doi/full/10.1080/1068316X.2020.1774589.

31 "Post-World War II Economic Expansion." *Wikipedia*. Accessed December 29, 2022. https://en.wikipedia.org/wiki/Post%E2%80%93World_War_II_economic_expansion.

32 Tanner, Michael, and Charles Hughes. "War on Poverty Turns 50: Are We Winning Yet?" *Cato Institute*. October 20, 2014. https://www.cato.org/policy-analysis/war-poverty-turns-50-are-we-winning-yet.

33 "Effects of Fatherless Families on Crime Rates." *Marripedia*. Accessed December 29, 2022. http://marripedia.org/effects_of_fatherless_families_on_crime_rates#fn 8; "Information on Poverty and Income Statistics: A Summary of 2014 Current Population Survey Data." *U.S. Department of Health and Human Services*. September 15, 2014. https://aspe.hhs.gov/reports/information-poverty-income-statistics-summary-2014-current-population-survey-data-0.

34 Wiseman, Ryan. "The Welfare State Has Done a Great Job of Destroying the Nuclear Family." *Bloomp*. August 2020. https://bloomp.net/welfare-harms-the-poor/9-welfare-state-has-done-great-job-of-destroying-nuclear-family.htm.

35 Lerman, Richard, and W. Bradford Wilcox. "For Richer, for Poorer, How Family Structures Economic Success in America." *Institute for Families Studies*. 2014. https://ifstudies.org/ifs-admin/resources/for-richer-or-poorer-hep-2014.pdf.

36 Ibid.

37 Ibid.

38 Ibid.

39 McLanahan, Sara, and Gary Sandefur. *Growing Up with a Single Parent: What Hurts, What Helps*. Cambridge, MA: Harvard Press, 1994.

40 See page 80 in Armor, David. *Maximizing Intelligence*. New Brunswick, NJ: Transaction Publishers, 2003.

41 Sun, Yongmin, and Yuanzhang Li. "Parents' Marital Disruption and Its Uneven Effect on Children's Academic Performance—A Simulation Model." *Social Science Research* 37, no. 2 (2008): 449–60. https://pubmed.ncbi.nlm.nih.gov/19069054/.

42 Manning, Wendy, and Kathleen Lamb. "Adolescent Well-Being in Cohabiting, Married, and Single-Parent Families." *Journal of Marriage and Family* 65, no. 4 (2003): 876–93. https://www.jstor.org/stable/3599897.

43 See page 79 in McLanahan, Sara, and Gary Sandefur. *Growing Up with a Single Parent: What Hurts, What Helps*.

44 Sandefur, Gary, Sara McLanahan, and Roger A. Wojtkiewicz. "The Effects of Parental Marital Status during Adolescence on High School Graduation." *Social Forces* 71, no. 1 (1992): 103–21. https://www.jstor.org/stable/2579968.

45 Ver Ploeg, Michele. "Children from Disrupted Families as Adults: Family Structure, College Attendance and College Completion." *Economics of Educa-*

tion Review 21, no. 2 (2002): 171–84. https://www.sciencedirect.com/science/article/abs/pii/S0272775700000509.

46 See Table C3 in "Living Arrangements of Children Under 18 Years/1 and Marital Status of Parents by Age, Sex, Race, and Hispanic Origin/2 and Selected Characteristics of the Child for all Children 2010." *US Census Bureau.* Accessed December 29, 2022. https://www.census.gov/data/tables/2010/demo/families/cps-2010.html.

47 Hill, Anne M., and June O'Neill. *Underclass Behaviors in the United States: Measurement and Analysis of Determinants.* New York, NY: City University of New York, Baruch College, 1990.

48 Manning, Wendy, and Kathleen Lamb. "Adolescent Well-Being in Cohabitating, Married, and Single-Parent Families."

49 Rector, Robert. "Marriage: America's Greatest Weapon Against Child Poverty." *The Heritage Foundation.* September 5, 2012. http://www.heritage.org/research/reports/2010/09/marriage-america-s-greatest-weapon-against-child-poverty.

50 Harper, Cynthia, and Sara S. McLanahan, "Father Absence and Youth Incarceration," *Journal of Research on Adolescence* 14, no. 3 (2004): 369–97. https://www.ojp.gov/ncjrs/virtual-library/abstracts/father-absence-and-youth-incarceration.

51 Loeber, Rolf, Magda Stouthamer-Loeber, Welmont Van Kammen, and David P. Farrington. "Initiation, Escalation, and Desistance in Juvenile Offending and their Correlates." *Journal of Criminal Law and Criminology* 82, (1991): 36–82. https://www.ojp.gov/ncjrs/virtual-library/abstracts/initiation-escalation-and-desistance-juvenile-offending-and-their; Demuth, Stephen, and Susan L. Brown. "Family Structure, Family Processes, and Adolescent Delinquency: The Significance of Parental Absence Versus Parental Gender." *Journal of Research in Crime and Delinquency* 41, no. 1 (2004): 58–81. https://journals.sagepub.com/doi/10.1177/0022427803256236; See also Wright and Wright, "Family Life and Delinquency and Crimes: A Policymaker's Guide to the Literature." For a comprehensive listing of the following researchers who year by year in the last decade report similar conclusions: H. B. Gibson (1969); Michael Rutter (1971); Karen Wilkinson (1980); R.J. Canter (1982); Joseph H. Rankin (1983); Ross L. Matsueda and Karen Heimer (1987); and Larry LeFlore (1988).

52 See analysis of the fifty states and the District of Columbia showing a correlation of .69 between juvenile violent crime arrest rates and the percentage of children residing in single-parent homes within the states or District. Using statewide figures for the states and the District of Columbia, Heritage staff used multiple regression analysis to estimate the effect of family structure on juvenile crime, holding constant the degree of urbanization. The juvenile violent crime arrest rate served as the dependent variable. Two independent variables were used in the regression: the percentage of children residing in single-parent families and the percentage of the population within the state or District residing within standard metropolitan areas. These data indicate that a 10% increase in single-parent variable leads to a 17% increase in juvenile crime. Both the family structure variable and the urbanization

variable were found to have a statistically significant effect on juvenile crime, with over a 99% level of significance. Detailed results are available from the author.

53 Loeber, Rolf, et al. "Initiation, Escalation, and Desistance in Juvenile Offending and Their Correlates"; Demuth, Stephen, and Susan L. Brown. "Family Structure, Family Processes, and Adolescent Delinquency." See also Wright and Wright, "Family Life and Delinquency and Crimes: A Policymaker's Guide to the Literature," for a comprehensive listing of the following researchers who year by year in the last decade report similar conclusions: H. B. Gibson (1969); Michael Rutter (1971); Karen Wilkinson (1980); R.J. Canter (1982); Joseph H. Rankin (1983); Ross L. Matsueda and Karen Heimer (1987); and Larry LeFlore (1988).

54 "The Consequences of Fatherlessness." *National Center for Fathering.* 2015. http://www.fathers.com/statistics-and-research/the- consequences-of-father-lessness/; Fagan, Patrick. "Rising Illegitimacy, America's Social Catastrophe." *The Heritage Foundation.* June 29, 1994. http://www.heritage.org/research/reports/1994/06/rising-illegimacy.

55 "11 Terms You Should Know to Better Understand Structural Racism." *Aspen Institute.* July 11, 2016. https://www.aspeninstitute.org/blog-posts/structural-racism-definition/.

56 Gonzales, Mike. "Black Lives Matter Leaders Resigns, but This Radical Marxist Agenda with Continue. *The Heritage Foundation.* June 4, 2021. https://www.heritage.org/progressivism/commentary/black-lives-matter-leader-resigns-radical-marxist-agenda-will- continue.

57 Wiseman, Ryan. "The Welfare State Has Done a Great Job of Destroying the Nuclear Family"; Gonzales, Mike and Andrew Olivastro. "The Agenda of Black Lives Matter Is Far Different from the Slogan." *The Heritage Foundation.* July 3, 2020. https://www.heritage.org/progressivism/commentary/the-agenda-black-lives-matter-far-different-the-slogan; "BLM's Leftist Agenda Has Little to Do with Black Lives." The Heritage Foundation. June 30, 2020. Video. https://www.youtube.com/watch?v=8J68p5l-gjQ.

58 Colton, Emma. "Marcellus Wiley Slams BLM After It Deletes Page on Nuclear Families: 'Heard Too Many People Tell Me I Was Wrong.'" *Washington Examiner.* September 22, 2020. https://www.washingtonexaminer.com/news/marcellus-wiley-slams-blm-after-it- deletes-page-on-nuclear-families-heard-too-many-people-tell-me-that-i-was-wrong.

59 Ibid.

60 Wiseman, Ryan. "The Welfare State Has Done a Great Job of Destroying the Nuclear Family." The traditional nuclear family structure is something found all over the earth, not just in Western cultures. It has been around in all human civilizations, societies, nations, languages, and tribes since ancient Sumer and before. The group dynamic that we refer to as the "nuclear family" is not found just with us humans but is found within other animal and bird species the world over. There is a reason that this group structure is found all over the earth, and among many species—it maximizes the well-being of the species practicing it. NOT practicing this dynamic decreases well-being and reduces chances of making it to the point of producing offspring. What BLM

refers to as "white supremacy" could be based on the fact that white people tend to be more suspicious of social welfare and are thus less likely to become dependent on those programs, thus the deleterious effects of those programs are less likely to hurt the white community.

61 D'Sousa, Dinesh. PragerU. December 4, 2017. Video. https://www.prageru. com/videos/fascism-right-or-left.

62 Ibid.

63 Wiseman, Ryan. "The Welfare State Has Done a Great Job of Destroying the Nuclear Family."

64 Blair, Douglas. "I'm a Former Teacher. Here's How Your Children Are Getting Indoctrinated by Leftist Ideology." *The Heritage Foundation*. August 17, 2020. https://www.heritage.org/education/commentary/im-former-teacher-heres-how-your-children-are- getting-indoctrinated-leftist.

65 Will, George. "Opinion: A Teacher Pushes Back Against K-12 Critical Race Theory Indoctrination." *The Washington Post*. June 23, 2021. https://www. washingtonpost.com/opinions/2021/06/23/teacher-pushes-back-against-k-12-critical-race-theory- indoctrination.

66 "Educational Freedom Wiki Pages: An Introduction to Educational Freedom." *Cato Institute*. Accessed December 29, 2022. https://www.cato.org/ education-wiki/educational-freedom-an-introduction.

67 Blair, Douglas. "I'm a Former Teacher. Here's How Your Children Are Getting Indoctrinated by Leftist Ideology"; Masella, Paolo, and Nicola Fuchs-Schundein. "Long-Lasting Effects of Socialist Education: Evidence from the German Democratic Republic." *VOX EU*. June 5, 2016. https://voxeu.org/ article/long-lasting-effects-socialist-education; Marotta, David John. "Looking Backward on Socialism: Free College Education for All." *Marotta Wealth Management*. August 13, 2020. https://www.marottaonmoney.com/looking-backward-on-socialism-free-college-education-for-all/; Harris, Douglas. "Why Managed Competition Is Better than a Free Market Schooling." Brookings Institute. March 17, 2017. https://www.brookings.edu/opinions/ why- managed-competition-is-better-than-a-free-market-for-schooling/.

68 "Educational Freedom Wiki Pages: An Introduction to Educational Freedom."

69 Ibid.

70 Ibid.

71 Ibid.

72 Serrano, Alfonso. "How Many Jobs Do Small Businesses Really Create?" *Fundera by Nerdwallet*. July 24, 2020. https://www.fundera.com/blog/small-businesses-job-creation.

73 Ibid.

74 Wiens, Jason, and Chris Jackson. "The Importance of Young Firms for Economic Growth." *Ewing Marion Kauffman Foundation*. September 24, 2014. https://www.kauffman.org/resources/entrepreneurship-policy-digest/the-importance-of-young-firms-for- economic-growth/.

75 Hethcock, Bill. "1,800 Companies Left California in a Year—With Most Bound for Texas." *San Antonio Business Journal*. December 17, 2018. https://

www.bizjournals.com/sanantonio/news/2018/12/17/1-800-companies-left-california-in-a-year-with.html.

76 Ibid.

77 Ibid.

78 Holiday, Kathryn. "The Road to Disinvestment: How Highways Divided the City and Destroyed Neighborhoods." *AIA Dallas.* Accessed December 29, 2022. https://www.aiadallas.org/v/columns-detail/The-Road-to-Disinvest-ment-How-Highways-Divided-the- City-and-Destroyed-Neighborhoods/pt/; Garcia, Nick. "These Two Highways Tore Dallas Neighborhoods Apart. Can the Damage Be Fixed?" *The Dallas Morning News.* June 7, 2021. https://www.dallasnews.com/news/transportation/2021/06/07/these-two-highways-tore-dallas-neighborhoods-apart-can- the-damage-be-fixed/.

79 Ibid.

80 "Scorecard." *Texas Association of Business.* Accessed December 29, 2022. https://www.txbiz.org/scorecard.

81 Milburn, Forrest. "Roll Call of Infamy: Dallas City Hall Corruption Scandals, Including Dwaine Caraway." *The Dallas Morning News.* April 5, 2019. https://www.dallasnews.com/news/politics/2019/04/05/roll-call-of-infamy-dallas-city-hall-corruption-scandals-including-dwaine-caraway/.

82 "It's 2020 but Banks' Redlining Practices Still Stifle Southern Dallas." *Dallas Weekly.* November 22, 2020. https://www.dallasweekly.com/articles/its-2020-but-banks-redlining-practices-still-stifle-southern-dallas/; Rodgers, Tim. "Watch: Great Story on WFAA About Banks Screwing Southern Dallas." *D Magazine.* December 1, 2020. Video. https://www.dmagazine.com/front-burner/2020/12/watch-great-story-on-wfaa-about-banks-screwing-southern-dallas/; "Banking Below 30: Activist Calls U.S. Department of Justice to Investigate Dallas Banks." WFAA. December 13, 2020. https://www.wfaa.com/video/news/local/banking-below-30-activist-calls-on-us-department-of-jus-tice-to-investigate-dallas- banks/287-46fd7bce-a14c-43db-9d65-d966f62a37a6.

83 Allen, John, David Armstrong, and Lawrence Wolken. *The Foundations of Free Enterprise* (College Station, Texas: Texas A&M University Center for Education, 1979).

84 Moffatt, Mike. "Free Enterprise and the Role of Government in America." *ThoughtCo.* January 27, 2020. https://www.thoughtco.com/free-enterprise-and-the-role-of-us-government-1146947.

85 "U.S. Economy." *US Diplomatic Mission to Germany.* May 2008. https://usa.usembassy.de/economy.htm.

86 Frey, William. "The New Great Migration: Black Americans Return to the South, 1965–2000." Brookings Institute. May 2004. https://www.brookings.edu/wp-content/uploads/2016/06/20040524_Frey.pdf; Frey, William. "Chapter 6 The Great Migration of Blacks, In Reverse." In *Diversity Explosion: How New Racial Demographics are Remaking America.* Brookings Institution Press, 2018.

87 Frey, William. "A 'New Great Migration' Is bringing Black Americans back to the South." Brookings Institute. September 12, 2022. https://www.brookings.edu/research/a-new-great-migration-is-bringing-black-americans-back-to-the-south/#footnote-1.

88 Ibid.
89 Koop, Avery. "Ranked: America's Best States to do Business in." *Visual Capitalist.* August 24, 2022. https://www.visualcapitalist.com/ranked-americas-best-states-to-do-business-in/.
90 "These Are the 5 WORST Cities for Blacks in America." Black Excellence Media. 2021. Video. https://www.youtube.com/c/BlackExcellenceonline.
91 Hepler, Lauren. "The Hidden Toll of California's Black Exodus." *CalMatters.* July 15, 2020. https://calmatters.org/projects/california-black-population-exodus/.

CHAPTER 10

1 Watson, Bruce. "Black Like Me, 50 Years Later." *Smithsonian Magazine.* October 2011. https://www.smithsonianmag.com/arts-culture/black-like-me-50-years-later-74543463/.
2 Manzoor, Sarfraz. "Rereading: Black Like Me by John Howard Griffin." *The Guardian.* October 27, 2011. https://www.theguardian.com/books/2011/oct/27/black-like-me-john-howard-griffin.
3 Felton, Emmanuel, John Harden, and Kevin Schaul. "Still Looking for a 'Black Mecca,' the New Great Migration." *The Washington Post.* January 14, 2022.
4 Demsas, Jerusalem. "What's Causing Black Flight?" *The Atlantic.* September 6, 2022. https://www.theatlantic.com/ideas/archive/2022/09/black-families-leaving-cities-suburbs/671331/.
5 Felton, Emmanuel, et al. "Still Looking for a 'Black Mecca,' the New Great Migration."
6 Frey, William. "A 'New Great Migration' Is Bringing Black Americans Back to the South." *Brookings.* September 12, 2022. https://www.brookings.edu/research/a-new-great-migration-is-bringing-black- americans-back-to-the-south/.
7 "Distressed Communities Index: The Space Between Us: The Evolution of American Communities in the New Century." *Economic Innovation Group.* October 2020. https://eig.org/wp- content/uploads/2020/10/EIG-2020-DCI-Report.pdf.
8 Crenshaw, Kimberlé. "Demarginalizing the Intersection of Race and Sex: A Black Feminist Critique of Antidiscrimination Doctrine, Feminist Theory and Antiracist Politics." *University of Chicago Legal Forum* 1, (1989): 139–167. https://chicagounbound.uchicago.edu/cgi/viewcontent.cgi?article=1052&context=uclf.
9 "Distressed Communities Index: The Space Between Us: The Evolution of American Communities in the New Century."
10 "New Research Finds 21st Century Economic Growth Failed to Lift the Most Vulnerable U.S. Communities Prior to Pandemic." *Economic Innovation Group.* October 14, 2020. https://eig.org/new- research-finds-21st-century-economic-growth-failed-to-lift-the-most-vulnerable-u-s-communities-prior-to-pandemic/.

11 "What Is Marginalized Communities." *IGI Global.* Accessed December 7, 2022. https://www.igi- global.com/dictionary/marginalized-communities/50719.

12 Crenshaw, Kimberlé. "Demarginalizing the Intersection of Race and Sex."

13 "Measures for Neighborhood Success." *The Urban Renaissance Network.* Accessed December 8, 2022. https://www.theturnnetwork.com/impact.

14 "Distressed Communities Index: The Space Between Us: The Evolution of American Communities in the New Century."

15 Jefferson, Thomas, et al. "Declaration of Independence: A Transcript." *National Archives.* Accessed December 8, 2022. https://www.archives.gov/founding-docs/declaration-transcript.

16 Hayek, Friedrich. "Quote: Individualism and Economic Order." *Good Reads.* Accessed December 8, 2022. https://www.goodreads.com/quotes/7223249-there-is-all-the-difference-in-the-world-between- treating.

17 Washington, Chanell, and Laquitta Walker. "Social Economic and Housing Statistics Division Working Paper 2022-07: The New Great Migration and Black Marriage Patterns in the South." *US Census Bureau.* Accessed December 8, 2022. https://www.census.gov/content/dam/Census/library/working-papers/2022/demo/sehsd-wp2022-07.pdf.

18 Washington, Chanell, and Laquitta Walker. "The New Great Migration and Black Marriage Patterns in the South." *US Census Bureau.* April 7, 2022. https://www.census.gov/library/working- papers/2022/demo/SEHSD-WP2022-07.html.

19 "Table: Population." *US Census Bureau.* Accessed December 8, 2022. https://www.census.gov/quickfacts/fact/table/US/PST045221.

20 "Race and Ethnicity." *Prison Policy Initiative.* Accessed December 8, 2022. https://www.prisonpolicy.org/research/race_and_ethnicity/.

21 Washington, Jesse. "Blacks Struggle with 72 Percent Unwed Mothers Rate." *NBC News.* November 7, 2010. https://www.nbcnews.com/id/wbna39993685.

22 Western, Bruce. "Incarceration, Marriage, and Family Life." *Princeton University Department of Sociology.* September 2004. https://www.russellsage.org/sites/all/files/u4/Western_Incarceration,%20Marriage,%20%26%20Family%20Life_0.pdf.

23 "Core Practices for Neighborhood Reinforcement and City Transformation." *The Urban Renaissance Network by Insight Strategic Concepts®.* Accessed December 8, 2022. https://www.theturnnetwork.com/about.

24 Crenshaw, Kimberlé. "Demarginalizing the Intersection of Race and Sex."

CHAPTER 11

1 Moore, Stephen, Jeff Yates, Peter Ferrara, and Steven Entin. "Fix Social Security by Creating Own America Personal Accounts for All Workers." *The Committee to Unleash Prosperity.* 2020. https://committeetounleashprosperity.com/wp-content/uploads/2020/10/Social-Security-Own-America-Accounts-CTUP-Final.pdf. p. 1.

2 Ibid.

3 Ibid.

4 Ibid., p. 4.

5 Ibid., p. 14.

6 "Life Expectancy in the US Dropped for the Second Year in a Row in 2021." *Centers for Disease Control and Prevention*. August 31, 2022. https://www.cdc. gov/nchs/pressroom/nchs_press_releases/2022/20220831.htm.

7 Ferrara, Peter. *Power to the People: The New Road to Freedom and Prosperity for the Poor, Seniors, and Those Most In Need of the World's Best Health Care* (Chicago: The Heartland Institute, 2015).

8 "The 2016 Annual Report of the Board of Trustees of the Federal Old-Age and Survivors Insurance and Federal Disability Insurance Trust Funds." *Social Security Administration*. June 22, 2016. https://www.ssa.gov/oact/ TR/2016/tr2016.pdf.

9 Moore, Stephen, et al. "Fix Social Security by Creating own America Personal Accounts for All Workers." p. 9.

10 Ibid., p. 4.

11 Ibid., p. 6.

12 Peterson, Beatrice, and Justin Gomez. "'Around the Table': Sen. Cory Booker Talks Water Crisis, Income Inequality." *ABC News*. November 27, 2019. https://abcnews.go.com/Politics/table-sen-cory-booker-talks-water- crisis-income/story?id=65807023.

13 Moore, Stephen, et al. "Fix Social Security by Creating Own America Personal Accounts for All Workers." pp. 14–15.

14 Ibid.

15 Ibid., p. 10.

CHAPTER 12

1 "Historical Background and Development of Social Security: Pre-Social Security Period." *Social Security Administration*. Accessed March 4, 2023. https://www.ssa.gov/history/briefhistory3.html.

2 Johnson, Derrick. "Viewing Social Security through the Civil Rights Lens." *National Association for the Advancement of Colored People*. August 14, 2020. https://naacp.org/articles/viewing-social-security- through-civil-rights-lens.

3 "The 2022 OASDI Trustees Report." *Social Security Administration*. June 2022. https://www.ssa.gov/OACT/TR/2022/IV_A_SRest.html#506116.

4 "Investment Holdings: Social Security Trust Funds Reports." *Social Security Administration*. Accessed March 4, 2023. https://www.ssa.gov/OACT/Prog-Data/investheld.html.

5 "Social Security's Funding Shortfall." *Congressional Research Service*. June 22, 2022. https://sgp.fas.org/crs/misc/IF10522.pdf.

6 "Social Security History: Frequently Asked Questions—Ratio of Covered Workers to Beneficiaries." *Social Security Administration*. Accessed March 4, 2023. https://www.ssa.gov/history/ratios.html.

7 "Social Security History: Life Expectancy for Social Security." *Social Security Administration*. March 4, 2023. https://www.ssa.gov/history/lifeexpect.html.

8   "2020 Profile of Older Americans." *Administration for Community Living.* May 2021. https://acl.gov/sites/default/files/aging%20and%20Disability%20In%20 America/2020Profileolderamerican s.final_.pdf

9   "Flemming v. Nestor." Oyez. Accessed December 15, 2022. https://www.oyez. org/cases/1959/54.

10 Holden, Sarah, Steven Bass, and Craig Copeland. "What Does Consistent Participation in 401 (k) Plans Generate? Changes in 401 (k) Plan Account Balances, 2010–19." *Employee Benefit Research Institute,* no. 562 (2022): 1–18. https://www.ebri.org/docs/default-source/ebri-issue- brief/ebri_ib_562_401k-long-30june22.pdf?sfvrsn=f36d382f_8.

11 "Social Security and Medicare Tax Rates." *Social Security Administration.* March 4, 2023. https://www.ssa.gov/oact/progdata/taxRates.html.

12 "Primary Insurance Amount." *Social Security Administration.* March 4, 2023. https://www.ssa.gov/oact/cola/piaformula.html.

13 Martin, Patricia, and John Murphy. "African Americans: Description of Social Security and Supplemental Security Income Participation and Benefit Levels Using the American Community Survey." *Social Security Administration.* January 2014. https://www.ssa.gov/policy/docs/rsnotes/rsn2014-01.html.

14 Aladangady, Aditya, and Akila Forde. "Wealth Inequality and the Racial Wealth Gap." *Board of Governors of the Federal Reserve System.* October 22, 2021. https://doi.org/10.17016/2380-7172.2861.

15 "Social Security and People of Color." *National Academy of Social Insurance.* March 8, 2022. https://www.nasi.org/learn/social-security/social-security-and-people-of-color/.

16 Derenoncourt, Ellora, et al. "Wealth of Two Nations: The U.S. Racial Wealth Gap, 1860–2020." *National Bureau of Economic Research.* June 6, 2022. https:// www.nber.org/papers/w30101.

17 Carloni, Dorian. "Revisiting the Extent to Which Payroll Taxes Are Passed Through to Employees." *Congressional Budget Office.* June 2021. https://www. cbo.gov/system/files/2021-06/57089-Payroll- Taxes.pdf.

18 "Social Security and Medicare Tax Rates."

19 Bagchi, Shantanu. "Can Removing the Tax Cap Save Social Security?" *The BE Journal of Macroeconomics* 17, no. 2 (2017). https://www.degruyter.com/docu-ment/doi/10.1515/bejm-2016- 0091/html?lang=en.

20 Bui, Truong, Jordan Campbell, and Zachary Christensen. "Unfunded Public Pension Liabilities Are Forecast to Rise to $1.3 Trillion in 2022." *Reason Foun-dation.* July 14, 2022. https://reason.org/data- visualization/2022-public-pen-sion- forecaster/#:~:text=Based%20on%20a%20%2D6%25%20return,the%20 Pension%20Integrity%20Project%20finds.

21 Hill, Latoya, Samantha Artiga, and Sweta Haldar. "Key Facts on Health and Health Care by Race and Ethnicity." *Kaiser Family Foundation.* January 26, 2022. https://www.kff.org/report-section/key-facts-on- health-and-health-care-by-race-and-ethnicity-health-status-outcomes-and-behaviors/.

22 Thune, Kent. "Average Return of the Stock Market." *Seeking Alpha.* January 2, 2023. https://seekingalpha.com/article/4502739-average-stock-market-return.

23 "Effective Interest Rates." *Social Security Administration*. Accessed March 4, 2023. https://www.ssa.gov/oact/progdata/effectiveRates.html.

24 Entin, Stephen. "Comparing the Returns from Tax-Favored Retirement Plans to Social Security Yields." *Tax Foundation*. June 8, 2016. https://taxfoundation. org/comparing-returns-tax-favored-retirement-plans- social-security-yields/.

25 Elkins, Kathleen. "A Brief History of the 401(k), Which Changed How Americans Retire." *CNBC*. January 5, 2017. https://www.cnbc.com/2017/01/04/ a-brief-history-of-the-401k-which-changed-how- americans-retire.html.

26 Vereckey, Betsy. "Study: How Target Date Funds Impact Investment Behavior." *MIT Sloan School of Management*. May 23, 2022. https://mitsloan.mit. edu/ideas-made-to-matter/study-how-target-date-funds- impact-investment-behavior.

27 Kagan, Julia. "Government Pension Fund of Norway (GPFN)." *Investopedia*. September 30, 2021. https://www.investopedia.com/terms/g/government-pension-fund-norway.asp.

28 Eccles, Robert. "Active Ownership vs. Active Returns: The Norway Sovereign Wealth Fund Dilemma." *Forbes*. January 29, 2022. https://www.forbes.com/ sites/bobeccles/2022/01/29/active-ownership-vs- active-returns-the-norway-sovereign-wealth-fund-dilemma/?sh=3a7f064225eb.

29 "CPFB: The CPF Story." Central Provident Fund Board. Accessed March 4, 2023. https://www.cpf.gov.sg/member/who-we-are/the-cpf-story#:~:text=CPF%20was%20established%20on%201,mortgages%20on%20 their%20HDB%20flats.

30 "CPF Overview: How CPF Works." *Central Provident Fund Board*. Accessed March 4, 2023. https://www.cpf.gov.sg/member/cpf-overview.

31 Mitchell, Olivia, and Stephen Zeldes. "'Social Security Privatization: A Structure for Analysis.'" *National Bureau of Economic Research*. March 1996. https:// www.nber.org/papers/w5512.

32 Kritzer, Barbara. "Chile's Next Generation Pension Reform." *Social Security Bulletin* 68, no. 2 (2008). https://www.ssa.gov/policy/docs/ssb/v68n2/ v68n2p69.html.

33 Haindl Rondonelli, Erik. "Chilean Pension Fund Reform and Its Impact on Saving." Regional Seminar on Fiscal Policy, no. 8 (1996). https://repositorio. cepal.org/handle/11362/34299..

34 "The Social Security Reformer: An Interactive Tool to Fix Social Security." Committee for a Responsible Federal Budget. Accessed March 4, 2023. https://www.crfb.org/socialsecurityreformer/.

35 "Data for Progress." *Data for Progress*. Accessed March 4, 2023. https://www. filesforprogress.org/datasets/2022/6/dfp_june22_ss_updated_tabs.pdf.

36 "Walker to Campaign with Rick Scott, Architect of GOP Plan to Slash Social Security and Medicare." *Democratic Party of Georgia*. October 11, 2022. https:// www.georgiademocrat.org/walker-to-campaign- with-rick-scott-architect-of-gop-plan-to-slash-social-security-and-medicare/.

37 Farley, Robert. "Democrats Misleadingly Claim 'Republicans' Plan' Would 'End' Social Security, Medicare." *FactCheck.org*. April 29, 2022. https://www.

factcheck.org/2022/04/democrats-misleadingly- claim-republicans-plan-would-end-social-security-medicare/.

38 Eccles, David, et al. "The Relationship Between Retirement Wealth and Householders' Lifetime Personal Financial and Investing Behaviors." *Journal of Consumer Affairs* 47, no. 3 (2013): 432–64. https://onlinelibrary.wiley.com/doi/abs/10.1111/joca.12022.

39 Sabelhaus, John, and Jeffrey Thompson. "Racial Wealth Disparities: Reconsidering the Roles of Human Capital and Inheritance." *Federal Reserve Bank of Boston*. September 2021. https://www.bostonfed.org/publications/research-department-working-paper/2022/racial-wealth- disparities-reconsidering-the-roles-of-human-capital-and-inheritance.aspx.